Advanced Swift

Chris Eidhof, Airspeed Velocity

Version 1.0 (March 2016)

For more books and articles visit us at http://objc.io
Email: mail@objc.io
Twitter: @objcio

7   Strings

8   Error Handling

9   Generics

10   Protocols

Foreword

1

I started OS X development in 2005. I started iOS development in 2008. When I co-wrote an advanced iOS book in 2011, I had years of production experience, decades of Objective-C best practice to draw on, and colleagues and mentors with more experience whom I could ask for advice.

Swift is close to two years old and still evolving dramatically. Best practices from six months ago are already obsolete. Can anyone write an advanced Swift book yet?

Yes — but you'd want some things from the authors. You'd want them to be have been there from the beginning. You'd want them to be involved in the community. You'd want them to dig into the *why* of Swift as much as the *how* of Swift. You'd want them to be answering hard questions. You'd want them to be *asking* hard questions.

Additionally, there's much more to Swift than the documentation. The authors need to know what's being discussed in the forums and on Twitter. They need to have dug through the standard library to really get how it works. They need to have followed it closely enough to see where Apple is going, to separate "not Swift-like" from "not Swift yet." That's what Airspeed Velocity and Chris do, and that's why you should read what they have to say.

If you've seen any of my Swift talks, you know Airspeed Velocity[1] is my favorite Swift blog. I love how it digs into the details, and that's what this book does. And like the blog, this book isn't afraid to say where Swift is still awkward. Sometimes there is no good Swift answer yet. Sometimes Swift only solves 80 percent.

Chris's blog[2] helped inspire me to dig into Swift's functional side, and *Functional Swift*[3] sets the bar for the subject. I highly recommend it. But, as you'll learn in this book, "Swift is not Haskell." There are plenty of higher-order functions and immutable data structures here, but there are also loops and **var** properties when those are the right tools. This is a book that lets Swift be Swift by embracing its strengths and acknowledging its weaknesses but always striving to find the Swift way.

Swift is a new world with new rules and new voices. There's still plenty of room to contribute and make an impact on the language and the community.

---

1 http://airspeedvelocity.net/
2 http://chris.eidhof.nl
3 https://www.objc.io/books/fpinswift/

We're all still learning what "good Swift" looks like and which patterns work best. Read what Airspeed Velocity and Chris have to say, and I hope you join the conversation.

Rob Napier (@cocoaphony[4])

Nov 2015

4 https://twitter.com/cocoaphony

Introduction

2

Advanced Swift is quite a bold title for a book, so perhaps we should start with what we mean by it.

When we began writing this book, Swift was barely a year old. We did so before the beta of 2.0 was released — albeit tentatively, because we suspected the language would continue to evolve as it entered its second year. Few languages — perhaps no other language — have been adopted so rapidly by so many developers.

But that left people with unanswered questions. How do you write "idiomatic" Swift? Is there a right way to do certain things? The standard library gave some clues, but even that has changed over time, dropping some conventions and adopting others.

To someone coming from another language, Swift can resemble everything you like about your language of choice. Low-level bit twiddling can look very similar to (and can be as performant as) C, but without many of the undefined behavior gotchas. The lightweight trailing closure syntax of map or filter will be familiar to Rubyists. Swift generics are similar to C++ templates, but with type constraints to ensure generic functions are correct at the time of definition rather than at the time of use. The flexibility of higher-order functions and operator overloading means you can write code that is similar in style to Haskell or F#. And the **@objc** keyword allows you to use selectors and runtime dynamism in ways you would in Objective-C.

Given these resemblances, it's tempting to adopt the idioms of other languages. Case in point: Objective-C example projects can almost be mechanically ported to Swift. Books were rapidly published showing Swift implementations of Java or C# design patterns. And a new wave of monad tutorial blog posts was born.

But then comes the frustration. Why can't we use protocol extensions with associated types like interfaces in Java? Why are arrays not covariant in the way we expect? Why can't we write "functor?" Sometimes the answer is because the part of Swift in question isn't yet implemented. But more often, it's either because there is a different Swift-like way to do what you want to do, or because the Swift feature you thought was like the equivalent in some other language is not quite what you think.

Swift is a complex language — most programming languages are. But it hides that complexity well. You can get up and running developing apps in Swift without needing to know about generics or overloading or the difference between static and dynamic dispatch. You may never need to call into a C library or write your own collection type. But after a while, you'll eventually need to know about these things — either to improve your code's performance, to make it more elegant or expressive, or to just get certain things done.

Learning more about these features is what this book is about. We intend to answer many of the "How do I do this?" or "Why does Swift behave like that?" questions we've seen come up on various forums. Hopefully once you've read it, you'll have gone from being aware of the basics of the language to knowing about many advanced features and having a much better understanding of how Swift works. Being familiar with the material presented is probably necessary, if not sufficient, for calling yourself an advanced Swift programmer.

Who Is This Book For?

This book targets experienced (though not necessarily expert) programmers, such as existing Apple-platform developers, or those coming from other languages such as Java or C++, who want to bring their knowledge of Swift to the same level as that of Objective-C or some other language. It's also suitable for new programmers who have started on Swift, grown familiar with the basics, and are looking to take things to the next level.

It's not meant as an introduction to Swift; it assumes you are familiar with the syntax and structure of the language. If you want some good, compact coverage of the basics of Swift, the best source is the official Apple Swift book (available on iBooks or at developer.apple.com/swift/resources/. If you're already a confident programmer, you could try reading both our book and the Apple Swift book in parallel.

This is also not a book about programming for OS X or iOS devices. Of course, since Swift is currently mainly used on Apple platforms, we have tried to include examples of practical use, but we hope this book will be useful for non-Apple-platform programmers as well.

Themes

We've organized the book under the heading of basic concepts. There are in-depth chapters on some fundamental basic concepts like optionals or strings, and some deeper dives into topics like C interoperability. But throughout the book, hopefully a few themes regarding Swift emerge:

Swift is both a high- and low-level language. Swift allows you to write code similarly to Ruby and Python, with map and reduce, and to write your own higher-order functions easily. Swift also allows you to write fast code that compiles directly to native binaries with performance similar to code written in C.

What's exciting to us, and what's possibly the aspect of Swift we most admire, is that you're able to do both these things *at the same time.* Mapping a closure expression over an array compiles to the same assembly code as looping over a contiguous block of memory.

However, there are some things you need to know about to make the most of this feature. For example, it will benefit you to have a strong grasp on how structs and classes differ, or an understanding of the difference between dynamic and static method dispatch. We'll cover topics such as these in more depth later.

Swift is a multi-paradigm language. You can use it to write object-oriented code or pure functional code using immutable values, or you can write imperative C-like code using pointer arithmetic.

This is both a blessing and a curse. It's great, in that you have a lot of tools available to you, and you aren't forced into writing code one way. But it also exposes you to the risk of writing Java or C or Objective-C in Swift.

Swift still has access to most of the capabilities of Objective-C, including message sending, runtime type identification, and KVO. But Swift introduces many capabilities not available in Objective-C.

Erik Meijer, a well-known programming language expert, tweeted the following in October 2015[1]: "At this point, @SwiftLang is probably a better, and more valuable, vehicle for learning functional programming than Haskell." Swift is a good introduction to a more functional style through its use of generics, protocols, value types, and closures. It is even possible to write operators that compose functions together. The early months of Swift brought

---

1 https://twitter.com/headinthebox/status/655407294969196544

many monad blog posts into the world. But with the release of Swift 2.0 and the introduction of protocol extensions, this trend has shifted.

Swift is very flexible. In the introduction to the book *On Lisp*, Paul Graham writes that:

> Experienced Lisp programmers divide up their programs differently. As well as top-down design, they follow a principle which could be called bottom-up design– changing the language to suit the problem. In Lisp, you don't just write your program down toward the language, you also build the language up toward your program. As you're writing a program you may think "I wish Lisp had such-and-such an operator." So you go and write it. Afterward you realize that using the new operator would simplify the design of another part of the program, and so on. Language and program evolve together.

Swift is a long way from Lisp. But still, we feel like Swift shares this characteristic of encouraging "bottom-up" programming — of making it easy to write very general reusable building blocks that you then combine into larger features, which you then use to solve your actual problem. Swift is particularly good at making these building blocks feel like primitives — like part of the language. A good demonstration of this is that the many features you might think of as fundamental building blocks, like optionals or basic operators, are actually defined in a library — the Swift standard library — rather than directly in the language.

Swift code can be compact and concise while still being clear. Swift lends itself to relatively terse code. There's an underlying goal here, and it isn't to save on typing. The idea is to get to the point quicker and to make code readable by dropping a lot of the "ceremonial" boilerplate you often see in other languages that obscure rather than clarify the meaning of the code.

For example, type inference removes the clutter of type declarations that are obvious from the context. Semicolons and parentheses that add little or no value are gone. Generics and protocol extensions encourage you to avoid repeating yourself by packaging common operations into reusable functions. The goal is to write code that is readable at a glance.

At first, this can be off-putting. If you have never used functions like map, filter , and reduce before, they might look harder to read than a simple **for** loop. But our hope is that this is a short learning curve and that the reward is code that is more "obviously correct" at first glance.

Swift tries to be as safe as practical, until you tell it not to be. This is unlike languages such as C and C++ (where you can be unsafe easily just by forgetting to do something), or like Haskell or Java (which are sometimes safe whether or not you like it).

Eric Lippert, one of the principal designers of C#, recently wrote about his 10 regrets of C#, including the lesson that:

> sometimes you need to implement features that are only for experts who are building infrastructure; those features should be clearly marked as dangerous—not invitingly similar to features from other languages.

Eric was specifically referring to C#'s finalizers, which are similar to C++ destructors. But unlike destructors, they run at a nondeterministic time (perhaps never) at the behest of the garbage collector (and on the garbage collector's thread). However Swift, being reference counted, *does* execute a class's **deinit** deterministically.

Swift embodies this sentiment in other ways. Undefined and unsafe behavior is avoided by default. For example, a variable cannot be used until it has been initialized, and using out-of-bounds subscripts on an array will trap, as opposed to continuing with possibly garbage values.

There are a number of "unsafe" options available (such as the unsafeBitcast function, or the UnsafeMutablePointer type) for when you really need them. But with great power comes great undefined behavior. You can write the following:

```
let uhOh = someArray.withUnsafePointer { ptr in
    // ptr is only valid within this block, but
    // there is nothing stopping you letting it
    // escape into the wild:
    return ptr
}
// later ...
uhOh[10]
```

It will compile, but who knows what it will do. But you can't say nobody warned you.

Swift is an opinionated language. We as authors have strong opinions about the "right" way to write Swift. You'll see many of them in this book, sometimes expressed as if they're facts. But they're just, like, our opinions, man. Feel free to disagree! Swift is still a young language and many things aren't settled. What's more is that many blog posts are flat-out wrong, or outdated (including several ones we wrote, especially in the early days). Whatever you're reading, the most important thing is to try things out for yourself, check how they behave, and decide how you feel about them. Think critically, and beware of out-of-date information.

Terminology

> 'When I use a word,' Humpty Dumpty said, in rather a scornful tone, 'it means just what I choose it to mean — neither more nor less.'
>
> — *Through the Looking Glass*, by Lewis Carroll

Programmers throw around terms of art a lot. To avoid confusion, what follows are some definitions of terms we use throughout this book. Where possible, we're trying to adhere to the same usage as the official documentation, or sometimes a definition that's been widely adopted by the Swift community. Many of these definitions are covered in more detail in later chapters, so don't worry if not everything is familiar on first reading. If you're already familiar with all of these terms, it's still best to skim through to make sure your accepted meanings don't differ from ours.

In Swift, we make the distinctions between values, variables, references, and constants.

A **value** is immutable and forever — it never changes. For example, 1, **true**, and [1,2,3] are all values. Those are examples of **literals**, but values can also be generated at runtime. The number that you get when you square the number five is a value.

When we assign a value to a name using **var** x = [1,2], we are creating a **variable** named x that holds the value [1,2]. By changing x, e.g. by performing x.append(3), we did not change the original value. Rather, we replaced the value that x holds with the new value [1,2,3] — at least *logically*, if not in the actual implementation (which might actually just tack a new entry on the back of some existing memory). We refer to this as **mutating** the variable.

We can declare **constant** variables (constants, for short) with **let** instead of **var**. Once a constant has been assigned a value, it can never be assigned a new value.

We also don't need to give a variable a value immediately. We can declare the variable first (**let** x: Int) and then later assign a value to it (x = 1). Swift, with its emphasis on safety, will check that all possible code paths lead to a variable being assigned a value before its value can be read. There is no concept of a variable having an as-yet-undefined value. Of course, if the variable was declared with **let**, it can only be assigned to once.

Structs and enums are **value types**. When you assign one struct variable to another, the two variables will then contain the same value. You can think of the contents as being copied, but it's more accurate to say that one variable was changed to contain the same value as the other.

A **reference** is a special kind of value: a value that "points to" a variable. Because two references can refer to the same variable, this introduces the possibility of that variable getting mutated by two different parts of the program at once.

Classes are **reference types**. You cannot hold an instance of a class (which we might occasionally call an **object** — a term fraught with troublesome overloading!) directly in a variable. Instead, you must hold a reference to it in a variable and access it via that reference.

Reference types have **identity** — you can check if two variables are referring to the exact same object, using ===. You can also check if they are equal, assuming == is implemented for the relevant type. Two objects with different identity can still be equal.

Value types don't have identity. You cannot check if a particular variable holds the "same" number 2 as another. You can only check if they both contain the value 2. === is really asking: "Do both these variables hold the same reference as their value?" In programming language literature, == is sometimes called *structural equality*, and === is called *pointer equality* or *reference equality*.

Class references are not the only kind of reference in Swift. For example, there are also pointers, accessed through withUnsafeMutablePointer functions and the like. But classes are the simplest reference type to use, in part because their reference-like nature is partially hidden from you by syntactic sugar. You don't need to do any explicit "dereferencing" like you do with pointers in some other languages. (We will cover the other kind of references in more detail in the chapters on CommonMark and interoperability.)

A variable that holds a reference can be declared with **let** — that is, the reference is constant. This means that the variable can never be changed to refer to something else. But — and this is important — it does *not* mean that the object it *refers to* cannot be changed. So when referring to a variable as a constant, be careful — it is only constant in what it points to. It does not mean what it points to is constant. (Note: if those last few sentences sound like doublespeak, don't worry, as we cover this again in the chapter on structs and classes). Unfortunately, this means that when looking at a declaration of a variable with **let**, you can't tell at a glance whether or not what's being declared is completely immutable. Instead, you have to *know* whether it's holding a value type or a reference type.

Here we hit another complication. While structs are value types, structs can be composed of multiple other types, and those types can be references. This means that while assigning one value type to another copies the value, it is a *shallow copy*. It will copy the reference, and not the value the reference points to.

We refer to types having **value semantics** to distinguish a value type that performs a *deep copy*. For example, a Swift array has value semantics if it contains structs as the elements. Yet this is still a tricky definition. If an array contains objects, the elements in the array are references to the objects. Thus, when copying an array that contains objects, the objects themselves do not get copied — only the references to the objects do. In the chapter on structs and classes, we describe this behavior in more detail.

Some classes are completely immutable — that is, they provide no methods for changing their internal state after they are created. This means that even though they are classes, they also have value semantics (because even if they are shared, they can never change). Be careful though — only **final** classes can be guaranteed not to be subclassed with added mutable state.

The collection types in the Swift standard library are structs that have value semantics. Internally, they are implemented using references. In the next chapter, we'll explain how this differs from the way the Foundation classes behave in Objective-C. The Swift structs do this efficiently via a technique called copy-on-write, which we describe the mechanics of in the chapter on structs and classes. But for now, it's important to know that this behavior does not come "for free" whenever structs have reference fields; it has to be implemented by the author of the struct. Copy-on-write is also not the only way to create value semantics, but it's the most common one.

In Swift, functions are also values. You can assign a function to a variable, have an array of functions, and call the function held in a variable. Functions that take other functions as arguments (such as map, which takes a function to transform every element of a sequence) or return functions are referred to as **higher-order functions**.

Functions do not have to be declared at the top level — you can declare a function within another function or in a **do** or other scope. Functions defined within an outer scope, but passed out from it (say, as the returned value of a function), can "capture" local variables, in which case those local variables are not destroyed when the local scope ends, and the function can hold state through them. This behavior is called "closing over" variables, and functions that do this are called **closures**.

Functions can be declared either with the **func** keyword or by using a shorthand { } syntax called a **closure expression**. Sometimes this gets shortened to "closures," but don't let it give you the impression that only closure expressions can be closures. Functions declared with the **func** keyword are closures too.

Functions are held by reference. This means assigning a function that has state via closed-over variables to another variable does not copy that state; it shares it, similar to object references. What's more is that when two closures close over the same local variable, they both share that variable, so they share state. This can be quite surprising, and we'll discuss this more in the chapter on functions.

Functions defined inside a class or protocol are **methods**, and they have an implicit self parameter. A function that, instead of taking multiple arguments, takes some arguments and returns another function representing the partial application of the arguments to that function, is a **curried function**. We'll see in the functions chapter how methods are actually curried functions.

Sometimes we call functions that are not methods **free functions**. This is to distinguish them from methods.

Free functions, and methods called on structs, are **statically dispatched**. This means the function that will be called is known at compile time. This also means the compiler might be able to **inline** the function, i.e. not call the function at all, but instead replace it with the code the function would execute. It can also discard or simplify code that it can prove at compile time won't actually run.

Methods on classes or protocols might be **dynamically dispatched**. This means the compiler does not necessarily know at compile time which function will run. This dynamic behavior is done either by using vtables (similar to how Java or C++ dynamic dispatch works), or in the case of **@objc** classes and protocols, by using selectors and objc_msgSend.

Subtyping and method **overriding** is one way of getting **polymorphic** behavior, i.e. behavior that varies depending on the types involved. A second way is function **overloading**, where a function is written multiple times for different types. (It's important not to mix up overriding and overloading, as they behave very differently.) A third way is via generics, where a function or method is written once to take any type that provides certain functions or methods, but the implementations of those functions can vary. Unlike method overriding, the results of function overloading and generics are known statically at compile time. We'll cover this more in the generics chapter.

Swift Style Guide

When writing this book, and when writing Swift code for our own projects, we try to stick to the following rules:

→ Readability is most important. This is helped by brevity.

→ Always add documentation comments to functions — *especially* generic ones.

→ Types start with UpperCaseLetters. Functions and variables start with lowerCaseLetters.

→ Use type inference. Explicit but obvious types get in the way of readability.

→ Don't use type inference in cases of ambiguity or when defining contracts (which is why, for example,**funcs** have an explicit return type).

→ Default to structs unless you actually need a class-only feature or reference semantics.

→ Mark classes as **final** unless you've explicitly designed them to be inheritable.

→ Use the trailing closure syntax, except when that closure is immediately followed by another opening brace.

→ Use **guard** to exit functions early.

→ Eschew force-unwraps and implicitly unwrapped optionals. They are occasionally useful, but needing them constantly is usually a sign something else is wrong.

→ Don't repeat yourself. If you find you have written a very similar piece of code more than a couple of times, extract it into a function. Consider making that function a protocol extension.

→ Favor map and reduce. But don't force it: use a **for** loop when it makes sense. The purpose of higher-order functions is to make code more readable. An obfuscated use of reduce when a simple **for** loop would be clearer defeats this purpose.

→ Favor immutability: default to **let** unless you know you need mutation. But use mutation when it makes the code clearer or more efficient. Wrap that mutation in a function to isolate unexpected side effects.

→ Swift generics tend to lead to very long function signatures. Unfortunately, we have yet to settle on a good way of breaking up long function declarations into multiple lines. We'll try to be consistent in how we do this in sample code.

→ Much to the dismay of half of this book's authorship, the "cuddled else" is official Swift style: } **else** {.

Collections

3

Arrays and Mutability

The most common collection we use in Swift is that of arrays. An array is simply a list of things. As an example, to create an array of numbers, we can write the following:

```
let fibs = [0, 1, 1, 2, 3, 5]
```

There are the usual operations on array, like the isEmpty and count methods. To get the first and last elements of an array, we can use first and last, which return nil if the array is empty. Arrays also allow for direct access of elements at a specific index through subscripting. Subscripting is not a safe operation; before getting an element, you need to verify the index is within bounds. Otherwise, your program crashes.

If we try to modify the array defined above (by using append, for example), we get a compiler error. This is because the array is defined as a constant, using let. In many cases, this is exactly the right thing to do; it prevents us from accidentally changing the array. If we want the array to be a variable, we have to define it using var:

```
var mutableFibs = [0, 1, 1, 2, 3, 5]
```

Now we can easily append a single element or a sequence of elements:

```
mutableFibs.append(8)
mutableFibs.appendContentsOf([13, 21])
```

There are a couple of benefits that come with making the distinction between var and let. Variables defined with let are easier to reason about because they are immutable. When you read a declaration like let fibs = ... , you know that the value of fibs will never change — it is enforced by the compiler. This helps greatly when reading through code. Note that in the case of classes, the value is a reference. Defining an object with let will make sure the reference never changes. However, the memory it points to (i.e. the instance variables) *can* change. We will go into more detail on the differences between structs and classes in Chapter 4.

Swift arrays have value semantics, which means that they are never shared. When creating a new variable and assigning an existing array to it, a copy is made. This is the case when creating variables, passing arrays to functions, and more. For example, in the following code snippet, x is never modified:

```
var x = [1,2,3]
var y = x
y.append(4)
```

The statement **var** y = x makes a copy of x, so appending 4 to y will not change x — the value of x will still be [1, 2, 3].

Contrast this with the approach to mutability taken by NSArray. NSArray has no mutating methods — to mutate an array, you need an NSMutableArray. But just because you have a non-mutating NSArray reference does *not* mean the array can't be mutated underneath you:

```
let a = NSMutableArray(array: [1,2,3])

// I don't want to be able to mutate b
let b: NSArray = a

// but it can still be mutated - via a
a.insertObject(4, atIndex: 3)
b  // now contains a 4
```

The correct way to write this is to create a copy of a when we introduce b:

```
let a = NSMutableArray(array: [1,2,3])

// I don't want to be able to mutate b
let b = a.copy() as! NSArray

a.insertObject(4, atIndex: 3)
b  // still is [1,2,3]
```

In the example above, it is very clear that we need to make a copy — a is mutable, after all. However, when passing around arrays between methods and functions, this is not always so easy to see, leading to much unnecessary copying.

In Swift, instead of needing two types, there is just one, and mutability is defined by declaring with **var** instead of **let**. But there is no reference sharing — when you declare a second array with **let**, you are guaranteed it will never change.

Making so many copies could be a performance problem, but in practice, all collection types in the Swift standard library are implemented using a technique called copy-on-write, which makes sure the data is only copied when necessary. So in our example, x and y shared internal storage up the point where y.append was called. In the chapter on structs and classes, we'll take a deeper look at value semantics, including how to implement copy-on-write for your own types.

Transforming Arrays

The release of Swift in 2014 led to a galaxy of explanations on the benefits of map, filter , and reduce. Still there are a number of points we want to make, which we will cover briefly.

Map

It's common to need to perform a transformation on every value in the array. Every programmer has written similar code hundreds of times: create a new array, loop over all elements in an existing array, perform an operation on an element, and append the result of that operation to the new array. For example, the following code squares an array of integers:

```
var squared: [Int]  = []
for fib in fibs {
    squared.append(fib * fib)
}
```

Swift arrays have a map method, adopted from the world of functional programming. Here's the exact same operation, using map:

```
let squared = fibs.map { fib in fib  * fib }
```

The version above has three main advantages. It's shorter, of course. There is also less room for error. But more importantly, it's clearer. All the clutter has been removed. Once you are used to seeing and using map everywhere, it acts as a signal — you see map, and you know immediately what is happening: a function is going to be applied to every element, returning a new array of the transformed elements.

The declaration of squared no longer needs to be made with **var**, because we aren't mutating it any longer — it will be delivered out of the map fully formed, so we can declare squared with **let**, if appropriate. And because the type of the contents can be inferred from the function passed to map, squared no longer needs to be explicitly typed.

map isn't hard to write — it's just a question of wrapping up the boilerplate parts of the **for** loop into a generic function. Here's one possible implementation (though in Swift, it's actually an extension of SequenceType, something we'll cover in the chapter on writing generic algorithms):

```
extension Array {
    func map<U>(transform: Element->U) -> [U] {
        var result: [U] = []
        result.reserveCapacity(self.count)
        for x in self {
            result.append(transform(x))
        }
        return result
    }
}
```

Element is the generic placeholder for whatever type the array contains. And U is a new placeholder that can represent the result of the element transformation. The map function itself does not care what Element and U are; they can be anything at all. What they are and what to do to them is left to the caller.

> Really, the signature for this function should be
> **func** map<U>(**@noescape** transform: Element **throws** -> U) **rethrows** -> [U]
> — we'll cover **@noescape** in the functions chapter and **rethrows** in the errors chapter. Neither of these are necessary; they just make it more pleasant for the caller to use.

Parameterizing Behavior with Functions

Even if you're already familiar with map, take a moment and consider the map code. What makes it so general yet so useful?

map manages to separate out the boilerplate functionality — which doesn't vary from call to call — from the functionality that always varies: the logic of how exactly to transform each element. It does this through a parameter the caller supplies: the transformation function.

This pattern of parameterizing behavior is found throughout the standard library. There are 13 separate functions that take a closure that allows the caller to customize the key step:

→ **map** and **flatMap** — how to transform an element

→ **filter** — should an element be included?

→ **reduce** — how to fold an element into an aggregate value

→ **sort** and **lexicographicCompare** — in what order should two elements come?

→ **indexOf** and **contains** — does this element match?

→ **minElement** and **maxElement** — which is the min/max of two elements?

→ **elementsEqual** and **startsWith** — are two elements equivalent?

→ **split** — is this element a separator?

The goal of all these functions is to get rid of the clutter of the uninteresting parts of the code, such as the creation of a new array, the **for** loop over the source data, and the like. Instead, the clutter is replaced with a single word that describes what is being done. This brings the important code – the logic the programmer wants to express – to the forefront.

Several of these functions have a default behavior. sort sorts elements in ascending order when they're comparable, unless you specify otherwise. contains can take a value to check for, so long as the elements are equatable. These help make the code even more readable. Ascending order sort is natural, so the meaning of array.sort() is intuitive. array.indexOf("foo") is clearer than array.indexOf { $0 == "foo" }.

But in every instance, these are just shorthand for the common cases. Elements don't have to be comparable or equatable, and you don't have to compare the whole element — you can sort an array of people by their ages (people.sort { $0.age < $1.age }) or check if the array contains anyone underage (people.contains { $0.age < 18 }). You can also compare some transformation of the element. For example, an admittedly inefficient case-insensitive sort could be performed via
people.sort { $0.name.uppercaseString < $1.name.uppercaseString }.

There are other functions of similar usefulness that would also take a closure to specify their behaviors but aren't in the standard library. You could easily define them yourself (and might like to try):

→ **accumulate** — combine elements into an array of running values (like reduce, but returning an array of each interim combination)

→ **allMatch** and **noneMatch** — test if all or no elements in a sequence match a criterion (can be built with contains, with some carefully placed negation)

→ **count** — count the number of elements that match (similar to filter , but without constructing an array)

→ **indicesOf** — return a list of indices matching a criteria (similar to indexOf, but doesn't stop on the first one)

→ **takeWhile** — filter elements while a predicate returns true, then drop the rest (similar to filter , but with an early exit, and useful for infinite or lazily-computed sequences)

→ **dropWhile** — drop elements until the predicate ceases to be true, and then return the rest (similar to takeWhile, but this returns the inverse)

Many of these we define elsewhere in the book.

You might find yourself writing something that fits a pattern more than a couple of times — something like this:

```
let someArray: [SomeObject] = []

var object: SomeObject?
for oneObject in someArray where oneObject.passesTest() {
    object = oneObject
    break
}
```

If that's the case, then consider writing a short extension to SequenceType. The method findElement wraps this logic. We use a closure to abstract over the part of our **for** loop that varies:

```
extension SequenceType {
    func findElement (match: Generator.Element->Bool) -> Generator.Element? {
        for element in self where match(element) {
            return element
        }
        return nil
    }
}
```

This then allows you to replace your **for** loop with the following:

```
let object = someArray.findElement { $0.passesTest() }
```

This has all the same benefits we described for map. The example with findElement is more readable than the example with the **for** loop; even though the **for** loop is simple, you still have to run the loop through in your head, which is a small mental tax. Using findElement introduces less chance of error, and it allows you to declare object with **let** instead of **var**.

It also works nicely with **guard** — in all likelihood, you're going to terminate a flow early if the element isn't found:

```
guard let object = someSequence.findElement({ $0.passesTest() })
    else { return }
// use object in body of function
```

We'll write more about extending collections and using functions later in the book.

Mutation and Stateful Closures

When iterating over an array, you could use map to perform side effects (e.g. inserting the elements into some lookup table). We don't recommend doing this. Take a look at the following:

```
array.map { item in
  table.insert(item)
}
```

This hides the side effect (the mutation of the lookup table) in a construct that looks like a transformation of the array. If you ever see something like the above, then it is a clear case for using a **for** loop instead of a function like map. There is a function called forEach that would be more appropriate in this case, but it has its own issues. We will look at forEach in a bit.

This is different from deliberately giving the closure *local* state, which is quite a useful technique, and it's what makes closures — functions that can capture and mutate variables outside their scope — so powerful a tool when combined with higher-order functions. For example, the accumulate function described above could be implemented with map and a stateful closure, like this:

```
extension Array {
    func accumulate<U>(initial: U, combine: (U, Element) -> U) -> [U] {
        var running = initial
        return self.map { next in
```

```
            running = combine(running, next)
            return running
        }
    }
}
```

This creates a temporary variable to store the running value and then uses map to create an array of the running value as it progresses:

```
[1,2,3,4]. accumulate(0, combine: +)
```

```
[1,  3,  6,  10]
```

Filter

Another very common operation is to take an array and create a new array that only includes original elements that match a certain condition. The pattern of looping over an array and filtering out the elements that match a condition is captured in the filter method on arrays:

```
fibs. filter  { num in num % 2 == 0 }
```

As a final way of writing this with less code, we can use Swift's built-in notation for shorthand argument names. Instead of naming the num argument, we can write the code above like this:

```
fibs. filter  { $0 % 2 == 0 }
```

For very short closures, this can be more readable. If the closure is more complicated, it's almost always a better idea to name the arguments explicitly, as we have done before. It's really a matter of personal taste — choose whichever is more readable at a glance. A good rule of thumb is this: if the closure fits neatly on one line, shorthand argument names are a good fit.

By combining map and filter , we can easily write a lot of operations on arrays without having to introduce a single intermediate array. The resulting code will become shorter and easier to read. For example, to find all squares under 100 that are even, we could map the range 0..<10 in order to square it, and then we could filter out all odd numbers:

```
(1..<10). map { $0 * $0 }. filter  { $0 % 2 == 0 }
```

```
[4,  16,  36,  64]
```

The implementation of filter looks much the same as map:

```
extension Array {
    func filter (includeElement: Element -> Bool) -> [Element] {
        var result: [Element] = []
        for x in self where includeElement(x) {
            result.append(x)
        }
        return result
    }
}
```

For more on the **where** clause used in the **for** loop, see the optionals chapter.

One quick performance tip: if you ever find yourself writing something like the following, stop!

```
bigarray. filter  { someCondition }.count > 0
```

filter creates a brand new array and processes every element in the array. But this is unnecessary. This code only needs to check if one element matches — in which case, contains will do the job:

```
bigarray.contains { someCondition }
```

This is much faster for two reasons: it doesn't create a whole new array of the filtered elements just to count them, and it exits early, as soon as it matches the first element. Generally, only ever use filter if you want all the results.

Often you want to do something that can be done by contains, but it looks pretty ugly. For example, you can check if every element of a sequence matches a predicate using !sequence.contains { !condition }, but it's much more readable to wrap this in a new function that has a more descriptive name:

```
extension SequenceType {
    public func allMatch(predicate: Generator.Element -> Bool) -> Bool {
        // every element matches a predicate if no element doesn't match it:
        return !self.contains { !predicate($0) }
    }
}
```

Reduce

Both map and filter take an array and produce a new, modified array.
Sometimes, however, you want to combine elements into a new value. For
example, if we want to sum up all the elements, we could write the following
code:

```
var total = 0
for num in fibs {
    total = total + num
}
```

The reduce function takes this pattern and abstracts two parts: the initial
value (in this case, zero), and the function for combining the intermediate
value (total) and the element (num). Using reduce, we can write the same
example, like this:

```
fibs.reduce(0) { total, num in total + num }
```

In Swift, all operators are functions, and we could have also written the same
example like this:

```
fibs.reduce(0, combine: +)
```

The output type of reduce does not have to be the same as the input type. For
example, if we want to convert a list of integers into a string, with each number
followed by a newline, we can do the following:

```
fibs.reduce("") { str, num in str + "\(num)\n" }
```

Here is the implementation:

```
extension Array {
    func reduce<U>(initial: U, combine: (U, Element) -> U) -> U {
        var result = initial
        for x in self {
            result = combine(result,x)
        }
        return result
    }
}
```

Another performance tip: reduce is very flexible, and it's common to see it used to build arrays and perform other operations. For example, you can implement map and filter using only reduce:

```
extension Array {
    func map2<U>(transform: Element -> U) -> [U] {
        return reduce([]) {
            $0 + [transform($1)]
        }
    }

    func filter2 (includeElement: Element -> Bool) -> [Element] {
        return reduce([]) {
            includeElement($1) ? $0 + [$1] : $0
        }
    }
}
```

This is kind of beautiful and has the benefit of not needing those icky imperative for loops. But Swift is not Haskell, and Swift arrays are not lists. What is happening here is that every time, through the combine function, a brand new array is being created by appending the transformed or included element to the previous one. This means that both these implementations are $O(n^2)$, not $O(n)$.

A Flattening Map

Sometimes, you want to map an array using a function, but that function returns another array and not a single element.

For example, let's say we have a function, links, which reads a Markdown file and returns an array containing all the URLs of the links. The function type looks like this:

```
func extractLinks(markdownFile: String) -> [NSURL]
```

If we have a bunch of Markdown files and want to fetch all the links into a single array, we could try to write something like markdownFiles.map(extractLinks). But this returns an array of arrays containing the URLs: one array per file. Now you could just perform the map, get back an array of arrays, and then write another loop to flatten the results into a single array:

```
let nestedArrays = markdownFiles.map(extractLinks)
var links: [NSURL] = []
for array in nestedArrays {
    links.appendContentsOf(array)
}
```

This looks a lot like the **for** loop we used to write (before using map), with all the same shortcomings. So instead, we can use flatMap. It works almost like map, except that it flattens the resulting array too. So markdownFiles.flatMap(links) returns all the URLs in an array of Markdown files as a single array.

The implementation for flatMap looks pretty similar to map, except it takes a function argument that returns an array. It uses appendContentsOf instead of append to flatten the results when appending:

```
extension Array {
    func flatMap<U>(transform: Element -> [U]) -> [U] {
        var result: [U] = []
        for x in self {
            result.appendContentsOf(transform(x))
        }
        return result
    }
}
```

Another great use case for flatMap is when combining elements from different arrays. To get all possible pairs of two arrays, we can flatMap over one array and then map over the other:

```
let suits = ["♠", "♥", "♣", "♦"]
```

```
let ranks = ["J","Q","K","A"]
```

```
let allCombinations = suits.flatMap { suit in
    ranks.map { rank in
        (suit, rank)
    }
}
```

Iteration using forEach

There is also a function, forEach, available on arrays (it is defined on SequenceType, to which Array conforms). This works almost like a **for** loop; however, there are some subtle differences. We can replace a **for** loop with forEach quite mechanically:

```
for element in [1,2,3] {
  print(element)
}

[1,2,3]. forEach { element in
  print(element)
}
```

This can be very useful if the action you want to perform is a single function call on each element in a collection. Passing a function or method directly to forEach instead of a closure expression can lead to clear and concise code. For example, if you're inside a view controller and want to add an array of subviews, you can just do theViews.forEach(view.addSubview).

Because forEach is implemented using a closure, you might get unexpected behavior when you rewrite a **for** loop that has a **return** in it. For example, consider the following, which is written using a **for** loop with a **where** condition:

```
extension Array where Element: Equatable {
    func indexOf(element: Element) -> Int? {
        for idx in self.indices where self[idx] == element {
            return idx
        }
        return nil
    }
}
```

Because we cannot directly write a **where**, we might (incorrectly) rewrite this using filter :

```
extension Array where Element: Equatable {
    func indexOf_foreach(element: Element) -> Int? {
        self.indices. filter { idx in
            self[idx] == element
        }. forEach { idx in
            return idx
```

```
        }
        return nil
    }
}
```

The **return** inside the forEach closure does not return out of the outer function: it only returns out of the closure itself. In some cases, the compiler generates a warning when doing this, but not always. At the time of writing, no warning is generated for this code.

Also, consider the following simple example:

```
(1..<10). forEach { number in
    print(number)
    if  number > 2 { return }
}
```

If you are reading the code above, it is not obvious that this prints out all the numbers in the input array. The **return** is not breaking the loop, but rather returning from the closure.

In some cases, such as the addSubview example above, forEach can be nicer. However, because of the non-obvious behavior with **return**, we recommend against most uses of forEach. Instead, just use a regular **for** loop.

Array Types

Slices

Instead of accessing an element of an array by subscript (e.g. fibs [0]), we can also access a range of elements by subscript. For example, to get all but the first element of an array, we can do the following:

```
fibs [1..< fibs . endIndex]
```

This gets us a slice of the array starting at the second element, including the last element. The type of the result is ArraySlice, not Array. The slice type is a *view* on arrays. It is backed by the original array, yet it provides a view on just the slice. This makes certain the array doesn't need to get copied. The ArraySlice type has the same methods defined as Array does, so you can use them as if they were arrays. If you do need to convert them into an array, you can just construct a new array out of the slice:

```
Array(fibs [1..< fibs.endIndex])
```

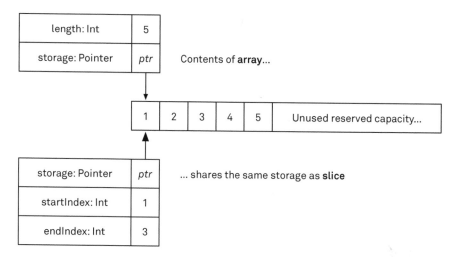

Figure 3.1: Array Slices

Bridging

Swift arrays can bridge to Objective-C. They can also be used with C, but we will cover that in a later chapter. Conversion can happen in two directions: a Swift array can (most of the time) be converted to an NSArray, and an NSArray can (always) be converted to a Swift array.

To create an NSArray out of a Swift array, the elements have to be convertible to AnyObjects. A Swift object is convertible to an AnyObject, and a limited number of structural types can also be converted to AnyObjects. For example, Int and Bool can convert automatically to an NSNumber. Other types, such as CGPoint (which could convert to an NSValue), don't work. Luckily, the compiler will tell you when it cannot figure out the automatic bridging.

For example, if we create a Swift array of integers, then convert it into an NSArray and check the type, we can verify that the integers get converted into NSNumbers:

```
var x = [1, 2, 3]
let z: NSArray = x
z[0] is NSNumber
```

true

Dictionaries and Sets

Another key data structure in Swift is that of dictionaries. A dictionary contains keys with corresponding values, and each key is present in the dictionary once. As an example, we will build some infrastructure for a settings screen. Before we start, we will first define the Settings protocol. Any type can conform to this by providing a UIView that renders the setting. In the case of a String, a UITextField is returned, and for booleans, a UISwitch is returned:

```
protocol Setting {
    func settingsView() -> UIView
}
```

We can now define a dictionary of keys and values. The keys are the names of the settings, and the values are, well, the values of the settings. We define the dictionary with **let**, which means that we can never modify it:

```
let defaultSettings: [String:Setting] = [
    "Airplane Mode": true,
    "Name": "My iPhone",
]
```

To get the value of a setting, we need to use subscripting (for example, defaultSettings["Name"]). Dictionary lookup always returns an *optional value*. When the value doesn't exist, it returns **nil** instead of a crash. Contrast this with arrays, which crash. The reasoning behind this difference in interfaces is that dictionaries are sparse (and will often not contain a value for a key), whereas array indexing is expected to succeed. We will go into more detail about this tradeoff at the end of this chapter. Swift makes a distinction between values that can be **nil** (optional values) and values that can never be **nil** (normal values). We will talk more about that in the chapter on optionals.

Mutation

Just like with arrays, dictionaries defined using **let** are immutable: no entries can be added or changed. And just like with arrays, we can define a mutable variant using **var**. To remove a value from a dictionary, we can just set it to **nil**.

If we want to take an immutable dictionary and make changes to it, we have to make a copy:

```
var localizedSettings = defaultSettings
localizedSettings["Name"] = "Mein iPhone"
localizedSettings["Do Not Disturb"] = true
```

```
let oldName = localizedSettings.updateValue("My iPhone", forKey: "Name")
// "Mein iPhone"
```

There are other built-in collections as well. There is Set, which can be bridged to NSSet. There's Range, which describes a range of consecutive index values. There's Repeat, which is a collection that contains the same value multiple times. We could even consider Optional, a collection with a maximum of one element.

Some Useful Dictionary Extensions

One useful extension that we can write ourselves is merging two dictionaries. For example, when displaying the settings to the user, we want to merge those with the settings that the user has stored. To read the settings, there is the function storedSettings:

```
func storedSettings() -> [String:Setting] {
```

We can add a merge function on dictionaries. Dictionaries conform to the SequenceType protocol, and by making the method generic, we can merge in dictionaries, but also any other type that conforms to SequenceType and can generate (Key,Value) pairs:

```
extension Dictionary {
    mutating func merge<S: SequenceType
        where S.Generator.Element == (Key,Value)>(other: S) {
        for (k, v) in other {
            self[k] = v
        }
    }
}
```

We can use this to merge our persisted settings into the default settings:

```
var settings = defaultSettings
settings.merge(storedSettings())
```

Another interesting extension is creating a dictionary from a sequence of (Key, Value) pairs. We can start with an empty dictionary and then just merge in the sequence. This makes use of the merge method defined above to do the heavy lifting:

```
extension Dictionary {
    init<S: SequenceType
        where S.Generator.Element == (Key,Value)>(_ sequence: S) {
        self = [:]
        self.merge(sequence)
    }
}
```

```
// All alarms are turned off by default
let defaultAlarms = (1..<5).map { ("Alarm \($0)", false) }
let alarmsDictionary = Dictionary(defaultAlarms)
```

Finally, a last useful extension is a map over the values of the dictionary. Because Dictionary is already a sequence, there is a map function that produces an array. However, sometimes we want to keep a dictionary but only map the values. If we want a dictionary containing the keys, and for every value, their views, we can write a mapValues method and use it (whereas mapping the entire dictionary is problematic, as it may generate duplicate keys):

```
extension Dictionary {
    func mapValues<NewValue>(transform: Value -> NewValue)
        -> [Key:NewValue] {
        return Dictionary<Key, NewValue>(map { (key, value) in
            return (key, transform(value))
        })
    }
}
```

```
let keysAndViews = settings.mapValues { $0.settingsView() }
```

Using Sets Inside Closures

Swift also includes the Set type in the standard library. A Set is an unordered collection of elements, with each element appearing only once. Set conforms to the ArrayLiteralConvertible protocol, which means that we can initialize it like this:

```
let mySet: Set<Int> = [1, 2, 2]
mySet

[2, 1]
```

Dictionaries and sets can be very useful data structures to use inside your functions, even when you're not exposing them to the caller. For example, if we want to write an extension on SequenceType to get all the unique elements out of the sequence, we could easily just put the elements inside a Set and return the contents of that set. However, that will not be *stable*: because a *Set* has no defined order, the input elements might get reordered in the result. Instead, we can write an extension that maintains the order by using a Set inside the method:

```
extension SequenceType where Generator.Element: Hashable {
    func unique() -> [Generator.Element] {
        var seen: Set<Generator.Element> = []
        return filter {
            if seen.contains($0) {
                return false
            } else {
                seen.insert($0)
                return true
            }
        }
    }
}
```

The method above allows us to find all unique elements in a sequence while still maintaining the original order. Inside the closure that we pass to filter , we refer to the variable seen: we can access and modify it within the closure. In the chapter on functions, we will look at this technique in more detail.

Collection Protocols

Looking at the definition of arrays, dictionaries, and sets, we can see they all conform to the CollectionType protocol. Digging deeper, we can see that CollectionType is a protocol that conforms to SequenceType. Taking another step, we can see that sequences use a GeneratorType to serve up their elements. To understand what's going on, we will start at the lowest level and work our way back up. In short, a generator encodes the knowledge needed to produce new values. A sequence encodes how to create a generator. A collection adds random access to that functionality.

Generators

The GeneratorType protocol is defined in two parts. First of all, it requires that any type conforming to the protocol has an associated Element type. For example, in the case of String.CharacterView, the element type is Character. In the case of an array, the element type is the same as the elements of the array. In the case of dictionaries, the element type is defined as (Key, Value), a pair containing both the key and the value.

The second part of the GeneratorType defines the function next, which returns an optional value of type Element. Whenever you have a value that conforms to the GeneratorType, you can keep calling next until you get a nil value. Taking these two parts, we end up with the following definition:

```
protocol GeneratorType {
    associatedtype Element
    mutating func next() -> Element?
}
```

The **associatedtype** definition in the protocol means that, in order to conform to the protocol, we need to specify an *associated type* as well (either explicitly, with a **associatedtype**, or implicitly).

The documentation tells us that we are free to copy values that are generators, but that a generator is single pass: we can only loop over it once. Therefore, generators do *not* have value semantics, so we will implement them as **class**es rather than **struct**s. (For a more in-depth look at the differences between structs and classes, see the structs and classes chapter.) The simplest generator we can write is one that just returns a constant value every time it gets asked for the next value:

```
class ConstantGenerator: GeneratorType {
    typealias Element = Int
    func next() -> Element? {
        return 1
    }
}
```

Alternatively, we could have specified the Element type implicitly by providing the following definition of ConstantGenerator:

```
class ConstantGenerator: GeneratorType {
    func next() -> Int? {
        return 1
    }
}
```

To use it, we can construct a new instance of ConstantGenerator and iterate over it using a **while** loop, printing an endless stream of ones:

```
var generator = ConstantGenerator()
while let x = generator.next() {
    // Use x
}
```

If we want to generate a list of Fibonacci numbers (starting with zero), we can track additional state in our generator: we store the upcoming two numbers. The next function then returns the first number in the state and updates the state for the consecutive call. This also produces an "infinite" stream of numbers (this keeps producing numbers until we reach integer overflow; then the program crashes):

```
class FibsGenerator: GeneratorType {
    var state = (0, 1)
    func next() -> Int? {
        let upcomingNumber = state.0
        state = (state.1, state.0 + state.1)
        return upcomingNumber
    }
}
```

An example of a generator that produces a finite stream is the following PrefixGenerator, which generates all prefixes of a string (including the string itself). It starts by setting the offset to startIndex, and with each call of next, it tries to increment the offset and returns the substring from the beginning until the offset:

```
class PrefixGenerator: GeneratorType {
    let string: String
    var offset: String.Index

    init (string: String) {
```

```
        self.string = string
        offset = string.startIndex
    }

    func next() -> String? {
        guard offset < string.endIndex else { return nil }
        offset = offset.successor()
        return string[string.startIndex..<offset]
    }
}
```

(string[string.startIndex..<offset] is a slicing operation that returns the substring between the start and the offset — we'll talk more about slicing later.)

All the generators above can be iterated over exactly once. If we want to iterate again, we have to create a new generator. This is also encoded in the definition: they are classes and not structs. They don't get copied when shared; instead, they get passed by reference.

Generators and Value Semantics

The Swift standard library AnyGenerator type has a bit of a checkered past. Originally there was a type, GeneratorOf, that did something similar and was a struct. In Swift 2.0, when AnyGenerator replaced GeneratorOf, it became a class, but in Swift 2.2, it switched back to being a struct. But it is a struct that does *not* have value semantics, because it stores the generator it wraps in a box reference type. Generators, being inherently stateful things, fit a little awkwardly into the Swift standard library, which, for the most part, contains structs with value semantics.

To illustrate the difference, suppose you take a simple generator, like one for a stride, and call next a few times:

```
let seq = 0.stride(through: 9, by: 1)
var g1 = seq.generate()
g1.next()  // returns 0
g1.next()  // returns 1
// g1 is now a generator ready to return 2
```

Now, say you take a copy of this generator:

```
var g2 = g1
```

Both the original and the copy are now separate and independent, and both return 3 when you call next:

```
g1.next()  // returns 2
g1.next()  // returns 3
g2.next()  // returns 2
g2.next()  // returns 3
```

This is because StrideThroughGenerator, a pretty simple struct, has value semantics.

As mentioned above, AnyGenerator does *not* have value semantics, even though it is a struct. To see why, we create an AnyGenerator that wraps g1:

```
var g3 = AnyGenerator(g1)
```

The above captures g1 by reference (using some techniques that we will cover in later chapters). Any calls to next on either g1 or g3 increment the same underlying generator instance:

```
g3.next()  // returns 4
g1.next()  // returns 5
g3.next()  // returns 6
g3.next()  // returns 7
```

Obviously, this could lead to bugs. It's also a little surprising, so chances are high that this behavior might change in the future. We have one simple rule to avoid heartache from all of this: try to avoid making copies of generators. Always create a fresh generator when you need one. This leads us to the next type in the hierarchy.

Sequences

Because iterating multiple times is very common, there is SequenceType. The SequenceType protocol builds on top of GeneratorType. It asks us to specify the type of the generator and a function that creates a new generator:

```
protocol SequenceType {
    associatedtype Generator: GeneratorType
    func generate() -> Generator
}
```

For example, to allow iterating over the prefixes more than once, we can wrap the PrefixGenerator in a sequence. We do not specify the GeneratorType explicitly, but instead let the compiler derive it from the type of the generate method:

```
struct PrefixSequence: SequenceType {
    let string: String

    func generate() -> PrefixGenerator {
        return PrefixGenerator(string: string)
    }
}
```

Now we have encoded the knowledge of how to create a PrefixGenerator for a specific string. And once we have implemented the SequenceType protocol, we can use a **for** loop to iterate over all the prefixes:

```
for prefix in PrefixSequence(string: "Hello") {
    print(prefix)
}
```

This is how a **for** loop works under the hood: the compiler creates a fresh generator for the sequence and calls next on that generator repeatedly, until **nil** is returned. **for** is essentially shorthand for the following:

```
var generator = PrefixSequence(string: "Hello").generate()
while let prefix = generator.next() {
    print(prefix)
}
```

If we think about the implementation of Array, we can easily imagine what a generator and a sequence would look like, and likewise for dictionaries, sets, and strings. If we were to implement our own data structure, we now know how to make it work in a **for** loop: we ensure it conforms to SequenceType, and then we're set.

In the chapter on protocols, we will have a look at how protocols and associated types work, along with their limitations.

Function-Based Generators and Sequences

There is an even easier way to make generators and sequences. Instead of creating a custom class, we can also use the built-in AnyGenerator and

AnySequence types, which take a function as a parameter. For example, we
could have also defined the Fibonacci generator like this, without the need of
an intermediate **class:**

```
func fibGenerator() -> AnyGenerator<Int> {
    var state = (0, 1)
    return AnyGenerator {
        let result = state.0
        state = (state.1, state.0 + state.1)
        return result
    }
}
```

The AnyGenerator initializer takes another function as parameter (the body
function). In this case, we have moved the state outside of that function, and
every time it gets called, the state changes. This works because the state
variable gets captured by the block.

Now, creating a sequence out of this is even easier:

```
let fibSequence = AnySequence(fibGenerator)
```

In the standard library, the SequenceType protocol is used for types that can
be iterated over in a **for** loop. However, there is no constraint that this is a
non-destructive operation: for that, there is the CollectionType protocol. When
using a type that conforms to SequenceType, we always need to look at the
documentation to know whether or not iteration is destructive. For example,
computing the Fibonacci numbers is not destructive (we can always
recompute it), but reading lines directly from the standard input is a
destructive operation (once we have read a line, there is no way to read it
again). Even though we can make a SequenceType for both these operations,
we still need to be careful when iterating in a **for** loop.

> If you find generators and sequences and the relationship between the
> two odd, you are not alone! Many people have expressed confusion
> about these two types and why there is a need for both of them. The
> Swift team has mentioned on the evolution mailing lists that in many
> ways, these types work the way they do because of limitations of
> the existing type system. We expect the way SequenceType and
> GeneratorType interact to change further with Swift 3.0 and beyond.

Collections

A collection builds on top of a sequence and adds repeatable iteration and access to the elements via an index.

To demonstrate how collections in Swift work, we'll implement one of our own. Probably the most useful container type not present in the Swift standard library is a queue. Swift arrays are able to easily be used as stacks, with append to push and popLast to pop. But they're not ideal to use as queues. You could use push combined with removeAtIndex(0), but removing anything other than the last element of an array is an $O(n)$ operation — because arrays are held in contiguous memory, every element has to shuffle down to fill the gap (unlike popping the last element, which can be done in constant time).

Designing a Protocol for Queues

Before we implement a queue, maybe we should define what we mean by it. A good way to do this is to define a protocol that describes what a queue is. Let's try the following definition:

```
/// A type that can `enqueue` and `dequeue` elements.
protocol QueueType {
    /// The type of elements held in `self`.
    associatedtype Element
    /// Enqueue `newElement` to `self`.
    mutating func enqueue(newElement: Element)
    /// Dequeue an element from `self`.
    mutating func dequeue() -> Element?
}
```

As simple as this is, it says a lot about what our definition of queue is: it's defined generically. It can contain any type, represented by the associated type Element. It imposes no restrictions on what Element is — just that what the queue contains must be defined as a specific type.

It's important to note that the comments above the methods are as much a part of a protocol as the actual method names and types. Here, what we don't say tells us as much as what we do: there is no guarantee of the complexity of enqueue or dequeue. We could have said, for example, that both should operate in constant ($O(1)$) time. This would give users constraining to this protocol a good idea of the performance characteristics of *any* kind of queue implementing this protocol. But it would rule out data structures, such as priority queues, that might have an $O(log_n)$ enqueueing operation.

It also doesn't offer a peek operation to check without dequeuing, which means it could be used to represent a queue that didn't have such a feature (such as, say, a queue interface over an operating system or networking call that could only pop, not peek). It doesn't specify whether the two operations are thread-safe. It doesn't specify the queue is a collection (though the implementation we're about to write will be).

It doesn't even specify that it's a FIFO queue — it could be a LIFO queue, and we could conform Array to it, with append for enqueue and dequeue implemented via isEmpty/popLast.

Arrays and Optionals

Speaking of which, here *is* something the protocol specifies: like Array's popLast (and unlike its removeLast), dequeue returns an optional. If the queue is empty, it returns **nil**. Otherwise, it removes and returns the last element.

This is slightly different to the removeLast method of Array, which will trap (return a fatal error and exit your program) if you call it when the array is empty. popLast() is essentially equivalent to isEmpty ? **nil** : removeLast(). Which one you'd want to use depends on your use case. When you're using the array as a stack, you'll probably always want to combine checking for empty and removing the last entry. On the other hand, you might use an array for something more complex than a simple stack. Through invariants, you might already know whether or not the stack is empty, in which case, dealing with the optional is fiddly. For queues, we only provide one version, dequeue, because this is likely the most common use case for queues.

Another example of this tradeoff, where the user is expected to take care to check that preconditions are met before calling various methods, is the **subscript** on Array that takes an index. Fetch the element at index 9, and you'd better be sure the array has at least 10 elements in it.

The reason for this is mainly driven by how array indices are used. It's pretty rare in Swift to actually need to calculate an index:

→ Want to iterate over the collection?
  for x **in** collection

→ Want to iterate over all but the first element of a collection?
```
for x in collection.dropFirst()
```

→ Want to iterate over all but the last 5 of a collection?
```
for x in collection.dropLast(5)
```

→ Want to iterate over all the indices of a collection?
```
for idx in collection.indices
```

→ Want to number all the elements in a collection?
```
for (num, element) in collection.enumerate()
```

→ Want to find the location of a specific element in a collection?
```
if let idx = collection.indexOf { someMatchingLogic($0) }
```

→ Want to transform all the elements in a collection?
```
array.map { someTransformation($0) }
```

→ Want to fetch only the elements matching a specific criterion?
```
collection. filter  { someCriteria($0) }
```

Traditional C-style **for** loops are slated for removal in Swift 3.0. If in Swift 2.0 you are using **for var** idx = 0;idx < array.count;++i, you will have to convert them to **while** loops instead. But there is usually a clearer way to write your loop, and manually fiddling with indices is a rich seam of bugs to mine, so it's often best avoided. And if it can't be, well, we'll see in the generics chapter that it's easy enough to write a new reusable general function that does what you need and in which you can wrap your carefully tested index calculations.

But sometimes you do have to use an index. And with array indices, the expectation is that when you do, you'll have thought very carefully about the logic behind the index calculation. So to have to unwrap the value of a subscript operation is probably overkill — it means you don't trust your code. But chances are you do trust your code, so you'll probably resort to force-unwrapping the result, because you *know* that the index must be valid. This is a) annoying, and b) a bad habit to get into. When force-unwrapping becomes routine, eventually you're going to slip up and force-unwrap something you don't mean to. So to avoid this habit becoming routine, arrays don't give you the option.

removeLast versus popLast is less clear-cut. When using an array as a stack, you might often want to pop the last element, so long as the array isn't empty:

```
while !array.isEmpty {
    // must be guarded by !.isEmpty()
```

```
    let top = array.removeLast()
    // process top entry
}
```

By making dequeue an optional, you gain the ability to do this operation on one short line, along with the safety of not being able to get it wrong:

```
while let x = q.dequeue() {
    // process queue element
}
```

Whether or not these benefits outweigh the inconvenience of having to unwrap when you already know the collection *can't* be empty is up to you.

A Queue Implementation

Now that we've defined what a queue is, let's implement it.

Below is a very simple queue, with just enqueue and dequeue methods implemented on top of a couple of arrays.

Since we have named our queue's generic placeholder Element, the same name as the required associated type, there is no need to define it. It is not necessary to name it Element though — the placeholder is just an arbitrary name of your choosing. If it were named Foo, you could either define **typealias** Element = Foo, or leave Swift to infer it implicitly from the return types of the enqueue and dequeue implementations:

```
/// An efficient variable-size FIFO queue of elements of type `Element`
struct Queue<Element>: QueueType {
    private var left: [Element]
    private var right: [Element]

    init () {
        left = []
        right = []
    }

    /// Add an element to the back of the queue in O(1).
    mutating func enqueue(element: Element) {
        right.append(element)
    }
```

```
/// Removes front of the queue in amortized O(1).
/// Returns nil in case of an empty queue.
mutating func dequeue() -> Element? {
    guard !(left.isEmpty && right.isEmpty) else { return nil }

    if left.isEmpty {
        left = right.reverse()
        right.removeAll(keepCapacity: true)
    }
    return left.removeLast()
}
}
```

This implementation uses a technique of simulating a queue through the use of two stacks (two regular Swift arrays). As elements are enqueued, they are pushed onto the "right" stack. Then when elements are dequeued, they are popped off the "left" stack, where they are held in reverse order. When the left stack is empty, the right stack is reversed onto the left stack.

You might find the claim that the dequeue operation is $O(1)$ slightly surprising. Surely it contains a reverse call that is $O(n)$? But while this is true, the overall *amortized* time to pop an item is constant — over a large number of pushes and pops, the time taken for them all is constant, even though the time for individual pushes or pops might not be.

The key to why this is lies in understanding how often the reverse happens and on how many elements. One technique to analyze this is the "banker's methodology." Imagine that each time you put an element on the queue, you pay a token into the bank. Single enqueue, single token, so constant cost. Then when it comes time to reverse the right-hand stack onto the left-hand one, you have a token in the bank for every element enqueued and you use those tokens to pay for the reversal. The account never goes into debit, so you never spend more than you paid.

This kind of reasoning is good for explaining why the "amortized" cost of an operation over time is constant, even though individual calls might not be. The same kind of justification can be used to explain why appending an element to an array in Swift is a constant time operation. When the array runs out of storage, it needs to allocate bigger storage and copy all its existing elements into it. But since the storage size doubles with each reallocation, you can use the same "append an element, pay a token, double the array size, spend all the tokens but no more" argument.

Conforming to CollectionType

It is not always easy to see how to conform to a protocol in Swift. When we look at CollectionType, we can see that the protocol extends from Indexable and SequenceType. At the time of writing, the protocol also has two associated types and nine methods. However, both associated types have a default, and many of the methods have a default implementation.

The default value for the Generator associated type is an IndexingGenerator<**Self**>. We can override this, but if we choose to stay with the default, we get the generate() implementation for free, because it is defined in a protocol extension:

```
extension CollectionType where Generator == IndexingGenerator<Self> {
    public func generate() -> IndexingGenerator<Self>
}
```

All the other methods in CollectionType also have a default implementation. The only thing we need to do is implement the requirements from the Indexable protocol: startIndex, endIndex, and a subscript that takes an index and returns the element for that index. If we implement these three requirements, we can make our types conform to CollectionType.

We now have a container that can enqueue and dequeue. To turn it into a collection, Queue needs to conform to CollectionType, like so:

```
extension Queue: CollectionType {
    var startIndex: Int { return 0 }
    var endIndex: Int { return left.count + right.count }

    subscript(idx: Int) -> Element {
        precondition((0..<endIndex).contains(idx), "Index out of bounds")
        if idx < left.endIndex {
            return left[left.count - idx.successor()]
        } else {
            return right[idx - left.count]
        }
    }
}
```

CollectionType defines an Index associated type, but just like with Element, Swift can infer it from the method and property definitions. We follow the same convention as arrays in returning a non-optional value and trapping on invalid indices. Note that since the indexing returns elements from the front first, Queue.first returns the next item that will be dequeued (so it serves as a kind of "peek").

With just a handful of lines, Queue now conforms to CollectionType (and, through that, to SequenceType too). Queues now have more than 40 methods and properties at their disposal:

```
var q = Queue<String>()
for x in ["1", "2", "foo", "3"] {
    q.enqueue(x)
}

// you can now for...in over queues
for s in q { print(s) }        // prints 1 2 foo 3

// pass queues to methods that take sequences
q.joinWithSeparator(",")       // "1,2,foo,3"
let a = Array(q)               // a = ["1", "2", "foo", "3]

// call methods that extend SequenceType
q.map { $0.uppercaseString }   // ["1", "2", "FOO", "3"]
q.flatMap { Int($0) }          // [1,2,3]
q. filter {                     // ["foo"]
    $0.characters.count > 1
}

// call methods that extend CollectionType
q.isEmpty                      // false
q.count                        // 4
q. first                       // "1"
q.last                         // "3"
```

We can now iterate over the queue using a **for** loop, sort the elements, map the elements, reduce the elements, and use any of the other methods that are defined by SequenceType.

Conforming to ArrayLiteralConvertible

When implementing a collection like this, it's nice to implement ArrayLiteralConvertible too. This will allow users to create a queue using the familiar [value1, value2, etc] syntax. This can be done easily, like so:

```
extension Queue: ArrayLiteralConvertible {
    init(arrayLiteral elements: Element...) {
        self.left = elements.reverse()
        self.right = []
    }
}
```

For our queue logic, we want to reverse the elements to have them ready for use on the left-hand buffer. Of course, we could just copy the elements to the right-hand buffer, but since we're going to be copying elements anyway, it's more efficient to copy them in reverse order so that they don't need reversing later when they're dequeued.

Now queues can be created easily from literals:

```
let q: Queue = [1,2,3]
```

It's important here to underline the difference between literals and types in Swift. [1, 2, 3] here is *not* an array. It's an "array literal" — something that can be used to create any type that conforms to ArrayLiteralConvertible. This particular literal contains other literals — integer literals — which can create any type that conforms to IntegerLiteralConvertible.

These literals have "default" types — types that Swift will assume if you don't specify. So array literals default to Array, integer literals default to Int, float literals default to Double, and string literals default to String. But this only occurs in the absence of you specifying otherwise. For example, the queue declared above is a queue of integers, but it could have been a queue of some other integer type:

```
let byteQueue: Queue<Int8> = [1,2,3]
```

Often, the type of the literal can be inferred from the context. For example, this is what it looks like if a function takes a type that can be created from literals:

```
func takesSetOfFloats(floats: Set<Float>) {
    // ...
}
```

```
// this literal will be interpreted as Set<Float>, not as Array<Int>
takesSetOfFloats([1, 2, 3])
```

Conforming to RangeReplaceableCollectionType

The next logical protocol for queues to adhere to is
RangeReplaceableCollectionType. This protocol requires three things:

→ A reserveCapacity method — we used this when implementing map.
Since the number of final elements is known up front, it can avoid
unnecessary element copies when the array reallocates its storage. The
collection is not required to actually do anything when asked to reserve
capacity; it can just ignore it.

→ An empty initializer — this is useful in generic functions, as it allows a
function to create new empty collections of the same type.

→ A replaceRange function — this takes a range to replace and a collection
to replace it with.

RangeReplaceableCollectionType is a great example of the power of protocol
extensions. You implement one uber flexible method, replaceRange, and from
that comes a whole bunch of derived methods for free:

→ append and appendContentsOf — replace endIndex..<endIndex
(i.e. replace the empty range at the end) with the new element/elements

→ removeAtIndex and removeRange — replace i ... i or subRange with an
empty collection

→ splice and insertAtIndex — replace atIndex..<atIndex (i.e. replace the
empty range at that point in the array) with a new element/elements

→ removeAll — replace startIndex..<endIndex with an empty collection

If a specific collection type can use knowledge about its implementation to
perform these functions more efficiently, it can provide custom versions that
will take priority over the default protocol extension ones.

We chose to have a very simple inefficient implementation. As we stated when
defining the data type, the left stack holds the element in reverse order. In
order to have a simple implementation, we need to reverse all the elements
and combine them into the right array so that we can replace the entire range
at once. Even the most efficient implementation would still be $O(n)$, but with a
much lower constant factor:

```
extension Queue: RangeReplaceableCollectionType {
    mutating func reserveCapacity(n: Int) {
```

```
        return
    }

    mutating func replaceRange
        <C: CollectionType where C.Generator.Element == Element>
        (subRange: Range<Int>, with newElements: C)
    {
        right = left.reverse() + right
        left.removeAll(keepCapacity: true)
        right.replaceRange(subRange, with: newElements)
    }
}
```

You might like to try implementing a more efficient version, which looks at whether or not the replaced range spans the divide between the left and right stacks.

There was no need to implement **init** in the above example, since we already implemented it when we defined the Queue struct, and Queue chooses to ignore reserveCapacity. With this implementation, appendContentsOf and append add to the back of the queue, which seems logical.

Indices

Up until now, we've been using integers as the index into our collections. Array does, and (with a bit of manipulation) our Queue type does too.

But not all indices are random access, and not all random-access indices are integers. The base minimum a type needs to conform to in Swift to be an index on a collection is ForwardIndexType, which only has two requirements: it needs a successor method, and it needs to conform to Equatable, which means it needs an == operator.

To show this, let's implement the most basic forward-only access collection of all, a singly linked list. To do this, we'll first demonstrate another way of implementing data structures using an indirect enum.

A linked list node is one of either two things: a node with a value and a reference to the next node, or a node indicating the end of the list. We can define it like this:

/// A simple linked list enum

```
enum List<Element> {
    case End
    indirect case Node(Element, next: List<Element>)
}
```

The use of the **indirect** keyword here indicates that the compiler should represent this value as a reference. Swift enums are value types. This means they hold their values directly in the variable, rather than the variable holding a reference to the location of the value. This has many benefits, as we'll see in the structs and classes chapter, but it also means they cannot contain a reference to themselves. The **indirect** keyword allows an enum case to be held as a reference and thus hold a reference to itself.

We prepend another element to the list by creating a new node, with the next: value set to the current node. To make this a little easier, we can create a method for it:

```
extension List {
    /// Return a new list by prepending a node with value `x` to the
    /// front of a list.
    func cons(x: Element) -> List {
        return .Node(x, next: self)
    }
}
```

```
// a 3-element list, of (3 2 1)
let l = List<Int>.End.cons(1).cons(2).cons(3)
```

We name this prepending method cons, because that is the name of the operation in LISP (it's short for "construct," and adding elements onto the front of the list is sometimes called "consing").

This list type has an interesting property: it is "persistent." The nodes are immutable — once created, you cannot change them. Consing another element onto the list doesn't copy the list; it just gives you a new node that links onto the front of the existing list.

This means two lists can share a tail:

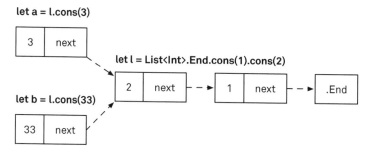

Figure 3.2: List Sharing

The immutability of the list is key here. If you could change the list (say, remove the last entry, or update the element held in a node), then this sharing would be a problem — a might change the list, and the change would affect b.

This list is a stack, with consing as a push, and unwrapping the next element a pop. As we've mentioned before, arrays are also stacks. Let's define a common protocol for stacks, as we did with queues:

```
/// A LIFO stack type with constant-time push and pop operations
protocol StackType {
    /// The type of element held stored in the stack
    associatedtype Element

    /// Pushes `x` onto the top of `self`
    ///
    /// - Complexity: Amortized O(1).
    mutating func push(x: Element)

    /// Removes the topmost element of `self` and returns it,
    /// or `nil` if `self` is empty.
    ///
    /// - Complexity: O(1)
    mutating func pop() -> Element?
}
```

We've been a bit more proscriptive in the documentation comments about what it means to conform to Stack, including giving some minimum performance guarantees.

Array can be made to conform to Stack, like this:

```
extension Array: StackType {
    mutating func push(x: Element) {
        append(x)
    }

    mutating func pop() -> Element? {
        return popLast()
    }
}
```

So can List:

```
extension List: StackType {
    mutating func push(x: Element) {
        self = self.cons(x)
    }

    mutating func pop() -> Element? {
        switch self {
        case .End: return nil
        case let .Node(x, next: xs):
            self = xs
            return x
        }
    }
}
```

But didn't we just say that the list had to be immutable for the persistence to work? How can it have mutating methods?

These mutating methods do not change the list. Instead, they just change the part of the list the variables refer to:

```
var stack = List<Int>.End.cons(1).cons(2).cons(3)
var a = stack
var b = stack

a.pop() // 3
a.pop() // 2
a.pop() // 1

stack.pop() // 3
stack.push(4)

b.pop() // 3
```

```
b.pop() // 2
b.pop() // 1

stack.pop() // 4
stack.pop() // 2
stack.pop() // 1
```

This shows us the difference between values and variables. The nodes of the list are values; they cannot change. A node of three and a reference to the next node cannot become some other value. It will be that value forever, just like the number three cannot change. It just is. Just because these values in question are structures with references to each other doesn't make them less value-like.

A variable a, on the other hand, can change the value it holds. It can be set to hold a value of an indirect reference to any of the nodes, or to the value End. But changing a doesn't change these nodes; it just changes which node a refers to.

This is what these mutating methods on structs do — they take an implicit **inout** argument of self, and they can change the value **self** holds. This doesn't change the list, but rather which part of the list the variable currently represents. We'll cover **inout** in more detail in the chapter on functions, and we'll cover mutating methods in more detail in the chapter on structs and classes.

In this sense, through **indirect**, the variables have become iterators into the list:

`let a = List<Int>.End.cons(1).cons(2).cons(3)`

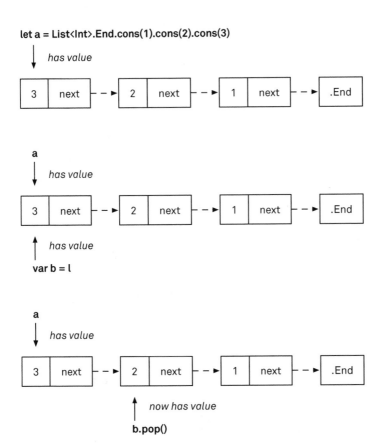

Figure 3.3: List Iteration

You can, of course, declare your variables with **let** instead of **var**, in which case the variables will be constant (i.e. you can't change the value they hold once set). But **let** is about the variables, not the values. Values are constant by definition.

Now this is all just a logical model of how things work. In reality, the nodes are actually places in memory that point to each other. And they take up space, which we want back if it's no longer needed. Swift uses automated reference counting (ARC) to manage this and frees the memory for the nodes that are not used anymore:

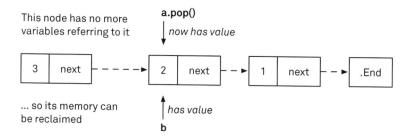

Figure 3.4: List Memory Management

We'll discuss ARC in more detail in the structs and classes chapter.

Conforming List to SequenceType

Since list variables are iterators into the list, this means you can use them to conform List to SequenceType:

```
extension List: SequenceType {
    func generate() -> AnyGenerator<Element> {
        // declare a variable to capture that tracks progression through the list:
        var current = self
        return AnyGenerator {
            // next() will pop, returning nil when the list is empty:
            current.pop()
        }
    }
}
```

And, to make things easier, you can conform them to ArrayLiteralConvertible as well:

```
extension List: ArrayLiteralConvertible {
    init (arrayLiteral elements: Element...) {
        self = elements.reverse().reduce(.End) { $0.cons($1) }
    }
}
```

Now you can use lists with for ... in:

```
let l: List = ["1", "2", "3"]
for x in l {
```

```
    print("\(x) ", terminator: "")
}
```

It also means that, through the power of protocol extensions, we can use List with dozens of standard library functions:

```
l.joinWithSeparator(",")              // "1,2,3"
l.contains("2")                       // true
l.flatMap { Int($0) }                 // [1, 2, 3]
l.elementsEqual(["1", "2", "3"])      // true
```

Conforming List to CollectionType

Next, we make List conform to CollectionType. This will bring us extensions like the first property, which would be nice to use to peek at the first element without popping it.

More importantly, conforming to CollectionType gives a guarantee that multiple passes over the sequence are OK. As the docs for SequenceType say:

> SequenceType makes no requirement on conforming types regarding whether they will be destructively "consumed" by iteration. To ensure non-destructive iteration, constrain your sequence to CollectionType.

This explains why the first property is only available on collections. Providing a computed property ought to be non-destructive. As an example of a destructively consumed sequence, consider this wrapper on the readLine function, which reads lines from the standard input:

```
let standardIn = AnySequence {
    return AnyGenerator {
        readLine()
    }
}
```

Now you can use this sequence with the various extensions of sequence type. For example, you could write a line-numbering version of the Unix cat:

```
let numberedStdIn = standardIn.enumerate()

for (i, line) in numberedStdIn {
    print("\(i+1): \(line)")
```

```
}
```

enumerate wraps a sequence in a new sequence of the elements, plus an incrementing number. Just like our wrapper of readLine, elements are *lazily* generated. The consumption of the base sequence only happens when you move through the enumerated sequence using its generator, and not when it is created. So if you run the above code from the command line, you will see it waiting inside the **for** loop. It prints the lines you type in as you hit return; it does *not* wait until the input is terminated with control-D.

An implementation of enumerate could look like this:

```
extension SequenceType {
    func enumerate() -> AnySequence<(Int,Generator.Element)> {
        // Swift currently needs a type-inference helping hand with this closure:
        return AnySequence { _ -> AnyGenerator<(Int, Generator.Element)> in
            // create a fresh counter and generator to begin enumeration
            var i = 0
            var g = self.generate()
            // capture these in a closure and return that in a new generator
            return AnyGenerator {
                // when the base sequence is exhausted, return nil
                guard let next = g.next() else { return nil }
                let result = (i,next)
                i += 1
                return result
            }
        }
    }
}
```

But nonetheless, each time enumerate serves up a line from standardIn, it is consuming the standard input. You can't iterate over it twice to get the same results.

We can safely iterate over some sequences multiple times, including some sequences that aren't also collections. For example, the StrideTo and StrideThrough types, as returned by stride, are not collections — the fact that you can stride over floating-point numbers would make it tricky (though probably not impossible) to render them as a collection, so they are just sequences. But they are certainly useable multiple times. As an author of a SequenceType extension, you don't need to take into account whether or not the sequence is destructively iterated. But as a *caller* of a method on a sequence type, you should bear it in mind.

We can non-destructively iterate over our list type, so conforming to CollectionType to indicate this would be good, if possible. But before we do this, let's separate out the nodes from the list and index types.

It is tempting to just conform the enum to CollectionType and ForwardIndexType directly, as we did with SequenceType. But this will lead to problems. For example, those two protocols need very different implementations of ==:

→ The index needs to know if two indices from the same list are at the same position. It should not need the elements themselves to conform to Equatable.

→ The collection, on the other hand, should be able to compare two different lists to see if they hold the same elements. It will need the elements to conform to Equatable.

By creating separate types to represent the index and collection, we will be able to implement different behavior for the two different == operators. And by having neither be the node enum, we will be able to make that node implementation private, hiding the details from users of the collection. The new ListNode type looks just like our first variant of List:

```
/// Private implementation detail of the List collection
private enum ListNode<Element> {
    case End
    indirect case Node(Element, next: ListNode<Element>)

    func cons(x: Element) -> ListNode<Element> {
        // each cons increments the tag by one
        return .Node(x, next: self)
    }
}
```

The index type wraps ListNode. An index can return its successor by traversing the node and creating a new index with the next node. But that only covers half of the requirements for conforming to ForwardIndexType. We need some additional information to allow us to implement the == operator for indices. As we've discussed, nodes are values, and values don't have identity. So how can we tell if two variables are pointing to the same node? To do this, we tag each index with an incrementing number. As we will see in a bit, storing the tags with the nodes will allow for very efficient operations. The way the list works, two indices in the same list must be the same if they have the same tag:

```
public struct ListIndex<Element> {
    private let node: ListNode<Element>
    private let tag: Int
}
```

Another thing to note is that ListIndex is a public struct but has private properties (node and tag). This means it is not publicly constructible — its "default" constructor of ListIndex(node:tag:) will not be accessible to users. So you can be handed a ListIndex from a List, but you can't create one yourself. This is a useful technique for hiding implementation details and providing safety.

ForwardIndexType requires the type to have a successor method that returns the next index:

```
extension ListIndex: ForwardIndexType {
    public func successor() -> ListIndex<Element> {
        switch node {
        case let .Node(_, next: next):
            return ListIndex(node: next, tag: tag.predecessor())
        case .End:
            fatalError("cannot increment endIndex")
        }
    }
}
```

ListIndex must also implement Equatable, so that you can determine if two indices are the same. As we discussed above, we do this by comparing the tag:

```
public func == <T>(lhs: ListIndex<T>, rhs: ListIndex<T>) -> Bool {
    return lhs.tag == rhs.tag
}
```

Now that ListIndex conforms to ForwardIndexType, it can be used by a List type that conforms to CollectionType:

```
public struct List<Element>: CollectionType {
    // Index's type could be inferred, but it helps make the rest of
    // the code clearer:
    public typealias Index = ListIndex<Element>

    public var startIndex: Index
    public var endIndex: Index
```

```
public subscript(idx: Index) -> Element {
    switch idx.node {
    case .End: fatalError("Subscript out of range")
    case let .Node(x, _): return x
    }
}
}
```

And, to make lists easier to construct, we implement ArrayLiteralConvertible:

```
extension List: ArrayLiteralConvertible {
    public init (arrayLiteral elements: Element...) {
        startIndex = ListIndex(node: elements.reverse().reduce(.End) {
            $0.cons($1)
        }, tag: elements.count)
        endIndex = ListIndex(node: .End, tag: 0)
    }
}
```

And now our list gains the extensions on CollectionType:

```
let l: List = ["one", "two", "three"]
l. first
l.indexOf("two")
```

As an added bonus, since the tag is the count of nodes prepended to .End, List gets a constant-time count property, even though forward-index-only indices normally make this an $O(n)$ operation:

```
extension List {
    public var count: Int  {
        return startIndex.tag - endIndex.tag
    }
}
```

The subtraction of the end index (which, up until now, will always be a tag of zero) is to support slicing, which we'll come to shortly.

Finally, since List and ListIndex are two different types, we can give List a different implementation of ==, this time comparing the elements:

```
public func == <T: Equatable>(lhs: List<T>, rhs: List<T>) -> Bool {
    return lhs.elementsEqual(rhs)
}
```

Implementing Custom Slicing

Similar to the default indexing generator, collections also get a default implementation of the slicing operation, [Range<Index>], which is how dropFirst works:

```
// equivalent of l.dropFirst()
let firstDropped = l[l.startIndex.successor()..<l.endIndex]
```

Since operations like l[somewhere..<l.endIndex] (slice from a specific point to the end) and l[l.startIndex..<somewhere] (slice from the start to a specific point) are very common, there are default operations in the standard library that do this in a more readable way:

```
let firstDropped = l.suffixFrom(l.startIndex.successor())
```

By default, the type of firstDropped will not be a list — it will be a Slice<List<String>>. Slice is a lightweight wrapper on top of any collection. The implementation could look something like this:

```
struct Slice<Base: CollectionType>: CollectionType {
    let collection: Base
    let bounds: Range<Base.Index>

    var startIndex: Base.Index { return bounds.startIndex }
    var endIndex: Base.Index { return bounds.endIndex }

    subscript(idx: Base.Index) -> Base.Generator.Element { return collection[idx] }

    typealias SubSequence = Slice<Base>
    subscript(bounds: Range<Base.Index>) -> Slice<Base> {
        return Slice(collection: collection, bounds: bounds)
    }
}
```

This default implementation returns a wrapper over the original collection, plus an index subrange, so it's twice as big as it needs to be in List's case:

```
// Size of a list is size of two nodes, the start and end:
sizeofValue(l)              // returns 32

// Size of a list slice is size of a list, plus size of a subrange
// (a range between two indices, which in List's case are also list nodes)
sizeofValue(l.dropFirst())   // returns 64
```

We can do better, because lists could instead return themselves as subsequences by holding different start and end indices. We can give a List a custom implementation that does this:

```
extension List {
    private init (subRange: Range<Index>) {
        startIndex = subRange.startIndex
        endIndex = subRange.endIndex
    }
    public subscript(subRange: Range<Index>) -> List<Element> {
        return List(subRange: subRange)
    }
}
```

Using this implementation, list slices are themselves lists, so their size is only 32 bytes:

```
sizeofValue(l.dropFirst())    // returns 32
```

This leads to another benefit of this list implementation. With many sliceable containers, including Swift's arrays and strings, a slice shares the storage buffer of the original collection. This has an unpleasant side effect: slices can keep the original collection's buffer alive in its entirety, even if the original collection falls out of scope. If you read a 1 GB file into an array or string, and then slice off a tiny part, the whole 1 GB buffer will stay in memory until both the collection and the slice are destroyed.

With List, it isn't quite as bad. As we've seen, the nodes are managed by ARC: when the slices are the only remaining copy, any elements dropped from the front will be reclaimed as soon as no one is referencing them:

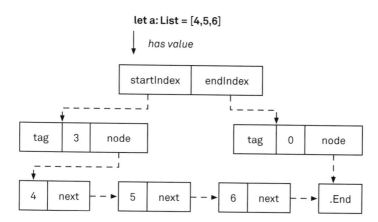

Figure 3.5: List Sharing and ARC

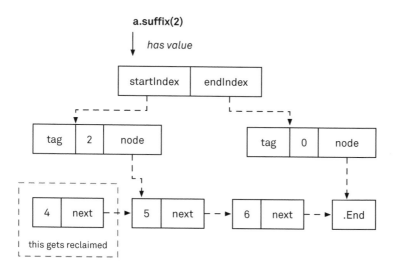

Figure 3.6: Memory Reclaiming

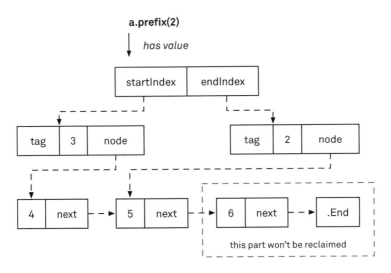

Figure 3.7: No Reclaiming of Memory

However, the back nodes won't be reclaimed, since the slice's last node still has a reference to what comes after it.

The default implementation of slicing demonstrates another thing to be aware of: even when using integer indices, do not assume a collection's index starts at 0.

For example, our Queue type uses the default slicing subscript, so if you create a queue and then slice it, you get a Slice<Queue<Element>> type back:

```
let q: Queue = ["a", "b", "c", "d", "e"]
let s = q[2..<5]
```

Now, given the implementation of Slice above, the start index will be the start of the subrange, and the end index the end of the subrange:

```
q.startIndex  // 0
q.endIndex    // 5
s.startIndex  // 2
s.endIndex    // 4
```

This is another reason to always prefer constructs like **for** x **in** collection or **for** index **in** collection.indices over old C-style loops. But when you are

looping over a collection, always remember to write
var i = collection.startIndex, rather than **var** i = 0.

Now that we know any collection can be sliced, we could revisit our prefix
generator code from earlier in the chapter and write a version that works with
any collection type:

```
class GPrefixGenerator<Base: CollectionType> {
    let base: Base
    var offset: Base.Index

    init (_ base: Base) {
        self.base = base
        self.offset = base.startIndex
    }

    func next() -> Base.SubSequence? {
        guard offset != base.endIndex else { return nil }
        offset = offset.successor()
        return base.prefixUpTo(offset)
    }
}
```

Forward Indices

We chose to implement a singly linked list because of the quality this data
structure is famous for: it can only be iterated forward. You cannot leap into
the middle of a linked list. You cannot start at the end and work backward.
You can only go forward.

For this reason, while our list collection has a . first property, it doesn't have a
. last property. To get the last element of a list, you have to iterate all the way to
the end, an $O(n)$ operation. Therefore, it would be misleading to provide a cute
little property for the last element — a list with a million elements takes a long
time to fetch the last element.

A general rule of thumb for properties is probably that "they must be
constant-time(-ish) operations only, unless it's incredibly obvious the
operation couldn't be done in constant time."

This is quite a wooly definition. "Must be constant-time operations" would be
nicer, but this wouldn't account for operations like "hello".uppercaseString,

which are obviously not constant time, but still reasonable candidates for a computed property.

Functions are a different matter. Our List type *does* have a reverse operation:

```
let reversed = l.reverse()
```

In this case, what is being called is the reverse function provided by the standard library as an extension on any SequenceType:

```
extension SequenceType {
    /// Return an `Array` containing the elements of `self` in reverse
    /// order.
    func reverse() -> [Self.Generator.Element]
}
```

This returns an array. But you might want to be able to stick with a list as the reverse of a list — in which case, we can overload the default implementation by extending List:

```
extension List {
    public func reverse() -> List<Element> {
        let reversedNodes: ListNode<Element> =
            self.reduce(.End) { $0.cons($1) }
        return List(
            startIndex: ListIndex(node: reversedNodes, tag: self.count),
            endIndex: ListIndex(node: .End, tag: 0))
    }
}
```

Now, when you call reverse on a list, you get another list. This will be chosen by default by Swift's overloading resolution mechanism, which always favors the most specialized implementation of a function or method on the basis that this almost always means it is a better choice. In this case, an implementation of reverse directly on List is more specific than a more general one that reverses any sequence type.

But it's possible you really want an array, in which case it would be more efficient to use the sequence-reversing version rather than reversing the list and then converting it to an array in two steps. If you still wanted to choose the version that returns an array, you could force Swift to call it by specifying the type you are assigning to (rather than letting type inference default it for you):

```
let reversedArray: [String] = l.reverse()
```

Or, you can use the **as** keyword if you pass the result into a function. For example, the following code tests that calling reverse on a list generates the same result as the version on an array:

```
l.reverse().elementsEqual(l.reverse as [String])
```

A quick testing tip: be sure to check that the overload is really in place and not accidentally missing. Otherwise, the above test will always pass, because you'll be comparing the two array versions.

You can test for this using **is** List, but assuming the overload is working, the compiler will warn you that your **is** is pointless (which would be true, so long as your overload has worked). To avoid that, you can cast via Any first:

```
l.reverse() as Any is List<Int>
```

Bidirectional Indices

BidirectionalIndexType adds a single but critical method to an index: predecessor. This gives your collection enough capabilities to get a default .last property, matching .first:

```
extension CollectionType where Index: BidirectionalIndexType {
    var last: Generator.Element? {
        guard !isEmpty else { return nil }
        return self[endIndex.predecessor()]
    }
}
```

An example of a bidirectionally indexed collection in the standard library is String.CharacterView. For Unicode-related reasons that we will go into in the chapter on strings, a character collection cannot have random-access indices, but you can move backward from the end, character by character.

It also adds a more efficient reverse operation — one that doesn't immediately reverse the collection but instead returns a lazy view:

```
extension CollectionType where Index : BidirectionalIndexType {
    /// Return a lazy `CollectionType` containing the elements of `self`
    /// in reverse order.
    func reverse() -> ReverseCollection<Self>
```

}

Just as with the enumerate wrapper on SequenceType, no actual reversing takes place. Instead, ReverseCollection holds the base collection and then returns a reversed index into the collection. In this index, successor and predecessor are reversed. This can be done with a fairly minimal wrapper around both the base collection and its index:

```
struct ReverseIndex<Base: BidirectionalIndexType> : BidirectionalIndexType {
    let idx: Base

    func successor() -> ReverseIndex<Base> {
        return ReverseIndex(idx: idx.predecessor())
    }
    func predecessor() -> ReverseIndex<Base> {
        return ReverseIndex(idx: idx.successor())
    }
}

func ==<T>(lhs: ReverseIndex<T>, rhs: ReverseIndex<T>) -> Bool {
    return lhs.idx == rhs.idx
}

struct ReverseCollection
    <Base: CollectionType where Base.Index: BidirectionalIndexType>
    : CollectionType
{
    let base: Base

    var startIndex: ReverseIndex<Base.Index> {
        return ReverseIndex(idx: base.endIndex)
    }
    var endIndex: ReverseIndex<Base.Index> {
        return ReverseIndex(idx: base.startIndex)
    }
    subscript(idx: ReverseIndex<Base.Index>) -> Base.Generator.Element {
        return base[idx.idx.predecessor()]
    }
}
```

Value semantics play a big part in the validity of this approach. On construction, the wrapper "copies" the base collection into its base variable. However, in the case of copy-on-write types such as Array (or immutable persistent structures like List, or types composed of two copy-on-write types like Queue), this is an efficient operation. But if the original source for base is altered, this does not change the copy held in base. This means that ReverseCollection has the same observable behavior as the version of reverse that returns an array.

Random-Access Indices

The top rung on the indices ladder is a random-access index – that is, one where you can jump to any point in the index in constant time. To do this, it adds two more functions on top of BidirectionalIndexType: distanceTo and advancedBy, both of which must operate in $O(1)$.

At first, this might seem like it doesn't add much. If you look at any index, even a forward-only one like with our List type, it has an advancedBy method just like any random-access index. But there is a big difference. For ForwardIndexType and BidirectionalIndexType, advancedBy and distanceTo are implemented as *extensions*. They operate by incrementing the index successively until they reach their destination. This clearly takes linear time — the longer the distance traveled, the longer it will take to run. Random-access indices, on the other hand, can just move straight to that point.

This ability is key in a number of algorithms, a couple of which we will look at in the chapter on generics. There, we will implement a generic binary search, but it's crucial this algorithm be constrained to random-access protocols only — otherwise it would be far less efficient than just searching from start to end through the collection.

Earlier, when we implemented our linked list, we wrote a custom version of count because we could get it from the tags. A collection that has random-access indices can compute the distance between its startIndex and endIndex in constant time. This also means the collection can compute the element count in constant time.

We have seen a number of different collections, which are all value types. In the chapter on structs and classes, we will go into more detail on the difference between value and reference types. By implementing protocols like SequenceType or CollectionType, our custom types can gain a lot of extra functionality for free. We have seen a number of operations on collections, such as map and filter , but also operations like reverse that return a (lazy) view on a collection. In the chapter on generics, we will look at extending existing collections with extra functionality. In the chapter on protocols, we will show how we can make our own protocols with extra functionality.

Optionals

Sentinel Values

An extremely common pattern in programming is to have an operation that might or might not return a value.

Perhaps not returning a value is an expected outcome when you've reached the end of a file you were reading, as in the following C snippet:

```
int ch;
while ((ch = getchar()) != EOF) {
    printf("Read character %c\n", ch);
}
printf("Reached end-of-file\n");
```

EOF is just a #define for -1. As long as there are more characters in the file, getchar returns them. But if the end of the file is reached, getchar returns -1.

Or perhaps returning no value means "not found," as in this bit of C++:

```
auto vec = {1, 2, 3};
auto iterator = std::find(vec.begin(), vec.end(), someValue);
if (iterator != vec.end()) {
    std::cout << "vec contains " << *iterator << std::endl;
}
```

Here, vec.end() is the iterator "one past the end" of the container; it's a special iterator that you can check against the container's end, but that you mustn't ever actually use to access a value. find uses it to indicate that no such value is present in the container.

Or maybe the value can't be returned because something went wrong during the function's processing. Probably the most notorious example is that of the null pointer. This innocuous-looking piece of Java code will likely throw a NullPointerException:

```
int i = Integer.getInteger("123")
```

It happens that Integer.getInteger doesn't parse strings into integers, but rather gets the integer value of a system property named "123." This property probably doesn't exist, in which case getInteger returns null. When the null then gets auto unboxed into an int, Java throws an exception.

Or take this example in Objective-C:

[[NSString alloc] initWithContentsOfURL:url encoding:NSUTF8StringEncoding error:&e]

Here, the NSString might be **nil**, in which case — and only then — the error pointer should be checked. There is no guarantee that the error pointer is valid if the result is non-**nil**.

In all of the above examples, the function returns a special "magic" value to indicate that it hasn't returned a real value. Magic values like these are called "sentinel values."

But this approach is problematic. The result returned looks and feels like a real value. An int of -1 is still a valid integer, but you don't ever want to print it out. v.end() is an iterator, but the results are undefined if you try to use it. And everyone loves seeing a stack dump when your Java program throws a NullPointerException.

So sentinel values are error prone — you can forget to check the sentinel value and accidentally use it instead. They also require prior knowledge. Sometimes there's an idiom, as with the C++ end iterator, but not always. Often you need to check the documentation. And there's no way for the function to indicate it *cannot* fail. If a call returns a pointer, that pointer might never be **nil**. But there's no way to tell except by reading the documentation, and even then, perhaps the documentation is wrong.

In Objective-C, it is possible to safely send messages to **nil**. If the message signature returns an object, it will return **nil** instead, and if the message should return a struct, all its values will be zeroed. However, consider the following snippet:

```
NSString *someString = ...;
if ([someString rangeOfString:@"swift"].location != NSNotFound) {
    NSLog(@"Someone mentioned swift!");
}
```

If someString is **nil**, the rangeOfString: message will return a zeroed NSRange. Hence, the .location will be zero, and NSNotFound is defined as NSIntegerMax. Therefore, the body of the if-statement will be executed if someString is **nil**.

Null references cause so much heartache that Tony Hoare, credited with their creation in 1965, calls them his "billion-dollar mistake":

At that time, I was designing the first comprehensive type system for references in an object oriented language (ALGOL W). My goal was to ensure that all use of references should be absolutely safe, with checking performed automatically by the compiler. But I couldn't resist the temptation to put in a null reference, simply because it was so easy to implement. This has led to innumerable errors, vulnerabilities, and system crashes, which have probably caused a billion dollars of pain and damage in the last forty years.

Solving the Magic Value Problem with Enumerations

Of course, every good programmer knows magic numbers are bad. Most languages support some kind of enumeration type, which is a safer way of representing a set of discrete possible values for a type.

Swift takes enumerations further with the concept of "associated values." These are enumeration values that can also have another value associated with them:

```
enum Optional<T> {
    case None
    case Some(T)
}
```

In some languages, these are called "tagged unions" (or "discriminated unions") — a union being multiple different possible types all held in the same space in memory, with a tag to tell which type is actually held. In Swift enums, this tag is the enum case.

The only way to retrieve an associated value is via a **switch** or an **if case let**. Unlike with a sentinel value, you can't accidentally use the value embedded in an Optional without explicitly checking and unpacking it.

So instead of returning an index, the Swift equivalent of find — called indexOf — returns an Optional<Index> with a protocol extension implementation somewhat similar to this:

```
extension CollectionType where Generator.Element: Equatable {
```

```swift
func indexOf(element: Generator.Element) -> Optional<Index> {
    for idx in self.indices where self[idx] == element {
        return .Some(idx)
    }
    // not found, return .None
    return .None
}
```

Since optionals are so fundamental in Swift, there is lots of syntax support to neaten this up: Optional<Index> can be written Index?; optionals conform to NilLiteralConvertible so that you can write **nil** instead of .None; and non-optional values (like idx) are automatically "upgraded" to optionals where needed so that you can write **return** idx instead of **return** .Some(idx).

Now there's no way that a user could mistakenly use the invalid value:

```swift
var array = ["one", "two", "three"]
let idx = array.indexOf("four")
// compile-time error: removeIndex takes an Int, not an Optional<Int>
array.removeAtIndex(idx)
```

Instead, you are forced to "unwrap" the optional in order to get at the index within, assuming you didn't get None back:

```swift
switch array.indexOf("four") {
case .Some(let idx):
    array.removeAtIndex(idx)
case .None:
    break // do nothing
}
```

This switch statement writes the enumeration syntax for optionals out longhand, including unpacking the "associated type" when the value is the Some case. This is great for safety, but it's not very pleasant to read or write. Swift 2.0 introduced the ? pattern suffix syntax to match a Some optional inside a switch, and you can use the **nil** literal to match None:

```swift
switch array.indexOf("four") {
case let idx?:
    array.removeAtIndex(idx)
case nil:
    break // do nothing
}
```

But this is still clunky. Let's take a look at all the other ways you can make your optional processing short and clear, depending on your use case.

A Tour of Optional Techniques

Optionals have a lot of extra support that is built into the language. Some of the examples below might look very simple if you have been writing Swift, but it is important to make sure you know all of these concepts well, as we will be using them again and again throughout the book.

if let

Optional binding with **if let** is just a short step away from the **switch** statement above:

```
if let idx = array.indexOf("four") {
    array.removeAtIndex(idx)
}
```

Just as with **switch** statements, an optional binding with **if** can have a **where** clause. So suppose you didn't want to remove the element if it happened to be the first one in the array:

```
if let idx = array.indexOf("four") where idx != array.startIndex {
    array.removeAtIndex(idx)
}
```

You can also bind multiple entries in the same **if** statement. What's more is that later entries can rely on the earlier ones being successfully unwrapped. This is very useful when you want to make multiple calls to functions that return optionals themselves. For example, these NSURL, NSData, and UIImage initializers are all "failable" — that is, they can return **nil** — if your URL is malformed, or the page returned an error, or the data download is corrupt. All three can be chained together like this:

```
let urlString = "http://www.objc.io/logo.png"
if let url = NSURL(string: urlString),
    data = NSData(contentsOfURL: url),
    image = UIImage(data: data)
{
    let view = UIImageView(image: image)
```

```
    XCPlaygroundPage.currentPage.liveView = view
}
```

Separate parts of a multi-variable **let** can have a **where** clause as well:

```
if  let  url  = NSURL(string: urlString) where url.pathExtension == "png",
    let  data = NSData(contentsOfURL: url),
    let  image = UIImage(data: data)
{
    let  view = UIImageView(image: image)
}
```

If you need to perform a check *before* performing various **if let** bindings, you can supply a leading boolean condition. Suppose you are using a storyboard and want to check the segue identifier before casting to a specific kind of view controller:

```
if  segue.identifier == "showUserDetailsSegue",
    let  userDetailVC = segue.destinationViewController
    as? UserDetailViewController
{
    userDetailVC.screenName = userScreenNameLabel.text
}
```

You can also use NSScanner, which returns a boolean value to indicate whether or not it successfully scanned something, after which you can unwrap the result:

```
let  stringScanner = NSScanner(string: "myUserName123")
var username: NSString?
let  alphas = NSCharacterSet.alphanumericCharacterSet()

if  stringScanner.scanCharactersFromSet(alphas, intoString: &username),
    let  name = username
{
    print(name)
}
```

while let

Very similar to the **if let** statement is **while let** — a loop that only terminates when a **nil** is returned.

The standard library's readLine function returns an optional string from the standard input. Once the end of input is reached, it returns **nil**. So to implement a very basic equivalent of the Unix cat command, you use **while let**:

```
while let line = readLine() {
    print(line)
}
```

Similar to **if let**, you can always add a **where** clause to your optional binding. So if you want to terminate this loop on either EOF or a blank line, add a clause to detect an empty string. Note that once the condition is **false**, the loop is terminated (you might mistakenly think that the **where** condition functions like a filter):

```
while let line = readLine() where !line.isEmpty {
    print(line)
}
```

As we saw in the chapter on collections, the **for** x **in** sequence loop requires sequence to conform to SequenceType. This provides a generate method that returns a type that conforms to GeneratorType, which in turn requires a next method. next returns values until the sequence is exhausted, and then it returns **nil**. **while let** is ideal for this:

```
let array = [1, 2, 3]
var generator = array.generate()
while let i = generator.next() {
    print(i)
}
```

So given that **for** loops are really just **while** loops, it's not surprising that they also support the same **where** clauses:

```
for i in 0..<10 where i % 2 == 0 {
    print(i)
}
```

> Note that the **where** clause above does not work like the **where** clause in a **while** loop. In a **while** loop, iteration stops once the value is **false**, whereas in a **for** loop, it functions like filter . If we rewrite the above **for** loop using **while**, it looks like this:

```
var generator = (0..<10).generate()
while let i = generator.next() {
    if i % 2 == 0 {
        print(i)
    }
}
```

This feature of **for** loops leads to an interesting behavior that avoids a particularly strange bug with variable capture that can happen in other languages. Consider the following code, written in Ruby:

```
a = []
for i in 1..3
    a.push(lambda { i })
end

for f in a
    print "#{f.call ()} "
end
```

Ruby lambdas are like Swift's closure expressions, and as with Swift, they capture local variables. So the above code loops from 1 to 3 — adding a closure to the array that captures i — and will print out the value of i when called. Then it loops over that array, calling each of the closures. What do you think will be printed out? If you're on a Mac, you can try it out by pasting the above into a file and running ruby on it from the command line.

If you run it, you'll see it prints out three 3s in a row. Even though i held a different value when each closure was created, they all captured the *same* i variable. And when you call them, i now has the value 3 — its value at the end of the loop.

This code in Python, using list comprehensions, also prints out three 3s:

```
a = [lambda: i for i in xrange(1, 4)]
for f in a:
    print f ()
```

Now for a similar Swift snippet:

```
var a: [() -> Int] = []

for i in 1...3 {
```

```
        a.append { i }
}

for f in a {
    print("\(f ()) ")
}
```

The output: 1, 2, and 3. This makes sense when you realize **for** ... **in** is really **while let**. To make the correspondence even clearer, imagine there *wasn't* a **while let**, and that you had to use a generator without it:

```
var g = (1...3). generate()
var o: Optional<Int> = g.next()
while o != nil {
    let i = o!
    a.append { i }
    o = g.next()
}
```

This makes it easy to see that i is a fresh local variable in every iteration, so the closure captures the correct value even when a *new* local i is declared on subsequent iterations.

By contrast, the Ruby and Python code is more along the lines of the following:

```
do {
    var g = (1...3). generate()
    var i: Int
    var o: Optional<Int> = g.next()
    while o != nil {
        i = o!
        a.append { i }
        o = g.next()
    }
}
```

Here, i is declared *outside* the loop — and reused — so every closure captures the same i. If you run each of them, they will all return 3. The **do** is there because, despite i being declared outside the loop, i is still scoped in such a way that it isn't *accessible* outside that loop — it's sandwiched in a narrow outer shell.

C# had the same behavior as Ruby until C# 5, when it was decided that this behavior was dangerous enough to justify a breaking change to work like Swift.

Doubly Nested Optionals

This is a good time to point out that the type an optional wraps can itself be optional, which leads to optionals nested inside optionals. To see why this isn't just a strange edge case or something the compiler should automatically coalesce, suppose you have an array of strings of numbers, which you want to convert into integers. You might run them through a map to convert them:

```
let stringNumbers = ["1", "2", "3", "foo"]
let maybeInts = stringNumbers.map { Int($0) }
```

You now have an array of Optional<Int> — i.e. Int? — because Int.init(String) is failable, since the string might not contain a valid integer. Here, the last entry will be a nil, since "foo" isn't an integer.

When looping over the array with for, you would rightly expect that each element would be an optional integer, because that's what maybeInts contains:

```
for maybeInt in maybeInts {
    // maybeInt is an Int?
    // three numbers and a `nil`
}
```

Now consider that the implementation of for ... in is shorthand for the while loop technique above. What is returned from next would be an Optional<Optional<Int>> — or Int?? — because next wraps each element in the sequence inside an optional. The while let unwraps it to check it isn't nil, and while it's non-nil, binds the unwrapped value and runs the body:

```
var generator = maybeInts.generate()
while let maybeInt = generator.next() {
    // maybeInt is an `Int?`
    // three numbers and a `nil`
}
```

When the loop gets to the final element — the nil from "foo" — what is returned from next is a non-nil value: .Some(nil). It unwraps this and binds what is inside (a nil) to maybeInt. Without doubly wrapped optionals, this wouldn't be possible.

By the way, if you ever want to loop over only the non-nil values with for, you can use if case pattern matching:

```
for case let i? in maybeInts {
    // i will be an Int, not an Int?
    // 1, 2, and 3
}
```

```
// or only the nil values:
for case nil in maybeInts {
    // will run once for each nil
}
```

This uses a "pattern" of x?, which only matches non-nil values. This is shorthand for .Some(x), so the loop could be written like this:

```
for case let .Some(i) in maybeInts {
}
```

This case-based pattern matching is a way to apply the same rules that work in switch statements to if, for, and while. It's most useful with optionals, but it also has other applications, for example:

```
let j = 5
if case 0..<10 = j {
    print("\(j) within range")
}
```

Since case matching is extensible via implementations of the ~= operator, this means you can extend if case and for case in various interesting ways:

```
struct Substring {
    let s: String
    init (_ s: String) { self.s = s }
}
```

```
func ~=(pattern: Substring, value: String) -> Bool {
    return value.rangeOfString(pattern.s) != nil
}
```

```
let s = "bar"
if case Substring("foo") = s {
    print("has substring \"foo\")")
}
```

This has incredible potential, but you need to take a little care. It is very easy to accidentally write ~= operators that match a little too much. Inserting the following into a common bit of library code would probably be a good April Fools' joke:

```
func ~=<T, U>(_: T, _: U) -> Bool { return true }
```

That is, it would be, right up until the person you do it to finds it and then comes and finds you.

if var and while var

Instead of **let**, you can use **var** with both **if** and **while:**

```
if var i = Int(s) {
    i += 1
    print(i)  // prints 2
}
```

But note that i will be a local copy; any changes to i will not affect the value inside the original optional. Optionals are value types, and unwrapping them unwraps the value inside. So this variant is like using **var** on a function argument: it's just shorthand if you want a local copy within the body to do some scratch work, and it doesn't change the original value.

Scoping of Unwrapped Optionals

Sometimes it feels frustrating to only have access to an unwrapped variable within the **if** block it has defined. But really, this is no different than other techniques.

For example, take the first method on arrays: a function that returns an optional of the first element, or **nil** when the array is empty. This is convenient shorthand for the following common bit of code:

```
if !a.isEmpty {
    // use a[0]
}
// outside the block, no guarantee that a[0] is valid
```

Instead, using the first method, you *have* to unwrap the optional in order to use it — you can't accidentally forget:

```
if let firstElement = a.first {
```

```
    // use firstElement
}
// outside the block, you can't use firstElement
```

The big exception to this is an early exit from a function. Sometimes you might write the following:

```
func doStuff(withArray a: [Int]) {
    if a.isEmpty { return }
    // now use a[0] safely
}
```

This early exit can help avoid annoying nesting or repeated guards later on in the function.

One option is to rely on Swift's deferred initialization capabilities. Consider the following example, which reimplements part of the pathExtension method:

```
func doStuffWithFileExtension(fileName: String) {
    let period: String.Index
    if let idx = fileName.characters.indexOf(".") {
        period = idx
    } else {
        return
    }

    let extensionRange = period.successor()..<fileName.endIndex
    let fileExtension = fileName[extensionRange]
    print(fileExtension)
}
```

Swift checks your code to confirm that there are only two possible paths: one in which the function returns early, and another where period is properly initialized. There is no way period could be **nil** (it isn't optional) or uninitialized (Swift won't let you use a variable that hasn't been initialized). So after the **if** statement, the code can be written without you having to worry about optionals at all.

But this is pretty ugly. Really, what is needed is some kind of **if** not **let** — which is exactly what **guard let** does:

```
func doStuffWithFileExtension(fileName: String) {
    guard let period = fileName.characters.indexOf(".") else { return }
```

```
    let extensionRange = period.successor()..<fileName.endIndex
    let fileExtension = fileName[extensionRange]
    print(fileExtension)
}
```

Anything can go in the **else** clause here, including multiple statements just like an **if else**. The only requirement is that the end of the **else** must leave the current scope. That might mean **return**, or calling fatalError (or any other function that declares **@noreturn**). If the **guard** were in a loop, it could be via **break** or **continue**.

Of course, **guard** is not limited to binding. Guard can take any condition you might find in a regular **if** statement. So the empty array example could be rewritten with it:

```
func doStuff(withArray a: [Int]) {
    guard !a.isEmpty else { return }
    // now, use a[0] safely
}
```

Unlike the optional binding case, this isn't a big win — in fact, it's slightly more verbose than the original return. But it's still worth considering doing this with any early-exit situation. For one, sometimes (though not in this case) the inversion of the boolean condition can make things clearer. Additionally, **guard** is a clear signal when reading the code; it says: "We only continue if the following condition holds." Finally, the Swift compiler will check that you are definitely exiting the current scope and raise a compilation error if you don't. For this reason, we'd suggest using **guard** even when an **if** would do.

Optional Chaining

In Objective-C, sending a message to **nil** is a no-op. In Swift, the same effect can be achieved via "optional chaining":

```
self.delegate?.callback()
```

Unlike with Objective-C, though, the compiler will warn you when your value might be optional. If your value is non-optional, you are guaranteed that the method will actually be called. If not, the ? is a clear signal to the reader that it might not be called.

When the method you call via optional chaining returns a result, that result will also be optional. Consider the following code to see why this must be the case:

```
// Assuming we have a variable i of type Int? and we want to find
// its successor
let j: Int
if i != nil {
    j = i!.successor()
} else {
    // no reasonable action to take at this point
    fatalError("no idea what to do now...")
}
```

If i is non-nil, j will have the next value up. But if i is nil, then j cannot be set to a value. So in the optional chaining case, j *must* be optional, to account for the possibility that i could have been nil:

```
let j = i?.successor()
```

As the name implies, you can chain optionals:

```
let j = Int("1")?.successor().successor()
```

However, this might look a bit surprising. Didn't we just say that the result of optional chaining is an optional? So why don't you need a ?. after the first successor()? This is because optional chaining is a "flattening" operation. If Int("1")?.successor() returned an optional and you called ?.successor() on it, then logically you would get an optional optional. But you just want a regular optional, so instead we write the second chained call without an optional to represent the fact that the optionality is already captured.

On the other hand, if the successor method itself returned an optional, then you would need a ? after it to express that you were chaining *that* optional. For example, let's imagine adding a method half on the Int type. This method returns the result of dividing the integer by two, but only if the number is big enough to be divided. When the number is smaller than two, it returns nil:

```
extension Int {
    func half() -> Int? {
        guard self > 1 else { return nil }
        return self / 2
    }
}
```

Because calling half returns an optional result, we need to keep putting in ?
when calling it repeatedly. After all, at every step, the function might return
nil:

```
20.half ()?. half ()?. half ()
```

```
Optional(2)
```

Optional chaining also applies to subscript and function calls, for example:

```
let dictOfArrays = ["nine": [0, 1, 2, 3, 4, 5, 6, 7]]
let sevenOfNine = dictOfArrays["nine"]?[7] // returns .Some(7)
```

Additionally, there's this:

```
let dictOfFuncs: [String: (Int, Int) -> Int] = [
    "add": (+),
    "subtract": (-)
]
dictOfFuncs["add"]?(1, 1) // returns .Some(2)
```

You can assign *through* an optional chain. Suppose you have an optional
variable, and if it's non-**nil**, you wish to update one of its properties:

```
if splitViewController != nil {
    splitViewController!.delegate = myDegelate
}
```

Instead, you can assign to the chained optional value, and if it isn't **nil**, the
assignment will work:

```
splitViewController?.delegate = myDelegate
```

nil-Coalescing Operator

Often you want to unwrap an optional, replacing **nil** with some default value.
This is a job for the **nil**-coalescing operator:

```
let stringteger = "1"
let i = Int(stringteger) ?? 0
```

So if the string is of an integer, i will be that integer, unwrapped. If it isn't, and Int. **init** returns **nil**, the default value of 0 will be substituted. So lhs ?? rhs is analogous to the code lhs != **nil** ? lhs! : rhs.

"Big deal!" Objective-C developers might say. "We've had the ?: for ages." And ?? is very similar to Objective-C's ?:. But there are some differences, so it's worth stressing an important point when thinking about optionals in Swift: optionals are *not* pointers.

Yes, most of the time you will encounter optionals combined with references when dealing with Objective-C libraries. But optionals, as we've seen, can also wrap value types. So i in the above example is just an Int, not an NSNumber.

Through the use of optionals, you can guard against much more than just null pointers. Consider the case where you want to access the first value of an array — but in case the array is empty, you want to provide a default:

```
let i = !array.isEmpty() ? array[0] : 0
```

Because Swift arrays provide a first property that is **nil** if the array is empty, you can use the **nil**-coalescing operator instead:

```
let i = array. first ?? 0
```

This is cleaner and clearer — the intent (grab the first element in the array) is up front, with the default tacked on the end, joined with a ?? that signals "this is a default value." Compare this with the ternary version, which starts first with the check, then the value, then the default. And the check is awkwardly negated (the alternative being to put the default in the middle and the actual value on the end). And, as is the case with optionals, it's impossible to forget that first is optional and accidentally use it without the check, because the compiler will stop you if you try.

Whenever you find yourself guarding a statement with a check to make sure the statement is valid, it's a good sign optionals would be a better solution. Suppose that instead of an empty array, you're checking a value that is within the array bounds:

```
let i = array.count > 5 ? a[5] : 0
```

Unlike first and last, getting an element out of an array by its index doesn't return an Optional. But it's easy to extend Array to add this functionality:

```
extension Array {
    subscript(safe idx: Int) -> Element? {
        return idx < endIndex ? self[idx] : nil
    }
}
```

This now allows you to write the following:

```
let i = array[safe: 5] ?? 0
```

Coalescing can also be chained — so if you have multiple possible optionals, and you want to choose the first non-optional one, you can write them in sequence:

```
let i: Int? = nil
let j: Int? = nil
let k: Int? = 42

let n = i ?? j ?? k ?? 0
```

Sometimes, you might have multiple optional values, and you want to choose between them in an order, but you don't have a reasonable default if they are all nil. You can still use ?? for this, but if the final value is also optional, the full result will be optional:

```
let m = i ?? j ?? k // m will be of type Int?
```

This is often useful in conjunction with if let. You can think of this like an "or" equivalent of if let:

```
if let n = i ?? j { }
// similar to if i != nil || j != nil
```

If you think of the ?? operator as similar to an "or" statement, you can think of an if let with multiple clauses as an "and" statement:

```
if let n = i, m = j { }
// similar to if i != nil && j != nil
```

Because of this chaining, if you are ever presented with a doubly nested optional and want to use the ?? operator, you must take care to distinguish between a ?? b ?? c (chaining) and (a ?? b) ?? c (unwrapping the inner and then outer layers):

```
let s1: String?? = nil
(s1 ?? "inner") ?? "outer"
let s2: String?? = .Some(nil)
(s2 ?? "inner") ?? "outer"
```

Optional map

Earlier, you saw this example:

```
func doStuffWithFileExtension(fileName: String) {
    guard let period = fileName.characters.indexOf(".") else { return }

    let extensionRange = period.successor()..<fileName.endIndex
    let fileExtension = fileName[extensionRange]
    print(fileExtension)
}
```

Suppose we were to change this slightly — instead of returning from the function in the **else** block, make fileExtension optional, and in the **else** block, set it to **nil**:

```
func doStuffWithFileExtension(fileName: String) {
    let fileExtension: String?
    if let idx = fileName.characters.indexOf(".") {
        let extensionRange = idx.successor()..<fileName.endIndex
        fileExtension = fileName[extensionRange]
    } else {
        fileExtension = nil
    }

    print(fileExtension ?? "No extension")
}
```

So now, if the filename contains a ., fileExtension will contain what follows it. But if it doesn't, fileExtension will be **nil**.

This pattern — take an optional, and transform it if it isn't **nil** — is common enough that there is a method on optionals to do this. It's called map, and it takes a closure that represents how to transform the contents of the optional. Here's the above function, rewritten using map:

```
func doStuffWithFileExtension(fileName: String) {
    let fileExtension: String? = fileName.characters.indexOf(".").map { idx in
```

```
        let extensionRange = idx.successor()..<fileName.endIndex
        return fileName[extensionRange]
    }

    print(fileExtension ?? "No extension")
}
```

This map is, of course, very similar to the map on arrays or other sequences. But instead of operating on a sequence of values, it operates on just one: the possible one inside the optional. You can think of optionals as being a collection of either zero or one values, with map either doing nothing to zero values or transforming one.

An optional map is especially nice when you already want an optional result. Suppose you wanted to write another variant of reduce for arrays. Instead of taking an initial value, it uses the first element in the array (in some languages, this might be called reduce1, but we'll call it reduce and rely on overloading):

```
[1, 2, 3, 4].reduce(+)
```

Because of the possibility that the array might be empty, the result needs to be optional — without an initial value, what else could it be? You might write it like this:

```
extension Array {
    func reduce(combine: (Element, Element) -> Element) -> Element? {
        // self.first will be nil if the array is empty
        guard let fst = first else { return nil }
        return self.dropFirst().reduce(fst, combine: combine)
    }
}
```

Since optional map returns nil if the optional is nil, reduce could be rewritten using a single return statement (and no guard):

```
extension Array {
    func reduce(combine: (Element, Element) -> Element) -> Element? {
        return first.map {
            self.dropFirst().reduce($0, combine: combine)
        }
    }
}
```

Given the similarities, the implementation of optional map looks a lot like collection map:

```
extension Optional {
    func map<U>(transform: Wrapped -> U) -> U? {
        if let value = self {
            return transform(value)
        }
        return nil
    }
}
```

Optional flatMap

As we saw in the chapter on collections, it's common to want to map over a collection with a function that returns a collection, but collect the results as a single array rather than an array of arrays.

Similarly, if you want to perform a map on an optional value, but your transformation function also has an optional result, you will end up with a doubly nested optional. An example of this is when you want to fetch the first element of an array of strings as a number, using first on the array, and then map to convert it to a number:

```
let x = stringNumbers.first.map { Int($0) }
```

The problem is that since map returns an optional (first might have been nil) and Int(String) returns an optional (the string might not be an integer), the type of x will be Int??.

flatMap will instead flatten the result into a single optional:

```
let y = stringNumbers.first.flatMap { Int($0) }
```

As a result, y will be of type Int?.

You could instead have written this with if let, because values that are bound later can be computed from earlier ones:

```
if let a = stringNumbers.first, b = Int(a) {
    print(b)
}
```

This shows that flatMap and **if let** are very similar. Earlier in this chapter, we saw an example that uses a multiple-if-let statement. We can rewrite it using using map and flatMap instead:

```
let view = NSURL(string: urlString)
    .flatMap { NSData(contentsOfURL: $0) }
    .flatMap { UIImage(data: $0) }
    .map    { UIImageView(image: $0) }

if let view = view {
    XCPlaygroundPage.currentPage.liveView = view
}
```

Optional chaining is also very similar to flatMap: i?.successor() is essentially equivalent to i.flatMap { $0.successor() }.

Since we've shown that a multiple-if-let statement is equivalent toflatMap, we could implement one in terms of the other:

```
extension Optional {
    func flatMap<U>(transform: Wrapped -> U?) -> U? {
        if let value = self, transformed = transform(value) {
            return transformed
        }
        return nil
    }
}
```

Filtering Out nils with flatMap

If you have a sequence and it contains optionals, you might not care about the **nil** values. In fact, you might just want to ignore them.

Suppose you wanted to process only the numbers in an array of strings. This is easily done in a **for** loop with optional pattern matching:

```
let numbers = ["1", "2", "3", "foo"]

var sum = 0
for case let i? in numbers.map({ Int($0) }) {
    sum += i
}
```

You might also want to use ?? to replace the **nil**s with zeros:

```
numbers.map { Int($0) }.reduce(0) { $0 + ($1 ?? 0) }
```

6

But really, you just want a version of map that filters out **nil** and unwraps the non-**nil** values. Enter the standard library's overload of flatMap on sequences, which does exactly that:

```
numbers.flatMap { Int($0) }.reduce(0, combine: +)
```

6

We've already seen two flattening maps: flattening a sequence mapped to arrays, and flattening an optional mapped to an optional. This is a hybrid of the two: flattening a sequence mapped to an optional.

This makes sense if we return to our analogy of an optional being a collection of zero or one thing(s). If that collection were an array, flatMap would be exactly what we want.

To implement our own version of this operator, let's first define a filterNil that filters out **nil** values and returns an array of non-optionals:

```
func filterNil <S: SequenceType, T where S.Generator.Element == T?>
    (source: S) -> [T]
{
    return source.lazy.filter { $0 != nil }.map { $0! }
}
```

Ewww, a free function? Why no protocol extension? Unfortunately, there's no way to constrain an extension on SequenceType to only apply to sequences of optionals. You would need a two-placeholder clause (one for S, and one for T, as given here), and protocol extensions currently don't support this.

Nonetheless, it does make flatMap simple to write:

```
extension SequenceType {
    func flatMap<U>(transform: Generator.Element->U?) -> [U] {
        return filterNil (self.lazy.map(transform))
    }
}
```

In both these functions, we've used **lazy** to defer actual creation of the array until the last moment. This is possibly a micro-optimization but might be worthwhile for larger arrays to avoid needlessly allocating multiple buffers to write the intermediary results into.

Equating and Comparing Optionals

Often, you don't care whether a value is **nil** or not — just whether it contains (if non-**nil**) a certain value:

```
if regex.characters.first == "^" {
    // match only start of string
}
```

In this case, it doesn't matter if the value is **nil** or not — if the string is empty, the first character can't be a caret, so you don't want to run the block. But you still want the protection and simplicity of first. The alternative, **if** !regex.isEmpty && regex.characters[regex.startIndex] == "^", is horrible.

The code above relies on two things to work. First, there is a version of == that takes two optionals, with an implementation something like this:

```
func ==<T: Equatable>(lhs: T?, rhs: T?) -> Bool {
    switch (lhs, rhs) {
    case (nil, nil): return true
    case let (x?, y?): return x == y
    case (_?, nil), (nil, _?): return false
    }
}
```

This overload *only* works on optionals of equatable types. Given this, there are four possibilities: they're both **nil**, or they both have a value, or either one or the other is **nil**. The **switch** exhaustively tests all four possibilities (hence no need for a **default** clause). It defines two **nil**s to be equal to each other, **nil** to never be equal to non-**nil**, and two non-**nil** values to be equal if their unwrapped values are equal.

But this is only half the story. Notice that we did *not* have to write the following:

```
// to compare two optionals, no need to declare "^" as optional:
if regex.characters.first == Optional("^") {
    // match only start of string
```

}

This is because whenever you have a non-optional value, Swift will always be willing to upgrade it to an optional value, in order to make the types match.

This implicit conversion is incredibly useful for writing clear, compact code. Suppose there was no such conversion, but to make things nice for the caller, you wanted a version of == that worked between both optional and non-optional types. You'd have to write three separate versions:

```
// both optional
func == <T: Equatable>(lhs: T?, rhs: T?) -> Bool
// lhs non-optional
func == <T: Equatable>(lhs: T, rhs: T?) -> Bool
// rhs non-optional
func == <T: Equatable>(lhs: T?, rhs: T) -> Bool
```

But instead, only the first version is necessary, and the compiler will convert to optionals where necessary.

In fact, we've been relying on this implicit conversion throughout the book. For example, when we implemented optional map, we transformed the inner value and returned it. But the return value of map is optional. The compiler automatically converted the value for us — we didn't have to write return Optional(transform(value)).

Swift code constantly relies on this implicit conversion. For example, dictionary subscript lookup by key returns an optional (the key might not be present). But it also takes an optional on assignment — subscripts have to both take and receive the same type. Without implicit conversion, you would have to write myDict["someKey"] = Optional(someValue).

Incidentally, if you're wondering what happens with key-based subscript assignment to dictionaries when you assign a nil, the answer is that the key is removed. This can be useful, but it also means you need to be a little careful when dealing with a dictionary with an optional value type. Consider this dictionary:

```
var dictWithNils: [String: Int?] = [
    "one": 1,
    "two": 2,
    "none": nil
]
```

The dictionary has three keys, and one of them has a value of **nil**. Suppose we wanted to set the value of the "two" key to **nil** as well. This will *not* do that:

```
dictWithNils["two"] = nil
```

Instead, it will *remove* the "two" key.

To change the value for the key, you would have to write one of the following (choose whichever you feel is clearer; they all work):

```
dictWithNils["two"] = Optional(nil)
dictWithNils["two"] = .Some(nil)
dictWithNils["two"]? = nil

dictWithNils["three"]? = nil
dictWithNils.indexForKey("three") // not found

nil
```

You can see that nothing would be updated/inserted.

Equatable and ==

Even though optionals have an == operator, this does not mean that they can conform to the Equatable protocol. This subtle but important distinction will hit you in the face if you try and do the following:

```
// two arrays of optional integers
let a: [Int?] = [1, 2, nil]
let b: [Int?] = [1, 2, nil]

// error: binary operator '==' cannot be applied to two [Int?] operands
a == b
```

The problem is that the == operator for arrays requires the elements of the array to be equatable:

```
func ==<Element : Equatable>(lhs: [Element], rhs: [Element]) -> Bool
```

Optionals don't conform to Equatable — that would require they implement == for any kind of type they contain, and they only can if that type is itself equatable. In the future, perhaps Swift will support conditional conformance — maybe something like this:

```
extension Optional: Equatable where T: Equatable {
    // no need to implement anything; == is already implemented so long
    // as this condition is  met
}
```

In the meantime, you could implement a version of == for arrays of optionals, like so:

```
func ==<T: Equatable>(lhs: [T?], rhs:  [T?]) -> Bool {
    return lhs.elementsEqual(rhs) { $0 == $1 }
}
```

switch-case Matching for Optionals:

Another consequence of optionals not being Equatable is that you can't check them in a **case** statement. **case** matching is controlled in Swift by the ~= operator, and the relevant definition looks a lot like the one that wasn't working for arrays:

```
func ~=<T: Equatable>(a: T, b: T) -> Bool
```

But it's simple to produce a matching version for optionals that just calls ==:

```
func ~=<T: Equatable>(pattern: T?, value: T?) -> Bool {
    return pattern == value
}
```

It's also nice to implement an interval match at the same time:

```
func ~=<I: IntervalType>(pattern: I,  value:  I.Bound?) -> Bool {
    return value.map { pattern.contains($0) } ?? false
}
```

Here, we use map to check if a non-**nil** value is inside the interval. Because we want **nil** not to match any interval, we return **false** in case of **nil**.

Given this, we can now match optional values with **switch**:

```
for i in ["2", "foo", "42", "100"] {
    switch Int(i) {
    case 42:
        print("The meaning of life")
    case 0..<10:
```

```
        print("A single digit")
    case nil:
        print("Not a number")
    default:
        print("A mystery number")
    }
}
```

```
A single digit
Not a number
The meaning of life
A mystery number
```

Comparing Optionals

Similar to ==, there is also an implementation of < for optionals, which relies on the type held in the optional conforming to Comparable. **nil** is always less than any non-**nil** value. It's important to realize that this means **nil** is less than *any* negative number when using <. If you sort using optional <, you'll find all the **nil** values gather up at one end:

```
let temps = ["-459.67", "98.6", "0", "warm"]
```

```
temps.sort { Double($0) < Double($1) }
```

```
["warm", "-459.67", "0", "98.6"]
```

This means you need to be careful to account for unexpected results:

```
let belowFreezing = temps.filter { Double($0) < 0 }
```

This kind of gotcha applies to optional == as well. The following code will evaluate to **true:**

```
let anyOne: Any = "1"
let anyTwo: Any = "99"
(anyOne as? Int) == (anyTwo as? Int)
```

This is because both sides are **nil** (they were strings, not integers), and two **nil**s are equal.

When to Force Unwrap

Given all these techniques for cleanly unwrapping optionals, when should you use !, the force-unwrap operator? There are many opinions on this scattered throughout the Internet, such as "never," "whenever it makes the code clearer," and "when you can't avoid it." We propose the following rule, which encompasses most of them:

> Use ! when you are so certain that a value will not be **nil** that you *want* your program to crash if it ever is.

As an example, take the implementation of flatten:

```
func flatten<S: SequenceType, T where S.Generator.Element == T?>
    (source: S) -> [T]
{
    return Array(source.lazy.filter { $0 != nil }.map { $0! })
}
```

Here, there is no possible way in the map that $0! will ever hit a **nil**, since the **nil** elements were all filtered out in the preceding filter step. This function could certainly be written to eliminate the force-unwrap operator by looping over the array and adding non-**nil** values into an array. But the filter/map version is cleaner and probably clearer, so the ! could be justified.

But these cases are pretty rare. If you have full mastery of all the unwrapping techniques described in this chapter, chances are there is a better way. Whenever you do find yourself reaching for !, it's worth taking a step back and wondering if there really is no other way. For example, we could have also implemented flatten using a single method call: source.flatMap { $0 }.

As another example, consider the following code that fetches all the keys in a dictionary with values matching a certain condition:

```
let ages = [
    "Tim":  53, "Angela": 54, "Craig": 44,
    "Jony": 47, "Chris": 37, "Michael": 34,
]

let people = ages
    .keys
```

```
        .sort()
        . filter  { name in ages[name]! < 50 }
```

(In theory, the sort would be better placed at the end, but as of the latest compiler, this does not work.)

Here, the ! is perfectly safe — since all the keys came from the dictionary, there is no possible way in which a key could be missing from the dictionary.

But you could also rewrite the statement to eliminate the need for a force unwrap altogether. Using the fact that dictionaries present themselves as sequences of key/value pairs, you could just filter this sequence and then run it through a map to remove the value:

```
let people = ages
        . filter  { (_, age) in age < 50 }
        .map { (name, _) in name }
        .sort()
```

This version even has a performance benefit: avoiding unnecessary key lookups.

Nonetheless, sometimes life hands you an optional, and you know *for certain* that it isn't **nil**. So certain are you of this that you would *rather* your program crash than continue, because it would mean a very nasty bug in your logic. Better to trap than to continue under those circumstances, so ! acts as a combined unwrap-or-error operator in one handy character. This approach is often a better move than just using the **nil** chaining or coalescing operators to sweep theoretically impossible situations under the carpet.

Improving Force-Unwrap Error Messages

That said, even when you are force unwrapping an optional value, you have options other than using the ! operator. When your program does error, you don't get much by way of description as to why in the output log.

Chances are, you will leave a comment as to why you are justified in force unwrapping. Why not have that comment serve as the error message too? Here is an operator, !!; it combines unwrapping with supplying a more descriptive error message to be logged when the application exits:

```
infix  operator !! { }
```

```
func !! <T>(wrapped: T?, @autoclosure failureText: ()->String) -> T {
    if let x = wrapped { return x }
    fatalError(failureText ())
}
```

Now you can write a more descriptive error message, including the value you expected to be able to unwrap:

```
let s = "foo"
let i = Int(s) !! "Expecting integer, got \"\(s)\""
```

The **@autoclosure** annotation makes sure that we only evaluate the second operand when needed. In the chapter on functions, we will go into this in more detail.

Asserting in Debug Builds

Still, choosing to crash even on release builds is quite a bold move. Often, you might prefer to assert during debug and test builds, but in production, you would substitute a valid default value, perhaps zero or an empty array.

Enter the interrobang operator, !?. We define this operator to assert on failed unwraps and also to substitute a default value when the assertion doesn't trigger in release mode:

```
infix operator !? { }
```

```
func !?<T: IntegerLiteralConvertible>
    (wrapped: T?, @autoclosure failureText: ()->String) -> T
{
    assert(wrapped != nil, failureText ())
    return wrapped ?? 0
}
```

Now, the following will assert while debugging, but print 0 in release:

```
let i = Int(s) !? "Expecting integer, got \"\(s)\""
```

Overloading for other literal convertible protocols enables a broad coverage of types that can be defaulted:

```
func !?<T: ArrayLiteralConvertible>
```

```
    (wrapped: T?, @autoclosure failureText: ()->String) -> T
{
    assert(wrapped != nil, failureText())
    return wrapped ?? []
}

func !?<T: StringLiteralConvertible>
    (wrapped: T?, @autoclosure failureText: ()->String) -> T
{
    assert(wrapped != nil, failureText)
    return wrapped ?? ""
}
```

And for when you want to provide a different explicit default, or for non-standard types, we can define a version that takes a pair — the default and the error text:

```
func !?<T>(wrapped: T?,
    @autoclosure nilDefault: () -> (value: T, text: String)) -> T
{
    assert(wrapped != nil, nilDefault().text)
    return wrapped ?? nilDefault().value
}

// asserts in debug, returns 5 in release
Int(s) !? (5, "Expected integer")
```

Since optionally chained method calls on methods that return Void return Void?, you can also write a non-generic version to detect when an optional chain hits a nil, resulting in a no-op:

```
func !?(wrapped: ()?, @autoclosure failureText: ()->String) {
    assert(wrapped != nil, failureText)
}

var output: String? = nil
output?.write("something") !? "Wasn't expecting chained nil here"
```

There are three ways to halt execution. The first option, fatalError, takes a message and stops execution unconditionally. The second option, assert, checks a condition and a message and stops execution if the condition evaluates to **false**. In release builds, the assert gets removed — the condition is not checked (and execution is never halted). The third option is precondition, which has the same interface as assert, but does not get removed from release builds, so if the condition evaluates to **false**, execution is stopped.

Living Dangerously: Implicit Optionals

Make no mistake: implicit optionals are still optionals — ones that are automatically force unwrapped whenever you use them. Now that we know that force unwraps will crash your application if they are ever **nil**, why on earth would you use them? Well, two reasons really.

Reason 1: Temporarily, because you are calling code that hasn't been audited for nullability into Objective-C.

Of course, on the first day you start writing Swift against your existing Objective-C, any Objective-C method that returns a reference will translate into an implicitly unwrapped optional. Since, until recently, there was no way to indicate that a reference was nullable from the Obj-C side, there was little option other than to assume any call returning a reference might return a **nil** reference. But few Objective-C APIs *actually* return null references, so it would be incredibly annoying to automatically expose them as optionals. Since everyone was used to dealing with the "maybe null" world of Objective-C objects, implicitly unwrapped optionals were a reasonable compromise.

So you see them in unaudited bridged Objective-C code. But you should *never* see a pure native Swift API returning an implicit optional (or passing one into a callback).

Reason 2: Because a value is **nil** *very* briefly, for a well-defined period of time, and is then never **nil** again.

For example, if you have a two-phase initialization, then by the time your class is ready to use, the implicitly wrapped optionals will all have a value. This is the reason Xcode/Interface Builder uses them.

Implicit Optional Behavior

As hard as implicit optionals try to hide their optional-ness from you, there are a few times when they behave slightly differently.

Sometimes they manifest as compiler errors. For example, you cannot pass an implicit optional into a function that takes the wrapped type as an **inout**:

```
func increment(inout x: Int) {
    x += 1
}
```

```
// regular Int
var i = 1
// increments i to 2
increment(&i)
```

```
// implicitly unwrapped Int
var j : Int! = 1
// error: cannot invoke 'increment' with an argument list of type '(inout Int !)'
increment(&j)
```

Other problems are more subtle. Especially strange are nested implicit optionals. While implicitly unwrapped optionals usually behave like non-optional values, you can still use most of the unwrap techniques to safely handle them like optionals — chaining, **nil**-coalescing, **if let**, and map all work the same:

```
var s: String! = "Hello"
s?.isEmpty // returns .Some(false)
if let s = s { print(s) }
s = nil
s ?? "Goodbye"
```

But doubly nested optionals are a bit tricky. If passing a doubly nested optional into a function, Swift will drill down to the inner value and pass that in. So the following will crash, because it unwraps the inner **nil**:

```
func useString(s: String) {
    print(s)
}
let s: String!! = nil
useString(s)
```

Optional chaining, on the other hand, operates on the *outer* value. So this will return **nil**:

```
let s: String!! = nil
s?.isEmpty // nil
```

Meanwhile, this will crash:

```
let s: String!! = .Some(nil)
s?.isEmpty // runtime error: unexpectedly found nil
// use double-?? to drill through into the inner optional:
s??.isEmpty // nil
```

Conclusion

Optionals are very useful when dealing with values that might or might not be nil. Rather than using magic values such as NSNotFound, we can use nil to indicate a value is empty. Swift has many built-in features that work with optionals so that you can avoid force unwrapping of optionals. Implicitly unwrapped optionals are useful when working with legacy code, but normal optionals should always be preferred (if possible). Finally, if you need more than just an optional (for example, you also need an error message if the result is not present), you can use errors, which we cover in the errors chapter.

Structs and Classes

In Swift, we can choose from three different options to store structured data: structs, enums, and classes. There is also a fourth way, capturing variables with closures, which we will discuss later in this chapter. In Swift's standard library, about 90 percent of the public types are defined as structs, with enums and classes making up 5 percent each. Part of this may be the nature of the types in the standard library, but it does give an indication as to the importance of structs in Swift. That said, we will mainly look at the differences between structs and classes in this chapter. We will not focus so much on enums because they behave in a way similar to structs.

Here are some of the major things that help distinguish between structs and classes:

→ Structs (and enums) are *value types*, whereas classes are *reference types*. When designing with structs, we can ask the compiler to enforce immutability. With classes, we have to enforce it ourselves.

→ How memory is managed differs. Structs can be held and accessed directly, whereas class instances are always accessed indirectly through their references. Structs are not referenced but instead copied. Structs have a single owner, whereas classes can have many owners.

→ Unless a class is marked as final, it can always be inherited from. With structs (and enums), inheritance is not possible. Instead, to share code using structs and enums, we need to use different techniques, such as composition, generics, and protocol extensions.

In this chapter, we will explore these differences in more detail. We'll start by looking at the differences between entities and values. Next, we will continue by discussing issues with mutability, and how **let** and **var** work differently for classes and value types. After that, we'll demonstrate how to wrap a reference type in a struct in order to use it as a value type. Then we'll compare the differences in how memory is managed — particularly how memory is managed for reference types. Given all those details, we'll look at solving the same problem using reference types and value types. We will look at inheritance, and finally, we will refactor a class-based design for a game into a struct-based design.

Value Types

We are often dealing with objects that need an explicit *lifecycle*: they are initialized, changed, and destroyed. For example, a file handle has a clear lifecycle: it is opened, actions are performed on it, and then we need to close it. If we open two file handles that otherwise have the same properties, we still want to keep them separate. In order to compare two file handles, we check whether they point to the same address in memory. Because we compare addresses, file handles are best implemented as reference types, using objects. This is what the NSFileHandle class in Foundation does.

Other types do not need to have a lifecycle. For example, a URL is created and then never changed. More importantly, it does not need to perform any action when it is destroyed (in contrast to the file handle, which needs to be closed). When we compare two URL variables, we do not care whether they point to the same address in memory, rather we check whether they point to the same URL. Because we compare URLs by their properties, we say that they are *values*. In Objective-C, they were implemented as immutable objects using the NSURL class. However, if they were built natively in Swift, we would implement them using structs.

In all software, there are many objects that have a lifecycle — file handles, notification centers, networking interfaces, database connections, and view controllers are some examples. For all these types, we want to perform specific actions on initialization and when they are destroyed. When comparing these types, we do not compare their properties, but instead compare their memory addresses. All of these types are implemented using objects, and all of them are reference types.

There are also many values at play in most software. URLs, binary data, dates, errors, strings, notifications, and numbers are only defined by their properties. When we compare them, we are not interested in their memory addresses. All of these types can be implemented using structs.

Values never change; they are immutable. This is (mostly) a good thing, because code that works with immutable data is much easier to understand. The immutability automatically makes such code thread-safe too: anything that cannot change can be safely shared across threads.

In Swift, structs are designed to build values. Structs cannot be compared by reference; we can only compare their properties. And although we can declare mutable struct *variables* (using **var**), it is important to understand that the mutability only refers to the variable, and not the underlying value. Mutating a property of a struct variable is conceptually the same as assigning a whole new struct (with a different value for the property) to the variable.

Structs have a single owner. For instance, if we pass a struct variable to a function, that function receives a copy of the struct, and it can only change its own copy. This is called *value semantics* (sometimes also called copy semantics). Contrast this with the way objects work: they get passed by reference and can have many owners. This is called *reference semantics*.

Because structs only have a single owner, it is not possible to create a reference cycle. With classes and functions, we need to always be careful to not create reference cycles. We will look at reference cycles in the section on memory.

The fact that values are copied all the time may sound inefficient; however, the compiler can optimize away many superfluous copy operations. It can do this because structs are very basic things. A struct copy is a shallow bitwise copy (except if it contains any classes — then it needs to increase the reference count for those). When structs are declared with **let**, the compiler knows for certain that none of those bits can be mutated later on. And there are no hooks for the developer to know *when* the struct is being copied, unlike with similar value types in C++. This simplicity gives the compiler many more possibilities for eliminating copy operations or optimizing a constant structure to be passed by reference rather than by value.

Copy optimizations of a value *type* that might be done by the compiler are not the same as the copy-on-write behavior of a type with value *semantics*. Copy-on-write has to be implemented by the developer, and it works by detecting that the contained class has shared references.

Unlike with elimination of value type copies, you do not get copy-on-write for free. But the two optimizations — the compiler potentially eliminating unnecessary "dumb" shallow copies, and the code inside types like arrays that perform "smart" copy-on-write — complement each other. We'll look at how to implement your own copy-on-write mechanism shortly.

If your struct is composed out of other structs, the compiler can enforce immutability. Also, when using structs, the compiler can generate really fast code. For example, the performance of operations on an array containing just structs is usually much better than an array containing objects. This is because structs usually have less indirection: the values are stored directly inside the array's memory. An array containing objects contains just the references to the objects. Finally, in many cases, the compiler can put structs on the stack, rather than on the heap.

When interfacing with Cocoa and Objective-C, we almost always need to use classes. For example, when implementing a delegate for a table view, there is no choice: we must use a class. Many of Apple's frameworks rely heavily on subclassing. However, depending on the problem domain, we can still create a class where the objects are values. For example, in the Core Image framework, the CIImage objects are immutable: they represent an image that never changes. We can even wrap classes inside structs, but we'll need to take special care to make sure we maintain value semantics.

It's not always easy to decide whether your new type should be a struct or a class. For example, if you are defining an Address type, you could build it as an object. Because objects are passed by reference, any changes to an address will change all variables pointing to that same object. In contrast, if you define Address as a struct, all changes are local. In the examples in the rest of this chapter, we will look in more detail at the implications of this behavior and provide some guidance for when to use structs.

Mutability

In many object-oriented languages, including Objective-C, data is mutable by default. For example, if we create a new instance of a class, we can mutate it:

```
let fileHandle = NSFileHandle(forReadingAtPath: "test.txt")
fileHandle?.seekToFileOffset(10) // Mutates
```

Often, when working with an object, you might assume some properties won't change during the duration of a method. For example, we might want some code to execute only if the file handle's position is zero. In the code below, we check that with a simple condition:

```
if fileHandle.offsetInFile == 0 {
    prepareHandle(fileHandle)
    // continue processing
}
```

But perhaps the prepareHandle function changes the file handle's offset, and after that call, the formatter has a different offset. If we want to be sure the file handle does not change, we either have to pass a copy to prepareHandle or check once again after the call. In the case of file handles, we cannot create a copy.

This problem becomes even bigger when dealing with multi-threaded code. Consider the following snippet:

```
let stream: NSInputStream = ...
dispatch_async(...)
while stream.hasBytesAvailable {
    // Process the stream
}
```

If the stream is shared across threads, then during the execution of the **while** block, the value of hasBytesAvailable might change. This can lead to unexpected results. For example, if another thread starts processing the same input stream directly after the condition but before the body of the **while** statement is executed, our code might crash.

In recent years, there has been an emerging consensus that immutability and value types can help resolve many of the issues that arise when doing multi-threaded programming. They make code easier to understand, increase confidence that the code is correct and doing what was intended, and can be safer in multi-threaded environments.

Many frameworks, including Cocoa, have immutable objects — instances of classes that just do not have any public methods that change the internal state of an object. For example, Cocoa has NSData, which has no methods for changing the data, and NSMutableData, which inherits from NSData and adds mutating methods.

However, there is often no enforcement of this immutability. Consider the following function. We might make the assumption that x is immutable and will not change during the duration of the call:

```
func processData(x: NSData) {
    // Do some work with x
}
```

But the assumption that x is guaranteed to be immutable is not correct. In the code below, we create a mutable object, and because NSMutableData is a subclass of NSData, we can pass it to a function that expects an argument of type NSData. Yet because the object is really an instance of NSMutableData, it could end up being mutated outside the function simultaneously, which also mutates x within the processData function:

```
processAsync {
```

```
    let y = NSMutableData() //...
    onMainThread {
        processData(y)
    }
    // Further changes to y
}
```

In the example above, we have control over both the caller and the callee, so we could solve the problem in two ways. For example, we could pass an immutable *copy* of the data to processData. A more robust solution, however, would be to make a copy *within* processData, because we might also get called by code over which we have no control. So we make a copy and then work with that:

```
func processData(x: NSData) {
    let data = x.copy() as! NSData
    // Do some work with data
}
```

There are two shortcomings to this. Firstly, we might make unnecessary copies. In the case where the data is already immutable (it's an NSData object), Foundation is smart and returns the same object. In the case where the data is mutable (an NSMutableData object) but will not be mutated again, a copy is still made. Secondly, we need to manually make a copy at every point where we expect to be called with a mutable value. In case we forget to secure our code and accidentally introduce a bug, we might not notice when running the code, because asynchronous bugs often do not happen deterministically.

In Swift, we can let the compiler help us with enforcing immutability. We can encode guarantees about immutability, both with structs and classes alike. First, let's consider a class with one mutable variable:

```
class Person {
    var name: String
    init (name: String) {
        self.name = name
    }
}
```

This allows us to create an instance of the class and change the name:

```
let p = Person(name: "John")
p.name = "Dave"
p.name.appendContentsOf(" Smith")
```

However, if we define the name using **let**, it can only be assigned once, during initialization. It can never be changed afterward:

```
class ImmutablePerson {
    let name: String

    init (name: String) {
        self.name = name
    }
}
```

The following code snippet does not compile, because the compiler enforces the immutability of the name property. We can neither change the property itself (e.g. assign a new value) nor change the value (e.g. appending something to the string):

```
let person = ImmutablePerson(name: "John")
person.name = "Dave" // Won't compile
person.name.appendContentsOf(" Smith") // Won't compile
```

However, defining all your properties as **let** is no guarantee for immutability. For example, consider the following class:

```
class File {
    let data: NSMutableData

    init (data: NSMutableData) {
        self.data = data
    }
}
```

Even with a **let** instance of the File class, we can still change the data property. We cannot change *which* object it is pointing to, but we *can* change that object itself:

```
let data = NSMutableData()
let file = File(data: data)
file.data = NSMutableData() // This is illegal
file.data.appendData(someOtherData) // This works
```

This might lead to unexpected results: even though a property is defined as **let** and is seemingly immutable, the internals of its value might change. There is a difference when compared to the previous example: Swift's String type is a struct, and NSMutableData is a class. Marking a struct variable as **let** makes it truly immutable, whereas marking an object as **let** only prevents the reference from being changed. The compiler will not allow us to change properties of a struct that is defined as **let**, but we can change properties of an object that is defined using **let**. In the next section, we will look at how this works.

Value Types

Value types imply that whenever a variable is copied, the value itself — and not just a reference to the value — is copied. For example, in almost all programming languages, scalar types are value types. This means that whenever a value is assigned to a new variable, it is copied rather than passed by reference:

```
var a = 42
var b = a
b += 1
```

After the code above executes, the value of b will be 43, but a will still be 42. This is so natural that it seems like stating the obvious.

But compare this to a very similar example with a simple class, like CIFilter from Apple's Core Image framework. The CIFilter class provides an output image and is typically configured with an input image and some other parameters. In this example, we create a Gaussian blur filter:

```
let inputParameters = [
    kCIInputRadiusKey: 10,
    kCIInputImageKey: image
]
let blurFilter = CIFilter(name: "CIGaussianBlur",
    withInputParameters: inputParameters)!

let secondBlurFilter = blurFilter
secondBlurFilter.setValue(20, forKey: kCIInputRadiusKey)
```

Objects are always passed by reference. Therefore, the variable secondBlurFilter points to the same instance of CIFilter: they are both a *reference* to the same object. Changing the inputRadius of one also changes the inputRadius of the other; after all, they are pointing to the same instance. Because both variables reference the same object, they now both have an updated input radius of 20.

Instead, if we want a second filter that is different, we need to manually copy the filter before assigning it to the new variable:

```
let otherBlurFilter = blurFilter.copy() as! CIFilter
otherBlurFilter.setValue(20, forKey: kCIInputRadiusKey)
```

As stated before, in Swift, both structs and enums are value types. We could create our own GaussianBlur struct, where we save the input image and radius in a variable:

```
struct GaussianBlur {
    var inputImage: CIImage
    var radius: Double
}

var blur1 = GaussianBlur(inputImage: image, radius: 10)
blur1.radius = 20
var blur2 = blur1
blur2.radius = 30
```

Because GaussianBlur is a value type, assigning blur1 to a new variable, blur2, will make a copy. Subsequent changes to the copy do not change the original: when we set blur2.radius, the value of blur1 remains unchanged. While this copying sounds wasteful, the compiler can often optimize copy operations away. Also, when the struct is implemented using copy-on-write, the actual copy of the data is only made once one of the values actually changes. In fact, this is how Swift arrays work: they are implemented using copy-on-write. Later on, we will look more closely at how to implement this technique.

If we wanted to add an outputImage property to our struct, we could do that using an extension. Here, we create a CIFilter, set the default parameters, and then configure it using the values in our struct. The code below will create a new filter every time the outputImage is accessed. However, this is not very efficient; if we access the property multiple times, a new filter will get created every time:

```
extension GaussianBlur {
    var outputImage: CIImage {
        let filter = CIFilter(name: "CIGaussianBlur", withInputParameters: [
            kCIInputImageKey: inputImage,
            kCIInputRadiusKey: radius
        ])!
        return filter.outputImage!
    }
```

```
}
```

A More Efficient Attempt

To improve performance, we could try a slightly different solution. This solution is *not correct*, but we will use it as the basis for a correct implementation in the next section. Instead of storing the values in the struct, we store an instance of CIFilter and modify that through custom properties. We declare the filter as a **var** because we will need this later on:

```
struct GaussianBlur {
    private var filter : CIFilter

    init (inputImage: CIImage, radius: Double) {
        filter  = CIFilter (name: "CIGaussianBlur", withInputParameters: [
            kCIInputImageKey: inputImage,
            kCIInputRadiusKey: radius
        ])!
    }
}
```

We can implement the inputImage and radius properties by directly accessing and modifying the filter's properties:

```
extension GaussianBlur {
    var inputImage: CIImage {
        get { return filter .valueForKey(kCIInputImageKey) as! CIImage }
        set { filter .setValue(newValue, forKey: kCIInputImageKey) }
    }

    var radius: Double {
        get { return filter .valueForKey(kCIInputRadiusKey) as! Double }
        set { filter .setValue(newValue, forKey: kCIInputRadiusKey) }
    }
}
```

Finally, to get the output image out, we can directly use the outputImage property on the filter:

```
extension GaussianBlur {
    var outputImage: CIImage {
        return filter .outputImage!
    }
}
```

We still have the same struct-based API, and as long as we only use a single filter, everything works fine:

```
var blur = GaussianBlur(inputImage: image, radius: 25)
blur.outputImage
```

However, once we start making copies of the struct, we will run into a problem:

```
var otherBlur = blur
otherBlur.radius = 10
```

By creating a variable, otherBlur, the blur struct gets copied. The way Swift structs work is that all value types get copied, but for reference types, the *reference* to the object, and not the object itself, gets copied. Even though otherBlur and blur are two different values, they both point to the same CIFilter instance. Now both values will have a radius of 10, because the radius setter changed the original object:

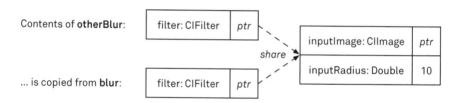

Figure 5.1: References are shared between blur and otherBlur

Copy-On-Write

One of the most powerful features of Swift is implementing structs with value semantics using mutable objects under the hood, which is exactly what we tried in the previous section. We get the benefits of value semantics, but we still have highly efficient code. However, as we have seen, this can lead to unwanted sharing. The approach we take in this section is to prevent sharing by copying the wrapped object every time the struct gets modified. This technique is called copy-on-write, and it is also how many of Swift's data structures work. In order to implement copy-on-write, we can use a nice trick and define a custom accessor for filter, which copies the CIFilter before returning:

```
extension GaussianBlur {
    private var filterForWriting: CIFilter {
```

```
        mutating get {
            filter = filter .copy() as! CIFilter
            return filter
        }
    }
}
```

This allows us to change the setters of our filter, which make a copy before changing the values:

```
extension GaussianBlur {
    var inputImage: CIImage {
        get { return filter .valueForKey(kCIInputImageKey) as! CIImage }
        set {
            filterForWriting.setValue(newValue, forKey: kCIInputImageKey)
        }
    }

    var radius: Double {
        get { return filter .valueForKey(kCIInputRadiusKey) as! Double }
        set {
            filterForWriting.setValue(newValue, forKey: kCIInputRadiusKey)
        }
    }
}
```

The approach above works as expected but comes at a performance cost: every time we change the filter, a new copy gets made, even if we only make in-place changes and don't share the struct:

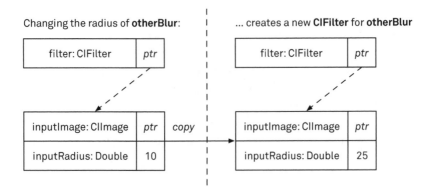

Figure 5.2: Changing the filter always makes a copy

Copy-On-Write, Efficiently

There is a function in Swift, isUniquelyReferencedNonObjC, which checks whether an instance of a class is uniquely referenced. We can use this to keep value semantics for the struct while avoiding unnecessary copies: only when the object is shared between multiple structs do we copy it before we modify the instance. Unfortunately, the isUniquelyReferencedNonObjC function only works with Swift objects, and CIFilter is an Objective-C class. To work around this, we create a simple wrapper type, Box, which wraps any type in a Swift class:

```
final class Box<A> {
    var unbox: A
    init (_ value: A) { unbox = value }
}
```

This function allows us to change our implementation. Instead of storing the filter directly, we store the boxed filter and turn filter into a computed property that takes care of the boxing and unboxing:

```
private var boxedFilter: Box<CIFilter> = {
    var filter = CIFilter (name: "CIGaussianBlur",
        withInputParameters: [:])!
    filter .setDefaults()
    return Box(filter)
}()

var filter : CIFilter {
    get { return boxedFilter.unbox }
    set { boxedFilter = Box(newValue) }
}
```

> There is another function, isUniquelyReferenced, which does not work on Objective-C types either; even though it accepts Objective-C types as input, it always returns **false**. Both functions share the same implementation, but they have different constraints on the input types.

Having this in place allows us to change the implementation of filterForWriting. It now checks whether or not the filter is shared and only makes a copy when it needs to. As long as the instance is the only owner, we can safely mutate the existing filter:

```
private var filterForWriting: CIFilter {
    mutating get {
        if !isUniquelyReferencedNonObjC(&boxedFilter) {
            filter = filter .copy() as! CIFilter
        }
        return filter
    }
}
```

This is exactly how Swift arrays work internally. When you create a new copy of an array, it is backed by the same data. Only once you start modifying one of the arrays will a copy of the buffer be made so that changes don't affect the other array.

We can verify this behavior by writing a few simple tests. First of all, if we create two structs that share the same properties, no copy is made:

```
let blur = GaussianBlur(inputImage: image, radius: 10)
var blur2 = blur
assert(blur. filter === blur2.filter)
```

When we change the radius of blur2, the filterForWriting implementation will detect that the filter object is shared. As a result, it will make a copy:

```
blur2.radius = 25
assert(blur. filter !== blur2. filter )
```

Finally, if we change blur2 again, its filter is already unique. Therefore, changing it once more will not make a new copy of the filter:

```
let existingFilter = blur2. filter
blur2.radius = 100
assert(existingFilter === blur2.filter)
```

This technique allows you to create custom structs that are value types while still being just as efficient as you would be working with objects or pointers. You do not need to worry about copying these structs manually — the compiler will take care of it for you, and the copy is only made when absolutely necessary.

When you define your own structs and classes, it is important to pay attention to the expected copying and mutability behavior. Structs are expected to have value semantics. When using a class inside a struct, we need to make sure that it is truly immutable. If this is not possible, we either need to take extra steps (like above), or just use a class, in which case consumers of our data do not expect it to behave like a value.

Most data structures in the Swift standard library are value types. For example, arrays, dictionaries, sets, and strings are all structs. This makes it simpler to understand code that uses those types. When we pass an array to a function, we know the function can't modify the original array: it only works on a copy of the array. Also, the way arrays are implemented, we know that no unnecessary copies will be made. Contrast this with the Foundation data types, where it is best practice to always manually copy types like NSArray and NSString. When working with Foundation data types, it is easy to forget to manually copy the object and instead accidentally write unsafe code.

When creating an immutable type, there might still be good reasons to use a class. For example, sometimes you might want an immutable type that is never shared, such as a singleton that represents a unique resource. By defining a restrictive interface, this is still very possible. Or you might need to interface with Objective-C, in which case structs will not work either.

It might also be interesting to wrap existing types in structs (or enums). In the chapter on wrapping CommonMark, we will provide an enum-based interface to a reference type. Even data types from Foundation, such as NSData, could be wrapped in a struct, allowing you to write safer and more efficient code.

Closures and Mutability

In this section, we will look at how closures store data.

For example, consider a function that generates a unique integer every time it gets called (until it reaches Int.max). It works by moving the state outside of the function. In other words, it *closes* over the variable i:

```swift
var i = 0
func uniqueInteger() -> Int {
    i += 1
    return i
}
```

Every time we call this function, the shared variable i will change, and a different integer will be returned. Functions are reference types as well — if we assign uniqueInteger to another variable, the compiler will not copy the function (or i). Instead, it will create a reference to the same function:

```
let otherFunction: () -> Int = uniqueInteger
```

Calling otherFunction will have exactly the same effect as calling uniqueInteger. This is true for all closures and functions: if we pass them around, they always get passed by reference, and they always share the same state.

Recall the generator example from the collections chapter, where we've seen this behavior before. When we used the generator, the generator itself (being a function) was mutating its state. In order to create a fresh generator for each iteration, we had to implement SequenceType, which was done by writing a function that returns a generator function.

If we want to have multiple different unique integer providers, we can use the same technique: instead of returning the integer, we return a closure that captures the mutable variable. The returned closure is a reference type, and passing it around will share the state. However, calling uniqueIntegerProvider repeatedly returns a fresh function that starts at zero every time:

```
func uniqueIntegerProvider() -> () -> Int {
    var i = 0
    return {
      i += 1
      return i
    }
}
```

Memory

Value types are very common in Swift. Most of the types in the standard library are either structs or enums, and memory management for them is very easy. Because they have a single owner, the memory needed for them is created and freed automatically. When using value types, you can't create cyclic references. For example, consider the following snippet:

```
struct Person {
    let name: String
    var parents: [Person]
}

var john = Person(name: "John", parents: [])
john.parents = [john]
print(john)
```

Because of the way value types work, the moment we put john in an array, a copy is created. If Person were a class, we would now have a cycle. With the struct version, john now has a single parent, which is the original value of john, with no parents.

> Swift structs are commonly stored on the stack rather than on the heap. However, there are exceptions. If a struct has a dynamic size, or if a struct is too large, it will be stored on the heap. Also, if a struct value is closed over by a function (like in the examples using closures), the value is stored on the heap so that it persists, even when the scope it's defined in will exit.

For classes, Swift uses automated reference counting to manage memory. In most cases, this means that things will work as expected. Every time you create a new reference to an object, the reference count gets increased by one. Once you let go of that reference (for example, the variable goes out of scope), the reference count decreases by one. If the reference count is zero, the object is deallocated.

For example, consider the following code:

```swift
class View {
    var window: Window
    init (window: Window) {
        self.window = window
    }
}

class Window {
    var rootView: View?
}
```

We can now create a variable, which allocates and initializes the object. The first line creates a new instance, and the reference count is one. The moment we set the variable to nil, the reference count of our Window instance is zero, and the instance gets deallocated:

```swift
var window: Window? = Window()
window = nil
```

When comparing Swift to a garbage-collected language, at first glance it looks like things are very similar when it comes to memory management. Most

times, you don't even think about it. However, consider the following
example:

```
var window: Window? = Window()
var view: View? = View(window: window!)
window?.rootView = view
view = nil
window = nil
```

First, the window gets created, and the reference count for the window will be
one. The view gets created and holds a strong reference to the window, so the
window's reference count will be two, and the view's reference count will be
one. Then, assigning the view as the window's rootView will increase the
view's reference count by one. Now, both the view and the window have a
reference count of two. After setting both variables to nil, they still have a
reference count of one. Even though they are not accessible from a variable
any longer, they strongly reference each other. This is called a *reference cycle*,
and when dealing with graph-like data structures, we need to be very aware of
this. Because of the reference cycle, these two objects will never be deallocated
during the lifetime of the program.

Weak References

To break the reference cycle, we need to make sure that one of the references is
either **weak** or **unowned**. A **weak** reference means that the reference will be **nil**
once the referred object gets deallocated. For example, we could make the
rootView property **weak**, which means it will not be strongly referenced by the
window and automatically becomes **nil** once the view is deallocated:

```
class View {
    var window: Window
    init (window: Window) {
        self.window = window
    }
}

class Window {
    weak var rootView: View?
}
```

In the code below, we create a window and a view. The view strongly
references the window, but because the window's rootView is declared as **weak**,
the window does not strongly reference the view. This way, we have broken the

reference cycle, and after setting both variables to **nil**, both views get deallocated:

```
var window: Window? = Window()
var view: View? = View(window: window!)
window?.rootView = view!
window = nil
view = nil
```

TOOD: is the following sentence true? Commenting it out for now. Weak references use a global table to keep track of when an object is deallocated; this is not stored in the object itself.

Unowned References

Weak references must always be optional types because they can become **nil**, but sometimes we might not want this. For example, maybe we know that our views will always have a window (so the property shouldn't be optional), but we do not want a view to strongly reference the window. For these cases, there is the **unowned** keyword, which assumes the reference is always valid:

```
class View {
    unowned var window: Window
    init (window: Window) {
        self.window = window
    }
}

class Window {
    var rootView: View?
}
```

Now, we can create a window, create views, and set the window's root view. There is no reference cycle, but we are responsible for ensuring that the window outlives the view. If the window is deallocated and the unowned variable is accessed, there will be a runtime crash:

```
var window: Window? = Window()
var view: View? = View(window: window!)
window?.rootView = view
view = nil
window = nil
```

For every **unowned** reference, the Swift runtime keeps a second reference count in the object. When all strong references are gone, the object will release all of its resources (for example, any references to other objects). However, the memory of the object itself will still be there until all **unowned** references are gone too. The memory is marked as invalid (sometimes also called *zombie* memory), and anytime we try to access an **unowned** reference a runtime error will occur.

There is a third option, **unowned**(unsafe), which does not have this runtime check. If we access an invalid reference that is marked as **unowned**(unsafe), we get undefined behavior.

When you do not need **weak**, it is recommended[1] that you use **unowned**. A **weak** variable always needs to be defined using **var**, whereas an **unowned** variable can be defined using **let** and be immutable. However, only use **unowned** in situations where you know that the reference will always be valid.

Structs and Classes in Practice

As stated in the introduction of this chapter, choosing whether or not you want a value or an entity to represent your data is very dependent upon the type of data and on your problem domain. In this section, we will look at transferring money between bank accounts and represent it in three different ways: once using classes, once using structs and a pure function, and once using structs with an **inout** parameter.

Classes

A natural way to model bank accounts is to use classes. Because accounts have identity, this is a great fit. We can create a simple class that only holds an integer for the funds in the account:

```
typealias USDCents = Int

class Account {
    var funds: USDCents = 0
    init (funds: USDCents) {
        self.funds = funds
```

1 https://twitter.com/jckarter/status/654819932962598913

```
    }
}
```

We create two sample accounts:

```
let alice = Account(funds: 100)
let bob = Account(funds: 0)
```

Writing the transfer function is easy. We choose to return Bool, indicating whether or not the transfer succeeded. The only reason why a transfer would fail is because of insufficient funds:

```
func transfer(amount: USDCents, source: Account, destination: Account)
    -> Bool
{
    guard source.funds >= amount else { return false }
    source.funds -= amount
    destination.funds += amount
    return true
}
```

Calling the transfer function is easy too. We pass in the amount and the two accounts, and the accounts will get modified in-place:

```
transfer(50, source: alice, destination: bob)
```

The code above is simple to write and simple to understand. There is only one issue with it: it is not thread-safe. Depending on your problem domain, this might not be an issue. But if you do work in a multi-threaded environment, you need to take great care not to call the function from multiple threads at the same time (for example, you could perform all calls on a serial queue). Otherwise, concurrent threads can make the system lose funds or add non-existing funds.

Pure Structs

We could also use a struct to model accounts. The definition is very similar to the previous example, but we can drop the initializer because the compiler automatically generates a default memberwise initializer:

```
struct Account {
    var funds: USDCents
}
```

The transfer function becomes more complicated, though. It still takes in an amount and two accounts. We create a mutable copy of the input account parameters by using **var**, which means they are mutable within the body of the function. However, such mutations do *not* change the original values that get passed in. To pass the changed account information back to the caller, we return a pair of updated accounts instead of the simple boolean value we used above. If the transfer does not succeed, we return **nil**:

```
func transfer(amount: USDCents, source: Account, destination: Account)
    -> (source: Account, destination: Account)?
{
    guard source.funds >= amount else { return nil }
    var newSource = source
    var newDestination = destination
    newSource.funds -= amount
    newDestination.funds += amount
    return (newSource, newDestination)
}
```

The great thing about a transfer function like this is that, just by looking at the type, we know it cannot change our accounts. Because Account is a struct, we know that there is no way the function can modify it. Again, working with value types makes our code easier to understand.

Also, because structs are values, we know that an account cannot be changed by another thread. At the very least, the two accounts are always in a consistent state.

At some point, we do have to store a mutable variable holding all the program's accounts. This is the single source of truth in our program. We could update the variable in the following way:

```
if let (newAlice, newBob) = transfer(50, source: alice, destination: bob) {
    // Update source of data
}
```

Again, we need to make sure that updates to the single source of truth are happening one after another. However, it is easier to do this in a single place rather than having to make sure that the function is never called in a non-thread-safe manner anywhere in your code. This comes at the cost of having a slightly more verbose program.

Structs with inout

A final example is to use structs and a function with **inout** parameters. This uses the same struct as above, but the transfer function looks different. Rather than marking our account parameters as **var**, we mark them as **inout**. This means that the values get copied in (so that within the body of the function, they cannot get mutated by other threads), and when the function returns, they get copied back into their original values:

```
func transfer
    (amount: USDCents, inout source: Account, inout destination: Account)
    -> Bool
{
    guard source.funds >= amount else { return false }
    source.funds -= amount
    destination.funds += amount
    return true
}
```

We need to prefix the **inout** arguments with an ampersand when we call the function, but note again that this is not by reference, despite the syntax similarity to passing in a C pointer. When the function returns, the modified values get copied back out to the caller:

```
var alice  = Account(funds: 100)
var bob = Account(funds: 0)
transfer(50, source: &alice, destination: &bob)
```

The advantage of this approach is that it guarantees consistency within the body of the function while still being almost as easy to write as the class-based approach.

In all three approaches, we need to think carefully about concurrency. In the first approach, it is very easy to make a mistake, and things can go wrong even within the transfer function. In the other two approaches, we still need to consider concurrency, but not within the transfer function itself — we can solve the problem in a single place.

Closures and Memory

In addition to classes, there is another reference type: closures. As we have seen in the section on mutability, a closure can capture variables. If these variables are reference types, the closure will maintain a strong reference to them. This is necessary for variable capture, but it also has a downside: it is very easy to introduce reference cycles.

To show when an object gets initialized and deinitialized, we can create a simple class that prints both stages:

```
class Example {
    init () { print("init") }
    deinit { print("deinit") }
}
```

To test when **deinit** gets called, we can create a new function. Inside the body of that function, we will initialize a new instance. The initializer gets called, and the reference count of example is one. Then the print statement in the body of the function will execute, and finally, because example goes out of scope, the reference count will be lowered by one. Because the reference count of example is now zero, it will get deallocated, and **deinit** will get called:

```
func newScope() {
    let example = Example()
    print("About to leave the scope")
}
```

We can verify this by calling our function. However, when we create a closure that references example, the closure will keep a strong reference to example until it goes out of scope itself. In this example, we return the closure from the function:

```
func capturingScope() -> () -> () {
    let example = Example()
    return { print(example) }
}
```

If we keep the closure around by assigning the return value to a variable, we can see that example will not get deallocated, because the closure still has a strong reference to it:

```
let z = capturingScope()
```

However, if we ignore the return value, the closure gets deallocated immediately because no one has a strong reference to it. This will cause example's reference count to drop to zero, which means it gets deallocated:

```
let _ = capturingScope()
```

When working with closures, we always need to be aware of what the closure references. Particularly if the closure is being referenced itself, it is easy to introduce a reference cycle, as we will see in the next section.

Reference Cycles

One of the issues with closures capturing their variables is the (accidental) introduction of reference cycles. The usual pattern is like this: object A references object B, but object B references a callback that references object A. For example, a view controller references an XML parser. The view controller configures the XML parser by setting a callback function. However, the callback function references the view controller, and a reference cycle is created.

In a diagram, it looks like this:

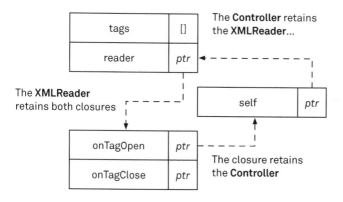

Figure 5.3: A retain cycle between the reader, controller, and closure

Translated to code, the XMLReader could look something like this:

```
class XMLReader {
    var onTagOpen: (tagName: String) -> ()
    var onTagClose: (tagName: String) -> ()

    init (url: NSURL) {
        // ...
```

```
            onTagOpen = { _ in }
            onTagClose = { _ in }
        }

    deinit {
        print("reader deinit")
    }
}
```

The controller initializes an XMLReader and also contains an empty array in which we will store the tag names that are read:

```
class Controller {
    let reader: XMLReader = XMLReader(url: NSURL())
    var tags: [String] = []

    deinit { print("controller deinit") }
}
```

The reference cycle originates in the viewDidLoad method. Here, we assign a new closure to the XMLReader's onTagOpen callback. This closure appends a tag to the view controller's tags array. However, that means the closure will hold a reference to the view controller, the XMLReader will hold a reference to the closure, and the view controller will hold a reference to the XMLReader, thereby creating a reference cycle:

```
func viewDidLoad() {
    reader.onTagOpen = {
        self.tags.append($0)
    }
}
```

We need to find a way to break this cycle. There are three places where we could break the cycle (each corresponding to an arrow in the diagram):

→ We could make the reference to the XMLReader weak. Unfortunately, this would make the XMLReader disappear, because there are no other references keeping it alive.

→ We could change the XMLReader to make the onTagOpen closure weak. This wouldn't work either, as closures cannot be marked as **weak**. And even if **weak** closures were possible, all users of the XMLReader would need to know this and somehow manually reference the closure.

→ We could make sure the closure does not reference the controller by using a capture list. This is the only correct option in the above example.

In the case of the (constructed) example above, it is not too hard to figure out that we have a reference cycle. However, it is not always this easy. Sometimes the number of objects involved might be much larger, and the reference cycle might be harder to spot.

Capture Lists

To break the cycle above, we want to make sure that the closure will not reference the controller. We can do this by using a *capture list* and marking the captured variable (**self**) as either **weak** or **unowned**. In this case, we know that the controller will outlive the XMLReader (the reader is owned by the controller), so we can use **unowned**:

```
func viewDidLoad() {
    reader.onTagOpen = { [unowned self] in
        self.tags.append($0)
    }
}
```

If we would have chosen to use a **weak** reference instead, **self** would be optional, and the call would look like this:

```
self?.tags.append($0)
```

Capture lists can also be used to initialize new variables. For example, if we wanted to have a **weak** variable that refers to the reader (myReader), we could initialize it in the capture list, like so:

```
reader.onTagOpen = { [unowned self, weak myReader = self.reader] tag in
    self.tags.append(tag)
    if tag == "stop" {
        myReader?.stop()
    }
}
```

This is almost the same as defining it just above the closure, except that with capture lists, the scope of the variable is just the scope of the closure; it is not available outside of the closure.

In the next chapter, we will also look at **@noescape**, which can help tremendously in avoiding reference cycles when dealing with closures.

Case Study: Game Design with Structs

Let's consider building a roguelike game, where a player can discover different levels and find items on the way. We will start with an extremely simple version of the game state. We implement our first version using classes: a Player class, a Health class, and a class for each of the items.

To persist the game, we can use something like NSUserDefaults, which provides simple key-value storage on iOS and OS X. We use dependency injection to make the persistence code testable; rather than working directly with NSUserDefaults.standardUserDefaults, each of our classes is passed an NSUserDefaults instance in its initializer. We can then pass different objects in our production code and our tests.

To make testing even easier, we create a Storage protocol as an abstraction over the concrete persistence API. Our game classes only care about the API defined in the protocol, regardless of the actual implementation. This allows us to easily swap out NSUserDefaults for a mock object in our tests, and it also gives us the flexibility to replace NSUserDefaults with a different persistence technology in the future. In this simplified version, the protocol has a subscript for getting and setting integers. Because the persisted values might not exist (for example, the first time we launch the game), the subscript returns an optional. Also, we make NSUserDefaults conform to the protocol:

```
protocol Storage {
    subscript(name: String) -> Int? { get set }
}

extension NSUserDefaults: Storage {
    subscript(name: String) -> Int? {
        get {
            return (objectForKey(name) as? NSNumber)?.integerValue
        }
        set {
            setObject(newValue, forKey: name)
        }
    }
}
```

Our player class has three properties. First, it owns the health object, which stores the player's food and experience points. It also stores a property, chocolates, which can optionally contain a box of chocolates (in a real game, there would be several different items, but for now, our game only contains a single item). Finally, we initialize the player with a Storage object (which is really just the NSUserDefaults object). This Storage object is used during initialization to load the stored game state. We also store the Storage object so that we can use it later to save the game state. We provide a default value so that we don't have to manually provide a value each time we initialize the Player, yet we still have the option to pass in a custom value (for example, when we're writing tests):

```swift
class Player {
    let health: Health
    var chocolates: BoxOfChocolates?
    let storage: Storage

    init (storage: Storage = NSUserDefaults.standardUserDefaults()) {
        self.storage = storage
        health = Health(storage: storage)
    }
}
```

The player has two additional methods that we won't cover: study and save. The study method uses health points to gain more experience, and the save method calls the save methods on both properties of the player (which use the Storage object to persist the game state).

For the Health class, we can also start with a very simple implementation. We store the foodPoints and experiencePoints as integers. In the initializer, we require a value that conforms to the Storage protocol. We then store this Storage object in the storage property so that we can use it when somebody calls save. For both foodPoints and experiencePoints, we add a **didSet** method that saves the player state when the property changes:

```swift
class Health {
    var foodPoints: Int = 100 {
        didSet { save() }
    }
    var experiencePoints: Int = 0 {
        didSet { save() }
    }

    var storage: Storage
```

```
init (storage: Storage) {
    self.storage = storage
    `foodPoints = storage["player.health"] ?? foodPoints
    experiencePoints = storage["player.experience"] ?? experiencePoints
}

func save() {
    storage["player.health"] = foodPoints
    storage["player.experience"] = experiencePoints
}
}
```

The BoxOfChocolates class is very similar to the Health class. It stores the number of chocolates as an Int, and it has similar implementations of save and init:

```
class BoxOfChocolates {
    private var numberOfChocolates: Int = 10 {
        didSet { save() }
    }
    var storage: Storage

    init (storage: Storage) {
        self.storage = storage
        numberOfChocolates = storage["player.chocolates"]
            ?? numberOfChocolates
    }
}
```

The eat method on BoxOfChocolates is more interesting: it takes a chocolate from the box and increases the player's foodPoints. The method also makes sure foodPoints is capped at 100, which is the maximum number of food points. Rather than storing a player reference inside the BoxOfChocolates (and possibly creating a reference cycle where the player refers to the box of chocolates, and the box of chocolates refers to the player), we pass in the player object to the eat method:

```
func eat(player: Player) {
    numberOfChocolates -= 1
    player.health.foodPoints = min(100, player.health.foodPoints + 10)
}
```

So far, so good. We have a nice design with all parts in separate objects. Because we override the **didSet** observers for the state properties, we know that everything will be safely stored. For example, if we say player.health.foodPoints += 1 somewhere in our code, this will trigger the **didSet** of the foodPoints variable.

Because we used dependency injection for the user defaults (and we even used a protocol), we have made that dependency very explicit. Now we can easily change the type of the dependency (for example, storing the state inside a JSON file somewhere). Also, we can easily provide a different implementation for testing.

However, there are also some downsides to this design. First of all, we have to override all the setters in order to persist our state the moment something changes. Second, and worse, we have a big dependency on Storage throughout all of our code. Even though we have made the dependency explicit, it still makes the code much harder to test and refactor. Finally, there might be unexpected sharing. The only owner of the Health object is the Player object. However, it's easy for any code to maintain a reference to the Health object. This makes it harder to refactor things.

To clean this design up, we can start by factoring out the Storage dependency. Instead of injecting it, we can provide a serialize method for each object, which serializes the object into a property list (a simple key-value dictionary). Additionally, we can provide an initializer, which initializes a value from such a property list. This allows us to factor out the Storage object completely (and will make the code much easier to test, because we don't need to build test doubles). However, the reason we stored the Storage object is so that we can always call save. Without it, we also need a different way to automatically call save on each change.

If we change the Player, Health, and BoxOfChocolates classes to structs, we can remove all the **didSet** property observers. Instead, we can have a single **didSet** on the player variable. This works, because updating a nested property (e.g. player.health.foodPoints) is a mutating function. It will mutate not only the health struct, but also the player struct. Semantically, it is the same thing as assigning a new value to the player variable (just with a much more natural syntax).

Our player struct now looks like this:

```
struct Player {
```

```swift
    var health: Health
    var chocolates: BoxOfChocolates?

    init (properties: PropertyList = [:]) {
        let healthProperties = properties["health"] as? PropertyList
        health = Health(properties: healthProperties ?? [:])
        if let chocolateProperties = properties["chocolates"] as? PropertyList {
            chocolates = BoxOfChocolates(properties: chocolateProperties)
        }

    }

    mutating func study() {
        health.foodPoints -= 2
        health.experiencePoints += 1
    }

    func serialize () -> PropertyList {
        var result: PropertyList = [
            "health": health.serialize ()
        ]
        result["chocolates"] = chocolates?.serialize()
        return result
    }
}

typealias PropertyList = [String:AnyObject]
```

The HealthStruct becomes very simple. It only stores the values and knows how to serialize and deserialize itself. The BoxOfChocolates struct is now almost the same (we'll leave it out because it's so similar):

```swift
struct Health {
    var foodPoints: Int = 100
    var experiencePoints: Int = 0

    init (properties: PropertyList) {
        foodPoints = properties["food"] as? Int ?? foodPoints
        experiencePoints = properties["experience"] as? Int ?? experiencePoints
    }

    func serialize () -> PropertyList {
        return [
            "food": foodPoints,
            "experience": experiencePoints
```

```
            ]
        }
    }
}
```

Instead of having the eat method on the BoxOfChocolates struct, we can now
move this to the player and write it as an extension on the Player struct:

```
extension Player {
    mutating func eat() {
        guard let count = self.chocolates?.numberOfChocolates where count > 0
            else { return }
        self.chocolates?.numberOfChocolates -= 1
        health.foodPoints = min(100, health.foodPoints + 10)
    }
}
```

The three structs are all simpler than their class-based counterparts. They no
longer have any dependencies and can easily be tested. Because of the way
structs work, we can now also observe the modification of any property (even
if it is deep inside a nested struct) by observing the player value. For example,
to recreate the automatic save behavior, we create a GameState class, which
stores and observes the player and is initialized in much the same way as we
initialized the Player before. Note that we use a different subscript on the
Serializer protocol (rather than returning integers, this subscript returns
property lists):

```
class GameState {
    var player: Player {
        didSet { save() }
    }
    var serializer : Serializer

    init (serializer : Serializer = NSUserDefaults.standardUserDefaults()) {
        self. serializer = serializer
        player = Player(properties: serializer ["player"] ?? [:])
    }

    func save() {
        serializer ["player"] = player.serialize ()
    }
}
```

The design with structs has a number of benefits. The code is shorter and
more to the point. There is no more dependency on Storage inside each of the

structs; instead, it has been moved to a single place. This also makes it easier to refactor: the structs could be initialized from JSON or Core Data. In the class-based approach, we had to override **didSet** for each property, but in the struct-based approach, we only do this once inside the GameState class. In the class-based approach, it would have been easy to make a mistake with the keys used for the key-value storage by accidentally using the same key in different classes. In our struct-based approach, it's much harder to make this mistake (because we store a nested dictionary of dictionaries, rather than a flat one).

Our struct-based implementation has a downside, too: it saves all of the data when a small part changes. Meanwhile, the class-based approach only persists those parts that changed. We could implement the same behavior using structs — however, saving everything at once isn't entirely a bad thing, as when reading through the struct code, it is easier to verify that it is correct.

Conclusion

We have looked at the differences between structs and classes in Swift. For entities (needing identity), classes are a better choice. For value types, structs are a better choice. When building structs that contain objects, we often need to take extra steps to ensure that they are really value types. We have looked at how to prevent reference cycles when dealing with classes. Often, a problem can be solved with either structs or classes, and what to choose depends on your needs. However, even problems that are classically solved using references can often benefit from values.

References

→ A Warm Welcome to Structs and Value Types[2]

→ Functional Swift[3]

→ Mike Ash[4]

2 http://www.objc.io/issue-16/swift-classes-vs-structs.html
3 http://www.objc.io/books/
4 https://www.mikeash.com/pyblog/friday-qa-2015-07-17-when-to-use-swift-structs-and-classes.html

Functions

To open this chapter, let's recap some things about functions. If you're already very familiar with first-class functions, feel free to skip ahead to the next section. But if you're even slightly hazy, skim through what's below.

To understand functions and closures in Swift, you really need to understand three things, in roughly this order of importance:

1. Functions can be assigned to variables and passed in and out of other functions as arguments, just as an Int or a String can be.

2. Functions can "capture" variables that exist outside of their local scope.

3. There are two ways of creating functions, either with the **func** keyword, or with { }. Swift calls the latter "closure expressions."

Sometimes people new to the topic of closures come at it in reverse order and maybe miss one of these points, or conflate the terms "closure" and "closure expression" — and this can cause a lot of confusion. It's a three-legged stool, and if you miss one of the three points above, you'll fall over when you try to sit down.

1. Functions can be assigned to variables and passed in and out of other functions as arguments.

In Swift, as in many modern languages, functions are referred to as "first-class objects." You can assign functions to variables, and you can pass them in and out of other functions to be called later.

This is *the most important thing* to understand. "Getting" this for functional programming is akin to "getting" pointers in C. If you don't quite grasp this part, everything else will just be noise.

Here is an example of assigning functions to variables and passing them to other functions:

```
// This is a function that takes an Int and prints it.
func printInt(i: Int) {
    print("you passed \(i)")
}

// This assigns the function you just declared to a variable.
// Note the absence of () after the function name.
let funVar = printInt
```

```
// Now you can call that function using your variable. Note the use of () after the
// variable name.
funVar(2)  // will print out "you passed 2"

// You can also write a function that takes a function as an argument.
func useFunction(funParam: (Int) -> () ) {
    // call the passed-in function:
    funParam(3)
}

// You can call this new function passing in either the original function:
useFunction(printInt)
// or the variable:
useFunction(funVar)
```

Why is being able to treat functions like this such a big deal? Because it allows you to easily write "higher-order" functions, which take functions as arguments and apply them in useful ways, as we saw in the chapter on collections.

You can also return functions from other functions:

```
// This is a function that returns another function.
// The returned function takes an Int and returns a String.
func returnFunc() -> (Int) -> String {
    func innerFunc(i: Int) -> String {
        return "you passed \(i) to the returned function"
    }
    return innerFunc
}

let myFunc = returnFunc()
myFunc(3)

you passed 3 to the returned function
```

2. Functions can "capture" variables that exist outside of their local scope.

When a function references variables outside the function's scope, those variables are "captured" and stick around after they would otherwise fall out of scope and be destroyed.

To see this, let's revisit our returnFunc function but add a counter that increases each time we call it:

```swift
func returnFunc() -> (Int) -> () {
    var counter = 0 // local variable declaration
    func innerFunc(i: Int) {
        counter += i   // counter is "captured"
        print("running total is now \(counter)")
    }
    return innerFunc
    // Normally counter, being a local variable,  would go out of scope
    // here and be destroyed. But instead, it  will  be kept alive  for
    // use by innerFunc.
}


let  f  = returnFunc()
f(3)  // will  print "running total  is  now 3"
f(4)  // will  print "running total  is  now 7"

// If  we call returnFunc() again, a fresh counter variable will  be
// created and captured.
let  g = returnFunc()
g(2)  // will  print "running total  is  now 2"
g(2)  // will  print "running total  is  now 4"

// This does not affect our  first  function, which still  has its  own
// captured version of counter.
f(2)  // will  print "running total  is  now 9"
```

Think of these functions combined with their captured variables as similar to instances of classes with a single method (the function) and some member variables (the captured variables).

In programming terminology, a combination of a function and an environment of captured variables is called a "closure." So f and g above are examples of closures, because they capture and use a non-local variable (counter) that was declared outside of them.

3. Functions can be declared using the {} syntax for closure expressions.

In Swift, you can declare functions in two ways. One is with the **func** keyword demonstrated above. The other way is to use a "closure expression." Consider this simple function to double a number:

```
func doubler(i: Int) -> Int { return i * 2 }
```

```
// The following runs doubler on each number, returning a new array of the results.
let a = [1, 2, 3, 4].map(doubler)
```

```
// `a` now contains [2, 4, 6, 8].
```

And here is the same function written using the closure expression syntax:

```
let doubler = { (i: Int) -> Int in return i*2 }
// doubler can be used just the same way as before
[1, 2, 3].map(doubler)
```

Functions declared as closure expressions can be thought of as function "literals" in the same way that 1 and "hello" are integer and string literals. They are also anonymous — they aren't named, unlike with the **func** keyword. The only way they can be used is if you assign them to a variable when they are created, as we do here with doubler.

The doubler declared using the closure expression, and the one declared earlier using the **func** keyword, are completely equivalent. They even exist in the same "namespace," unlike in some languages.

Why is the { } syntax useful then? Why not just use **func** every time? Well, it can be a lot more compact, especially when writing quick functions to pass into other functions, such as map. Here is our doubler map example written in a much shorter form:

```
[1, 2, 3].map { $0 * 2 }
```

```
[2, 4, 6]
```

This looks very different because we've leveraged several features of Swift to make code more concise. Here they are one by one:

1. If you are passing the closure in as an argument and that's all you need it for, there's no need to store it in a local variable first. Think of this like passing in a numeric expression, such as 5*i, to a function that takes an Int as a parameter.

2. If the compiler can infer a type from the context, you don't need to specify it. In our example, the function passed to map takes an Int (inferred from the type of the array elements) and returns an Int (inferred from the type of the multiplication expression).

3. If the closure expression's body contains just a single expression, it will automatically return the value of the expression, and you can leave off the **return.**

4. Swift automatically provides shorthand names for the arguments to the function — $0 for the first, $1 for the second, etc.

5. If the last argument to a function is a closure expression, you can move the expression outside the parenthesis of the function call. This *trailing closure syntax* is nice if you have a multi-line closure expression, as it more closely resembles a regular function definition or other block statement such as **if** (expr) { }.

6. Finally, if a function has no arguments other than a closure expression, you can leave off the parentheses after the function name altogether.

Using each of the above rules, we can boil down the expression to the form above:

```
[1, 2, 3].map({ (i: Int) -> Int in return i * 2 } )
[1, 2, 3].map({ i in return i * 2 } )
[1, 2, 3].map({ i in i * 2 } )
[1, 2, 3].map({ $0 * 2 } )
[1, 2, 3].map() { $0 * 2 }
[1, 2, 3].map { $0 * 2 }
```

If you're new to Swift's syntax, and to functional programming in general, these compact function declarations might seem daunting at first. But as you get more comfortable with the syntax and the functional programming style, they will start to feel more natural, and you'll be grateful for the ability to remove the clutter so you can see more clearly just what the code is doing. Once you get used to reading code written like this, it'll be much clearer to you at a glance than the equivalent code written with a conventional **for** loop.

Sometimes, Swift needs a helping hand with inferring the types. And sometimes, you may get something wrong and the types are not what you think they should be. If ever you get a mysterious error when trying to supply a closure expression, it is a good idea to write out the full form (version one above), complete with types. In many cases, that will help clear up where things are going wrong. Once you have the long form compiling, take the types out again one by one until the compiler complains. And if the error was yours, you'll have fixed your code in the process.

Swift will also insist you be more explicit sometimes. For example, you cannot completely ignore input parameters. Suppose you wanted an array of random numbers. A quick way to do this is to map a range with a function that just generates random numbers. But you must supply an argument nonetheless. You can use _ in such a case to indicate to the compiler that you acknowledge there is an argument but that you don't care what it is:

```
// Generate 100 random numbers.
(0..<100).map { _ in arc4random() }
```

When you need to explicitly type the variables, you don't have to do it inside the closure expression. For example, try defining isEven without any types:

```
let isEven = { $0 % 2 == 0 }
```

Above, the type of isEven is inferred to be Int -> Bool in the same way that let i = 1 is inferred to be Int — because Int is the default type for integer literals.

> This is because of a typealias, IntegerLiteralType, in the standard library:
>
> ```
> protocol IntegerLiteralConvertible {
>     associatedtype IntegerLiteralType
>
>     /// Create an instance initialized to `value`.
>     init(integerLiteral value: Self.IntegerLiteralType)
> }
>
> /// The default type for an otherwise unconstrained integer literal.
> typealias IntegerLiteralType = Int
> ```

If you were to define your own typealias, it would override the default one and change this behavior:

```
typealias IntegerLiteralType = UInt32
let i = 1  // i will be of type UInt32.
```

This is almost certainly a bad idea.

If, however, you needed a version of isEven for a different type, you could type the argument and return value inside the closure expression:

```
let isEven = { (i: Int8) -> Bool in i % 2 == 0 }
```

But you could also supply the context from *outside* the closure:

```
var isEven: Int8 -> Bool = { $0 % 2 == 0 }
// or
isEven = { $0 % 2 == 0 } as Int8->Bool
```

Since closure expressions are most commonly used in some context of existing input or output types, this isn't often necessary, but it's useful to know.

Of course, it's much better to define a generic version of isEven that works on *any* integer:

```
// As a protocol extension on all integer types:
extension IntegerType {
    func isEven() -> Bool {
        return self % 2 == 0
    }
}
```

```
// Or as a top-level function:
func isEven<T: IntegerType>(i: T) -> Bool {
    return i % 2 == 0
}
```

If you wanted to assign that top-level function to a variable, this is also when you would have to lock down which specific types it is operating on. A variable cannot hold a generic function, only a specific one:

```
// Assign a specific version of the generic `isEven` function to a variable:
let int8isEven: Int8 -> Bool = isEven
```

One final point on naming. It's important to keep in mind that functions declared with **func** can be closures, just like ones declared with { }. Remember, a closure is a function combined with any captured variables. While functions created with { } are called "closure expressions," people often refer to this syntax as just "closures." But don't get confused and think that functions declared with the closure expression syntax are different from other functions — they aren't. They are both functions, and they can both be closures.

Flexibility through Functions

In the chapter on collections, we talked about parameterizing behavior by passing functions as arguments. Let's look at another example of this: sorting.

If you want to sort an array in Objective-C using Foundation, you are met with a long list of different options. These provide a lot of flexibility and power, but at the cost of complexity — even the simplest probably needs a trip to the documentation to know how to use it.

Sorting collections in Swift is simple:

```
var myArray = [3, 1, 2]

myArray.sort()

[1, 2, 3]
```

There are really four sort methods: sort and sortInPlace, times two for the overloads that default to sorting comparable things in ascending order. But the overloading means that when you want the simplest case, sort() is all you need. If you want to sort in a different order, just supply a function:

```
myArray.sort(>)

[3, 2, 1]
```

You can also supply a function if your elements don't conform to Equatable but *do* have a < operator, like optionals:

```
let numberStrings = ["3", "1", "2"]
numberStrings.map { Int($0) }.sort(<)

[Optional(1), Optional(2), Optional(3)]
```

Or, you can supply a more complicated function if you want to sort by some arbitrary calculated criteria:

```
let animals = ["elephant", "zebra", "dog"]
animals.sort { lhs, rhs in
    let l = lhs.characters.reverse()
    let r = rhs.characters.reverse()
    return l.lexicographicalCompare(r)
}
```

It is this last ability — the ability to use any comparison function to sort a collection — that makes the Swift sort so powerful, and makes this one function able to replicate much (if not all) of the functionality of the various different sorting methods in Foundation.

To demonstrate this, let's reproduce a complex example from the documentation of sortedArrayUsingDescriptors. This sorting method is very flexible and a great example of the power of Objective-C's dynamic nature. Support for selectors and dynamic dispatch is still there in Swift, but the standard library favors a more function-based approach instead. We'll show a few techniques where functions as arguments, and treating functions as data, can be used to get the same dynamic effects.

Suppose you have an array of dictionaries containing first and last names:

```
let last = "lastName", first = "firstName"

let people = [
    [ first : "Jo", last: "Smith"],
    [ first : "Joe", last: "Smith"],
    [ first : "Joe", last: "Smyth"],
    [ first : "Joanne", last: "Smith"],
    [ first : "Robert", last: "Jones"],
]
```

(Lest you glare at us with a look of disapproval, yes, these elements would ideally be represented as structs and not dictionaries, but bear with us for the sake of an example.)

You want to sort this array first by last name, then by first name. You want to do this case insensitively and using the user's locale. Here's how you can do this with sortedArrayUsingDescriptors:

```
let lastDescriptor = NSSortDescriptor(key: last, ascending: true,
```

```
        selector: #selector(NSString.localizedCaseInsensitiveCompare(_:)))
```

```
let firstDescriptor = NSSortDescriptor(key: first, ascending: true,
        selector: #selector(NSString.localizedCaseInsensitiveCompare(_:)))
```

```
let descriptors = [lastDescriptor, firstDescriptor]
```

```
let sortedArray = (people as NSArray) .sortedArrayUsingDescriptors(descriptors)
```

This is a pretty cool use of selectors, especially when you realize the array of
sort descriptors can be built at runtime, say based on a user clicking a column
heading.

How can we replicate this functionality using Swift's sort? It's simple to
replicate *parts* of the sort, for example, if you want to sort an array using
localizedCaseInsensitiveCompare:

```
var strings = ["Hello", "hallo", "Hallo", "hello"]
```

```
strings.sortInPlace {
    return $0.localizedCaseInsensitiveCompare($1) == .OrderedAscending
}
```

If you want to sort using just a single key from a dictionary, that's also simple.
This is done by using the comparison operator that is defined for optionals
(the lookup result is optional, because the last name might not be present):

```
let sortedArray = people.sort { $0[last] < $1[last] }
```

This approach doesn't work so great when combined with methods like
localizedCaseInsensitiveCompare, though — it gets ugly fast:

```
let sortedArray = people.sort { lhs, rhs in
    return rhs[first ]. flatMap {
        lhs[ first ]?. localizedCaseInsensitiveCompare($0)
    } == .OrderedAscending
}
```

And this still doesn't account for sorting first by last name, then by first name.
To do that, we can use the standard library's lexicographicalCompare method.
This takes two sequences and performs a phonebook-style comparison by
moving through each pair of elements until it finds one that isn't equal. So we
can build two arrays of the elements and use lexicographicalCompare to

compare them. It also takes a function to perform the comparison. We'll put our use of localizedCaseInsensitiveCompare in the function, cleaned up a little this time using **guard:**

```
let sortedArray = people.sort { p0, p1 in
    let left  =  [p0[last],  p0[first ]]
    let right  = [p1[last],  p1[first ]]

    return left.lexicographicalCompare(right) {
        // same logic as Optional <
        guard let l = $0 else { return false }
        guard let r = $1 else { return true }
        return l.localizedCaseInsensitiveCompare(r) == .OrderedAscending
    }
}
```

At this point, we've replicated the functionality of the original sort in roughly the same number of lines. But there's still a lot of room for improvement: the building of arrays on every comparison is very inefficient, the comparison is hardcoded, and the optional handling is pretty messy.

First, look at the optional handling. It would be nice to have a simple way of comparing two optional values *using a method.* Similar to the < operator on optionals, **nil** is less than anything except **nil.** Otherwise, we compare the contents:

```
extension Optional {
    func compare(rhs: Wrapped?,
        _ comparator: Wrapped -> Wrapped -> NSComparisonResult)
        -> Bool
    {
        switch (self, rhs) {
        case (nil, nil), (_?, nil): return false
        case (nil, _?): return true
        case let (l?, r?): return comparator(l)(r) == .OrderedAscending
        }
    }
}
```

This logic is similar to the code for == that we saw in the optionals chapter, adapted for less-than semantics.

Curried Functions

Optional.compare makes use of a handy feature of methods to simplify calling it. You can pass in a method implemented by the types being operated on, like so:

```
let a: String? = "Fred"
let b: String? = "Bob"
a.compare(b, String.localizedCaseInsensitiveCompare)
```

Here, String.localizedCaseInsensitiveCompare is a method of type String -> String -> NSComparisonResult — that is, a function that takes a string and returns a function. You pass it an *instance* of a string, and you get back a new function that compares that instance to another string.

This is why, in the case of two non-**nil** values, we must first call the passed-in function to get back a version specific to the left-hand side, then call *that* function, passing in the right-hand side:

```
return comparator(l)(r) == .OrderedAscending
```

Functions of this form are called *curried* functions. They can sometimes be useful when you want to create families of functions that you can pass into another higher-order function, such as map.

Suppose you frequently want to check if a number, i, is a multiple of another value. What it might be a multiple *of* can change, but the rule for how to determine it is always the same: i % n == 0.

You might write a function like this:

```
func isMultipleOf(n n: Int, i: Int) -> Bool {
    return i % n == 0
}

isMultipleOf(n: 2, i: 3)  // false
isMultipleOf(n: 2, i: 4)  // true
```

However, perhaps you find yourself frequently wanting to use this function with higher-order functions, such as map and filter :

```
let nums = 1...10
// Use isMultipleOf to filter out the even numbers:
```

```
let evens = nums.filter { isMultipleOf(n: 2, i: $0) }
// `evens` is [2, 6, 8, 10]
```

That use of isMultipleOf looks a little clunky and hard to read, so maybe you define a new function, isEven, in terms of isMultipleOf, to make it a bit clearer:

```
let isEven = { isMultipleOf(n: 2, i: $0) }
isEven(2)  // true
isEven(3)  // false
let evens = r. filter (isEven)
```

Now, suppose you declare isMultipleOf a little differently, as a curried function:

```
func isMultipleOf(n n: Int) -> Int -> Bool {
    return { i in i % n == 0 }
}
```

isMultipleOf is now a function that takes a number, n, and returns a new function that takes a number and checks if it's a multiple of n.

You can use it to declare isEven, like this:

```
let isEven = isMultipleOf(n: 2)
```

Or, you could use it directly with filter , like this:

```
let evens = r. filter (isMultipleOf(n: 2))
// Just like before, evens is [2, 4, 6, 8, 10].
```

Functions as Data

Our sort is now nice and compact, but it's still hardcoded in terms of how to compare the different keys. What else could we do to make this closer to the flexibility of the descriptors-based sort?

The problem really lies with lexicographicalCompare. As written, it operates on two sequences — which is great when you have two sequences and you want to compare them using a single comparator function.

But we have the opposite problem. We have two *values*, and we want to compare them using a sequence of comparators. We need to turn lexicographicalCompare inside out and pass it a sequence of functions — something like this:

```
/// Return true if `self` precedes `other` in a lexicographical ("dictionary")
/// ordering, based on applying each element of `isOrderedBeforeSequence` as
/// the comparison between elements until the first element of
/// `isOrderedBefore` detects inequality.
///
/// - Requires: each element of `isOrderedBeforeSequence` is a
///     strict weak ordering over the elements of `self` and `other`.
///     (http://en.wikipedia.org/wiki/Strict_weak_order#Strict_weak_orderings)
func lexicographicalCompare<T>
    (comparators: [(T,T) -> Bool]) -> (T, T) -> Bool
{
    return { lhs, rhs in
        for isOrderedBefore in comparators {
            if isOrderedBefore(lhs,rhs) { return true }
            if isOrderedBefore(rhs,lhs) { return false }
        }
        return false
    }
}
```

This version of lexicographicalCompare iterates over the sequence of comparator functions, checking if it determines that the left-hand argument is less than or equal to the right-hand argument. By flipping the order of the arguments, we can determine if the left-hand argument is greater than the right-hand argument.

If neither element is less than the other, then they must be equal, and the comparison can continue to the next comparator in the sequence. This rule — if a value is neither less than or greater than another value — is governed by the requirement that the comparators be a strict weak ordering, as mentioned in the comment. We cover this in more detail in the protocols chapter.

By defining it in a curried way, we can feed it the comparator functions, and then it returns us a function of type (T, T) -> Bool, which is exactly what sort expects.

Now, we can declare an array of comparison functions, each one of which compares a value for a different key within the dictionary:

```
let comparators: [(([String: String], [String: String]) -> Bool] = [
    { $0[last]. compare($1[last], String.localizedCaseInsensitiveCompare) },
    { $0[first]. compare($1[first], String.localizedCaseInsensitiveCompare) },
]
```

Now we can use this within the sort:

```
let sortedArray = people.sort(lexicographicalCompare(comparators))
```

We had to give the comparators variable an explicit type because it is declared standalone. If you were happy to hardcode the sort order, the type could be inferred from the surrounding context:

```
let sortedArray = people.sort(lexicographicalCompare([
    { $0[last]. compare($1[last], String.localizedCaseInsensitiveCompare) },
    { $0[first]. compare($1[first], String.localizedCaseInsensitiveCompare) }
]))
```

You can think of functions declared inline this way as function "literals" — like writing the integer literal 1 or string literal "foo" into your code.

Now, we have restored the sort-coded nature of the comparison. Just as with the descriptors solution, you could build the array of comparators at runtime based on user interaction, and the sort function will change behavior accordingly.

This also gives us the ability to vary the sort order between different elements — for example, to sort by ascending last name, but then descending first name:

```
let sortedArray = people.sort(lexicographicalCompare([
    { $0[last] < $1[last] },
    { $0[first] > $1[first] },
]))
```

This approach of using functions as data — holding them in array and building those arrays at runtime — opens up a new level of dynamic behavior, and it is one way in which a statically typed compile-time-oriented language like Swift can still replicate some of the dynamic behavior of languages like Objective-C or Ruby.

This approach has also given us a clean separation between the sorting method and the comparison method. The algorithm that Swift's sort uses is a hybrid of multiple sorting algorithms — as of writing, it is an introsort (which is itself a hybrid of a quicksort and a heapsort), but it switches to an insertion sort for small collections to avoid the upfront startup cost of the more complex sort algorithms.

Introsort is not a "stable" sort. That is, it does not necessarily maintain relative ordering of values that are otherwise equal according to the comparison function.

But if you implemented a stable sort, the separation of the sort method from the comparison would allow you to swap it in easily:

```
let  sortedArray = people.stableSort { lhs, rhs in
    lexicographicalCompare(lhs, rhs, comparators)
}
```

Local Functions and Variable Capture

If you wanted such a stable sort, one choice might be a merge sort. Such a sort is made up of two parts: a division into sublists of one element, followed by a merge of those lists. Often, it's nice to define merge as a separate function. But this leads to a problem — merge requires some temporary scratch storage:

```
extension Array where Element: Comparable {
    private mutating func merge(lo: Int, _ mi: Int, _ hi: Int) {
        var tmp: [Element] = []
        var i = lo, j = mi
        while i != mi && j != hi {
            if self[j] < self[i] {
                tmp.append(self[j])
                j += 1
            } else {
                tmp.append(self[i])
                i += 1
            }
        }

        tmp.appendContentsOf(self[i..<mi])
        tmp.appendContentsOf(self[j..<hi])
        replaceRange(lo..<hi, with: tmp)
    }

    mutating func mergeSortInPlace() {
        let n = count
        var size = 1

        while size < n {
            for lo in 0.stride(to: n-size, by: size*2) {
```

```
            merge(lo, (lo+size), min(lo+size*2,n))
        }
        size *= 2
    }
  }
}
```

Of course, you could allocate this storage externally and pass it in as a parameter, but this is a little ugly. It's also complicated by the fact that arrays are value types — passing in an array you created outside would not help. You would probably have to resort to allocating your own buffer.

Or, you could define merge as an inner function and have it capture the storage defined in the outer function's scope:

```swift
extension Array where Element: Comparable {
    mutating func mergeSortInPlace() {
        // define the temporary storage for use by all merges
        var tmp: [Element] = []
        // and make sure it's big enough
        tmp.reserveCapacity(count)

        func merge(lo: Int, _ mi: Int, _ hi: Int) {
            // wipe the storage clean while retaining its capacity
            tmp.removeAll(keepCapacity: true)

            // the same code as before
            var i = lo, j = mi
            while i != mi && j != hi {
                if self[j] < self[i] {
                    tmp.append(self[j])
                    j += 1
                } else {
                    tmp.append(self[i])
                    i += 1
                }
            }

            tmp.appendContentsOf(self[i..<mi])
            tmp.appendContentsOf(self[j..<hi])
            replaceRange(lo..<hi, with: tmp)
        }

        let n = count
        var size = 1
```

```
        while size < n {
            for lo in 0.stride(to: n-size, by: size*2) {
                merge(lo, (lo+size), min(lo+size*2,n))
            }
            size *= 2
        }
    }
}
```

Since closures (including inner functions) capture variables by reference, every call to merge within a single call to mergeSortInPlace will share this storage. But it is still a local variable — separate concurrent calls to mergeSortInPlace will use separate instances. Using this technique can give a significant speed boost to the sort without needing major changes to the original version.

Functions as Delegates

Delegates. They're everywhere. Drummed into the heads of Objective-C (and Java) programmers is this message: use protocols (interfaces) for callbacks. You define a protocol, the delegate implements that protocol, and it registers itself as the delegate so that it gets callbacks.

A more generalized pattern for callbacks is to have an observer interface and an observable interface that receives observers and then calls them back when an event fires — maybe something like this:

```
protocol Observable {
    mutating func register(observer: Observer)
}

protocol Observer {
    func receive(event: Any)
}

// and then implement it like this:
struct EventGenerator: Observable {
    var observers: [Observer] = []

    mutating func register(observer: Observer) {
        observers.append(observer)
    }
```

```swift
    func fireEvents(event: Any) {
        for observer in observers {
            observer.receive(event)
        }
    }
}

struct EventReceiver: Observer {
    func receive(event: Any) {
        print("Received: \(event)")
    }
}

var g = EventGenerator()
let r = EventReceiver()
g.register(r)

var gen = EventGenerator()
let receiver = EventReceiver()
gen.register(receiver)
gen.fireEvents("hi!")
gen.fireEvents(42)
```

```
Received: hi!
Received: 42
()
```

The above works fine, but what's that? Any? Begone, foul untyped thing. Generics to the rescue, right? How about something like this:

```swift
protocol ObserverType {
    associatedtype Event
    func receive(event: Event)
}

struct StringEventReceiver: ObserverType {
    func receive(event: String) {
        print("Received: \(event)")
    }
}
```

This fixes the typing issue. When implementing Observable, you can set the type of the event, and observers' receive methods must match that type. Great.

Except you'll now hit a problem with Observable. ObserverType is a protocol with an associated type. So you can no longer declare it like this:

```
protocol Observable {
    // error:  protocol 'ObserverType' can only be used as a generic constraint
    // because it has Self or  associated type requirements
    mutating func register(observer: ObserverType)
}
```

When you are dealing with protocols that either have a **Self** requirement or an associated type, you cannot use the protocol name as a standalone type anymore. (We will look into this in more detail in the chapter on protocols.) Instead, you must declare a generic method that takes any type that *conforms* to ObserverType:

```
protocol Observable {
    mutating func register<O: ObserverType>(observer: O)
}
```

The protocol Observable now compiles, but it's still untyped. ObserverTypes of any type — receiving a String or an Int or a Foo — can now register. Really, we want Observable to generate a specific type of event, so we add an Event alias to it too:

```
protocol Observable {
    associatedtype Event
    mutating func register
        <O: ObserverType where O.Event == Event>(observer: O)
}
```

Erasing Types Using Closures

Now, we can *almost* implement a StringEventGenerator specifying that Event must be of type String:

```
struct StringEventGenerator: Observable {
    var observers: [???] = []

    // because Event is only used inside a placeholder constraint, Swift won't
    // infer  its  type,  so we need an explicit typealias type for  the associated type
    typealias Event = String

    mutating func register
```

```
        <O: ObserverType where O.Event == String>(observer: O) {
            observers.append(observer)
    }
}
```

But what type should the array of observers be? Inside register, O could be of *any* type, but Swift arrays must contain a single specific type.

One solution could be to wrap the type passed to register in a closure that captures the observer and calls receive on it. Then, when we want to call receive, we can just call the closure. So the type of the observers array would be [String -> ()]:

```
struct StringEventGenerator: Observable {
    var observers: [String -> ()] = []

    typealias Event = String

    mutating func register
        <O: ObserverType where O.Event == String>(observer: O)
    {
        observers.append { observer.receive($0) }
    }

    func fireEvents(event: String) {
        for observer in observers {
            observer(event)
        }
    }
}
```

We now have a type-safe observable/observer pair:

```
var gen1 = StringEventGenerator()
let rec1 = StringEventReceiver()
gen1.register(rec1)
gen1.fireEvents("hi!")
```

Replacing Protocol Callbacks with Functions

The way we stored the observers in an array suggests another way to implement the Observable protocol, which is to do away with the ObserverType altogether and just have register receive a function to call back:

```
protocol Observable {
    associatedtype Event
    // Remove any reference to ObserverType, just register a function
    mutating func register(observer: Event -> ())
}
```

Then, the implementation is much the same as before, but without needing to wrap the argument to register in a closure — it already is one:

```
struct StringEventGenerator: Observable {
    var observers: [String -> ()]  = []

    mutating func register(observer: String -> ())  {
        observers.append(observer)
    }

    func fireEvents(event: String) {
      for observer in observers {
        observer(event)
      }
    }
}
```

Now, to hook up the receiver, we could make use of the curried method call we saw earlier:

```
// StringEventReceiver no longer needs to conform to ObserverType:
struct StringEventReceiver {
    func receive(event: String) {
        print("Received: \(event)")
    }
}

var g = StringEventGenerator()
let r0 = StringEventReceiver()

// StringEventReceiver.receive(r0) returns a function, where receive is
// called on r0
let callback = StringEventReceiver.receive(r0)

// And now, we can register this function to observe g:
g.register(callback)
```

But there's a shorter way to write this. instance.method, without the argument parentheses, amounts to the same thing:

```
let r = StringEventReceiver()
g.register(r.receive)
```

However, there is no need to have the callback be on an object. A standalone closure can now also be registered:

```
g.register { print("Closure received \($0)") }
```

And since registering is just about passing in a closure, you can register the same object to listen multiple times, on different methods:

```
extension StringEventReceiver {
    func receiveDifferently(event: String) {
        print("Received \(event) differently")
    }
}

let receiver = StringEventReceiver()
g.register(receiver.receive)
g.register(receiver.receiveDifferently)
```

When a protocol only has a single method defined, replacing it by a callback can simplify things a lot. However, when a protocol defines multiple functions that are closely related (for example, providing the data for a table view), it can be helpful to keep them grouped together rather than having individual callbacks. This way, it can be enforced that a single object or struct implements all the functions.

Another difference between function callbacks and delegate protocols is unregistering. If we provide an API for registering function callbacks, we will also need to return a way to deregister them, either using a token, or by returning a deregister callback. In the case of object-based delegates, this is much simpler: we can simply remove an object from the list of delegates (because objects have identity).

Giving Value Types Reference Semantics Using Closures

Let's suppose we have a simple struct with a single **mutating** method:

```
struct StringStoringReceiver {
    var str = ""
    mutating func receive(event: String) {
        str += str.isEmpty ? event : ", \(event)"
    }
}
```

```
var stringR = StringStoringReceiver()
```

If we now try to pass the partially applied receive method to the register method, we get a compile-time error:

```
// Error: partial application of 'mutating' method is not allowed
g.register(r.receive)
```

However, there is an easy way to work around this. Instead of passing the function directly, we can create new closure. This will capture r, and because it's defined using **var**, we can update it. The type of the closure is just String -> (), without it being marked as **mutating**:

```
g.register { stringR.receive($0) }
```

Now we can fire events and r will get updated:

```
g.fireEvents("hi!")
g.fireEvents("one")
g.fireEvents("two")
stringR.str
```

```
hi!, one, two
```

inout Parameters and Mutating Methods

The "&" that you use at the front of an **inout** argument in Swift might give you the impression — especially if you have a C or C++ background — that **inout** parameters are essentially pass-by-reference. But they aren't. **inout** is pass-by-value-and-copy-back, *not* pass-by-reference.

> An **inout** parameter has a value that is passed in to the function, is modified by the function, and is passed back out of the function to replace the original value.

This has a few significant implications. The biggest advantage is that using **inout** is much safer than using references. To demonstrate, first let's take a very straightforward bit of code that increments an **inout** argument:

```
func inc(inout i : Int) {
    i += 1
}

var x = 0
inc(&x)
x
```

```
1
```

This prints out 1, because x is passed **inout** and incremented inside inc. When the inc function returns, the value of i is copied into x.

Next is our familiar closure variable capture scenario. This declares a variable inside the inc function. Keeping the variable inside the function is very much like an instance variable for objects — it is shared between calls of f:

```
func inc() -> () -> Int {
    // declare a variable i
    var i = 0
    // and capture it in a closure that increments i when called
    return {
      i += 1
      return i
    }
}

let h = inc()
print(h()) // prints 1
print(h()) // prints 2
```

```
1
2
```

Now, let's try and combine these two approaches, i.e. a version of inc that takes an **inout** argument and then captures *that argument* in a closure that increments it:

```
// Take an inout argument
func inc(inout i : Int) -> () -> Int {
```

```
    // and capture it in a returned function
    return { i += 1; return i }
}
```

If **inout** were pass-by-reference, you might expect a variable passed in to inc to continue to be incremented whenever the closure capturing it is called. But this is *not* what happens:

```
var x = 0
let fx = inc(&x)
print(fx ())   // prints 1
print(x)      // remains 0

1
0
```

Instead, inside inc, i was captured, but it occurred halfway through the pass-by-value-copy-back process. As a result, it captured the value 0 of the variable i. But when the function inc ended, what was copied back was the as-of-yet *unchanged* value of 0. Subsequent calls to f just increment the captured copy.

Finally, we can show the copying back in action by calling the closure capturing i one time inside inc before returning:

```
func inc1(inout i: Int) -> () -> Int {
    // store a copy of the closure
    let f: () -> Int = {
      i += 1
      return i
    }
    // and call it once before exiting, incrementing i
    f()
    // then return it
    return f
}

var x = 0
let f = inc1(&x)
x

1
```

Now, because the closure incremented i once before returning, and thus before i was copied back into x, x is incremented.

This might all seem both like an edge case and unimportant. But it's critical for safety. inc knows nothing about the scope of the variable that was passed in. If **inout** were pass-by-reference, consider what would happen under these circumstances:

```
// Declare a variable we will assign the closure to
let f: () -> Int

// Open up a local scope
do {
    // Declare a local variable
    var x = 0

    // Call inc passing in that local variable. Store the closure
    // outside the scope
    f = inc(&x)

// Local scope ends, x is destroyed
}

// Now, f is called, referencing x
print(f ())    // what might this print?
```

Swift is all about ruling this kind of nonsense right out. Unless you used a function with the word "unsafe" in the title, you shouldn't be able to accidentally crash a program like this.

And indeed you can't — the above code is perfectly safe, because the closure will actually be capturing a variable declared inside inc as passed-by-value. Just before inc returns, the value of i is written back to x.

When & Doesn't Mean inout

Speaking of unsafe functions, you should be aware of the other meaning of &, which is not to confirm you're passing a variable **inout**, but rather to convert to an unsafe pointer.

If a function takes an UnsafeMutablePointer as a parameter, then you can pass a **var** into it using &, similar to an **inout** argument. But here you *really are* passing by reference — by pointer in fact.

Here is inc, written to take an unsafe mutable pointer instead of an **inout**:

```
func incref(i : UnsafeMutablePointer<Int>) -> () -> Int {
    // store a copy of the pointer in a closure
    return {
        i.memory += 1
        return i.memory
    }
}
```

Now, suppose you pass in an array under similar scoped circumstances. As we'll cover in later chapters, Swift arrays implicitly decay to pointers to make C interoperability nice and painless:

```
let fun: () -> Int
do {
    var array = [0]
    fun = incref(&array)
}
fun()
```

This opens up a whole exciting world of undefined behavior. In testing, the above code printed different values on each run — sometimes 0, sometimes 1, and sometimes 140362397107840.

The moral here is: know what you're passing in to. When appending an &, you could be invoking nice safe Swift **inout** semantics, or you could be casting your poor variable into the brutal world of unsafe pointers. When dealing with unsafe pointers, be very careful about the lifetime of variables. We will go into more detail on this in the chapter on interoperability.

Computed Properties and Subscripts

There are two special kinds of methods that differ from regular methods: computed properties and subscripts. A computed property looks like a regular property, but it does not use any memory to store its value. Instead, the value is computed on the fly every time the property is accessed. A subscript is really just a method with unusual defining and calling conventions.

Let's look at the various ways to define properties. We'll start with a struct that represents a file in the filesystem. It has a method, computeSize, which asks the file manager for the size of the file:

```swift
struct File {
    let path: String

    func computeSize() -> Int? {
        let fm = NSFileManager.defaultManager()
        guard let dict = try? fm.attributesOfItemAtPath(self.path),
            let size = dict["NSFileSize"] as? Int
            else { return nil }
        return size
    }
}
```

If we treat computeSize as an expensive method (in a later version, we might recursively compute the size of all directory contents as well), we could consider caching the computed size in a private property. Note that, because we're using a **struct**, we have to mark the method as **mutating**. Otherwise, we cannot write the size property:

```swift
private var cachedSize: Int?
```

```swift
mutating func cachedComputeSize() -> Int? {
    guard cachedSize == nil else { return cachedSize! }
    let fm = NSFileManager.defaultManager()
    guard let dict = try? fm.attributesOfItemAtPath(self.path),
        let size = dict["NSFileSize"] as? Int
        else { return nil }
    cachedSize = size
    return size
}
```

Because the method is now **mutating**, the caller now also needs to use **var** for the variable where it stores the file, otherwise it cannot call the method:

```swift
var file = File("/Users/chris/Desktop")
print( file .cachedComputeSize())
```

Initializing a value lazily is such a common pattern that Swift has a special **lazy** keyword to define a lazy property. Note that a lazy property is automatically **mutating** and therefore must be declared as **var** (it works exactly like above). Consequently, we can only access this property on a File defined using **var**, just like in the previous example:

```swift
lazy var size: Int? = {
    let fm = NSFileManager.defaultManager()
```

```
    guard let dict = try? fm.attributesOfItemAtPath(self.path),
        let size = dict["NSFileSize"] as? Int
        else { return nil }
    return size
}()
```

Notice how we defined the lazy property: it's a closure expression that returns the value we want to store — in our case, an optional integer. When the property is first accessed, the closure is executed (note the parentheses at the end), and its return value is stored in the property. This is a common pattern for lazy properties that require more than a one-liner to be initialized.

If we don't want to cache the file size, but still prefer to access it like a property instead of a method, we can turn it into a computed property. Note, however, that every time we access the property, it is computed again:

```
var size: Int? {
    let fm = NSFileManager.defaultManager()
    guard let dict = try? fm.attributesOfItemAtPath(self.path),
        let size = dict["NSFileSize"] as? Int
        else { return nil }
    return size
}
```

By default, if we declare a property like above, only a getter is generated. If we want to provide both a getter and a setter, we have to specify them separately. For example, we could add a property to get and set the file's contents:

```
extension File {
    var data: NSData? {
        get {
            return NSData(contentsOfFile: path)
        }
        set {
            let theData = newValue ?? NSData()
            theData.writeToFile(path, atomically: true)
        }
    }
}
```

Setting the file's contents is now as simple as setting the property:

```
var file = File(path: "test.txt")
file.data = someData
```

For properties, we can also implement the **willSet** and **didSet** callbacks. These get called before and after the setter, respectively. One useful case is when working with Interface Builder: we can implement **didSet** to know when an IBOutlet gets connected, and then we can configure our views there. For example, if we want to set a label's text color once it's available, we can do the following:

```
class SettingsController: UIViewController {
    @IBOutlet weak var label: UILabel? {
        didSet {
            label?.textColor = .blackColor()
        }
    }
}
```

Overloading Subscripts with Different Arguments

In Swift, we have seen special syntax for subscripts. For example, we can perform a dictionary lookup like so: dictionary[key]. These subscripts are very much like normal functions except that they have special syntax. They can be either read-only (using **get**) or read-write (using **get set**). Just like normal functions, we can overload them by providing multiple variants with different types. For example, we can use array subscripting to get out a single element or a slice:

```
let fibs = [0, 1, 1, 2, 3, 5]
```

```
let first = fibs[0] // 0
fibs[1..<3]
```

```
[1, 1]
```

We can add subscripting support to our own types, and we can also extend existing types with new subscript overloads. In Swift, the Range type represents bounded intervals: every Range has a start and an end. As we demonstrated above, we can use this to find a subsequence of an array (or to be more precise: of any CollectionType). We will extend CollectionType to support half-bounded intervals — ranges where there is only one end specified (either the startIndex or the endIndex). To represent these, we will create two new **struct**s:

```
struct RangeStart<I: ForwardIndexType> { let start: I }
struct RangeEnd<I: ForwardIndexType> { let end: I }
```

We can define two convenience operators to write half-bounded intervals. These are **prefix** and **postfix** operators, and they have only one operand. This will allow us to write RangeStart(x) as x..< and RangeEnd(x) as ..< x:

```
postfix operator ..< { }
postfix func ..<< I : ForwardIndexType>(lhs: I) -> RangeStart<I> {
    return RangeStart(start: lhs)
}

prefix operator ..< { }
prefix func ..<< I : ForwardIndexType>(rhs: I) -> RangeEnd<I> {
    return RangeEnd(end: rhs)
}
```

We can extend CollectionType to support half-bounded ranges by adding two new subscripts:

```
extension CollectionType {
    subscript(r: RangeStart<Self.Index>) -> SubSequence {
        return self[r.start ..< self.endIndex]
    }
    subscript(r: RangeEnd<Self.Index>) -> SubSequence {
        return self[self.startIndex..<r.end]
    }
}
```

This allows us to write half-bounded subscripts like this:

```
fibs [2..<]
```

```
[1, 2, 3, 5]
```

We can use this to implement a search function that looks for a pattern in a collection. It traverses the string and finds the first occurrence of the pattern:

```
extension CollectionType where Generator.Element: Equatable,
    SubSequence.Generator.Element == Generator.Element {
    func search
        <S: SequenceType where S.Generator.Element == Generator.Element>
        (pat: S) -> Index?
    {
        return self.indices.indexOf {
            self[$0 ..<]. startsWith(pat)
        }
    }
```

```
}
```

This allows us to search a string for the first occurrence of ", ", and based on that index, return the string up until that index:

```
let greeting = "Hello, world"
if let idx = greeting.characters.search(", ".characters) {
    // Print everything that comes before ", "
    print(String(greeting.characters[..<idx]))
}
```

```
Hello
```

Advanced Subscripts

Now that we have seen how to add simple subscripts, we can take things a bit further. Instead of taking a single parameter, subscripts can also take more than one parameter (just like functions). The following extension allows for dictionary lookup (and updating) with a default value. During a lookup, when the key is not present, we return the default value. In the setter, we ignore it (because newValue is not optional):

```
extension Dictionary {
    subscript(key: Key, or defaultValue: Value) -> Value {
        get {
            return self[key] ?? defaultValue
        }
        set(newValue) {
            self[key] = newValue
        }
    }
}
```

This allows us to write a very short function to compute the frequencies in a sequence. We start with an empty dictionary, and for every element we encounter, we increase the frequency by 1. If the element was not present in the dictionary before, the default value of 0 is returned during lookup:

```
extension SequenceType where Generator.Element: Hashable {
    func frequencies() -> [Generator.Element: Int] {
        var result: [Generator.Element: Int] = [:]
        for x in self {
            result[x, or: 0] += 1
```

```
        }
        return result
    }
}
```

Automatic Closures and Memory

We are all familiar with the short-circuiting of the &&-operator. It takes two operands: first, the left operand is evaluated. Only if the left operand evaluates to true is the right operand evaluated. After all, if the left operand evaluates to false, there is no way the entire expression can evaluate to true. Therefore, we can short-circuit and don't have to evaluate the right operand. For example, if we want to check if a condition holds for the first element of an array, we could write the following code:

```
if  !evens.isEmpty && evens[0] > 10 {
    // Perform some work
}
```

In the snippet above, we rely on short-circuiting: the array lookup happens only if the first condition holds. Without short-circuiting, this code crashes on an empty array.

In almost all languages, short-circuiting is built into the language for the && and || operators. However, it is often not possible to define your own operators or functions that have short-circuiting. If a language supports closures, we can fake short-circuiting by providing a closure instead of a value. For example, let's say we wanted to define an and function in Swift with the same behavior as the && operator:

```
func and(l: Bool, _ r: () -> Bool) -> Bool {
    guard l else { return false }
    return r ()
}
```

The function above first checks the value of l and returns false if l evaluates to false. Only if l is true does it return the value that comes out of the closure r. Using it is a little bit more complicated than using the && operator, because the right operand now has to be a function:

```
if  and(!evens.isEmpty, { evens[0] > 10 }) {
    // Perform some work
```

```
}
```

In Swift, rather than building the short-circuiting into the and function directly, we can use the **@autoclosure** attribute to automatically create a closure around an argument. The definition of and is almost the same as above, except for the added **@autoclosure** annotation:

```
func and(l: Bool, @autoclosure _ r: () -> Bool) -> Bool {
    guard l else { return false }
    return r ()
}
```

However, the usage of and is now much simpler, as we do not need to wrap the second parameter in a closure. Instead, we can just call it as if it took a regular Bool parameter:

```
if and(!evens.isEmpty, evens[0] > 10) {
    // Perform some work
}
```

This allows us to define our own functions and operators with short-circuiting behavior. For example, operators like ?? and !? (as defined in the chapter on optionals) are now straightforward to write. In the Swift Standard Library, functions like assert and fatalError also use autoclosures, in order to only evaluate the arguments when really needed. Autoclosures can also come in handy when writing logging functions, e.g. so that the logged string is not evaluated when logging is turned off.

The noescape Annotation

As we saw in the previous chapter, we need to be careful about memory when dealing with closures. Recall the capture list example, where we needed to mark **self** as **weak** in order for the closure to not keep a strong reference to the controller:

```
reader.onTagOpen = { [unowned self, weak myReader = self.reader] tag in
    self.tags.append(tag)
    if tag == "stop" {
        myReader?.stop()
    }
}
```

We never marked anything as **weak** when we used functions like map, however. Since map is executed synchronously and the closure is not retained anywhere, this is not necessary, because no reference cycle will be created. If we look at the type of the closure passed to map, we can also see that it is annotated with the **@noescape** attribute:

```
@noescape transform: (Self.Generator.Element) throws -> T
```

This is a signal to both the compiler and to callers of the method that the closure will not escape the scope of map. In other words: once map is done, the closure is not referenced any longer. There are no asynchronous callbacks that will call the transform closure, nor are there any global variables or properties storing the closure. This is all statically verified by the compiler.

For the compiler, it means that some code can be optimized slightly. For the caller of the method, it means there is no need to worry about memory management any more than writing regular code: there is no need for **weak** or **unowned** annotations, and there is no need to write **self**. when you access the caller's properties or methods inside the closure expression.

When you are writing a function that takes a closure, be sure to annotate it with **@noescape** when you can. This makes life significantly simpler for callers of the function. They don't need to write **self**., and they don't need to think about **weak** or **unowned** annotations.

By default, all parameters annotated as **@autoclosure** are automatically also **@noescape**. In the rare case that you would want an **@autoclosure** that can escape the scope, you can mark a parameter as **@autoclosure**(escaping). This can be useful when working with asynchronous code.

Conclusion

Functions are first-class objects in Swift. Treating functions as data can make our code more flexible. We have seen how we can replace some common object-oriented patterns with simple functions instead. We have looked at **mutating** functions and **inout** parameters, as well as computed properties (which really are a special kind of function). Finally, we have looked at the **@autoclosure** and **@noescape** annotations. In the chapters on generics and protocols, we will look at more ways to use functions in Swift to gain even more flexibility.

Strings

No More Fixed Width

Things used to be so simple. ASCII strings were a sequence of integers between 0 and 127. If you stored them in an 8-bit byte, you even had a bit to spare! Since every character was of a fixed size, ASCII strings could be random access.

But this is only if you were writing in English for a U.S. audience; other countries and languages needed other characters (even English-speaking Britain needed a £ sign). Most of them needed more characters than would fit into seven bits. ISO/IEC 8859 takes the extra bit and defines 16 different encodings above the ASCII range, such as Part 1 (ISO/IEC 8859-1, aka Latin-1), covering several Western European languages, and Part 5, covering languages that use the Cyrillic alphabet.

But this is still limiting. If you want use ISO/IEC 8859 to write in Turkish about Ancient Greek, you are out of luck, since you would need to pick either Part 7 (Latin/Greek) or Part 9 (Turkish). And eight bits is still not enough to encode many languages. For example, Part 6 (Latin/Arabic) does not include the characters needed to write Arabic-script languages such as Urdu or Persian. Meanwhile, Vietnamese — which is based on the Latin alphabet but with a large number of diacritic combinations — only fits into eight bits by replacing a handful of ASCII characters from the lower half. And this isn't even an option for other East Asian languages.

When you run out of room with a fixed-width encoding, you have a choice: either increase the size, or switch to variable-width encoding. Initially, Unicode was defined as a 2-byte fixed-width format, now called UCS-2. This was before reality set in, and it was accepted that even two bytes would not be sufficient, while four would be horribly inefficient for most purposes.

So today, Unicode is a variable-width format, and it's variable in two different senses: in the combining of code units into code points, and in the combining of code points into characters.

Unicode data can be encoded with many different widths of "code unit," most commonly 8 (UTF-8) or 16 (UTF-16) bits. UTF-8 has the added benefit of being backwardly compatible with 8-bit ASCII — something that has helped it overtake ASCII as the most popular encoding on the web.

A "code point" in Unicode is a single value in the Unicode code space with a possible value from 0 to 0x10FFFF. A given code point might take a single code unit if you are using UTF-32, or it might take between one and four if you are using UTF-8. The first 256 Unicode code points match the characters found in Latin-1.

Unicode "scalars" are another unit. They are all the code points *except* the "surrogate" code points, i.e. the code points used for the leading and trailing codes that indicate pairs in UTF-16 encoding. Scalars are represented in Swift string literals as "\u{xxxx}", where xxxx represents hex digits. So the euro sign, €, can be written in Swift as "\u{20AC}".

But even when encoded using 32-bit code units, what a user might consider "a single character" — as displayed on the screen — might require multiple code points composed together. Most string manipulation code exhibits a certain level of denial about Unicode's variable-width nature. This can lead to some unpleasant bugs.

Swift's string implementation goes to heroic efforts to be as Unicode-correct as possible, or at least when it's not, to make sure you acknowledge the fact. This comes at a price. String in Swift is not a collection. Instead, it is a type that presents multiple ways of viewing the string: as a collection of Character values; or as a collection of UTF-8, UTF-16, or Unicode scalars.

The Swift Character type is unlike the other views, in that it can encode an arbitrary number of code points, composed together into a single "grapheme cluster." We'll see some examples of this shortly.

For all but the UTF-16 view, the index into these collections is *not* random access. Some of the views can also be slower than others when performing heavy text processing. In this chapter, we'll look at the reasons behind this, as well as some techniques for dealing with both functionality and performance.

Grapheme Clusters and Canonical Equivalence

A quick way to see the difference between Swift.String and NSString in handling Unicode data is to look at the two different ways to write "é." Unicode defines U+00E9, "LATIN SMALL LETTER E WITH ACUTE," as a single value. But you can also write it as the plain letter "e," followed by U+0301, "COMBINING ACUTE ACCENT." In both cases, what is displayed is é, and a user probably has a reasonable expectation that two strings displayed as "résumé" would not only be equal to each other but also have a "length" of six characters, no matter which technique was used to produce the "é" in either one. They would be what the Unicode specification describes as "canonically equivalent."

And in Swift, this is exactly the behavior you get:

```
let single = "Pok\u{00E9}mon"
let double = "Pok\u{0065}\u{0301}mon"
```

They both display identically:

```
(single, double)
```

```
("Pokémon", "Pokémon")
```

And both have the same character count:

```
single.characters.count == double.characters.count
```

true

Only if you drop down to a view of the underlying representation can you see that they are different:

```
single.utf16.count // 7
double.utf16.count // 8
```

Contrast this with NSString: the two strings are not equal, and the length property — which many programmers probably use to count the number of characters to be displayed on the screen — gives different results:

```
let nssingle = NSString(characters: [0x0065,0x0301], length: 2)
nssingle.length      // 2
let nsdouble = NSString(characters: [0x00e9], length: 1)
nsdouble.length      // 1
nssingle == nsdouble // false
```

Here, == is defined as the version for comparing two NSObjects:

```
func ==(lhs: NSObject, rhs: NSObject) -> Bool {
    return lhs.isEqual(rhs)
}
```

In the case of NSString, this will do a literal comparison, rather than one accounting for equivalent but differently composed characters.

NSString.isEqualToString will do the same. If you really want to perform a canonical comparison, you must use NSString.compare. Didn't know that? Enjoy your future undiagnosable bugs and grumpy international user base.

Of course, there's one big benefit to just comparing code units: it's a lot faster! This is an effect that can still be achieved with Swift strings, via the utf16 view:

```
single.utf16.elementsEqual(double.utf16)
```

The existence of precomposed characters is what enables the opening range of Unicode code points to be compatible with Latin-1, which already had characters like "é" and "ñ." While they might be a pain to deal with, it makes conversion between the two quick and simple.

Ditching them wouldn't have helped, because composition doesn't just stop at pairs; you can compose more than one diacritic together. For example, Yoruba has the character "ọ́," which could be written three different ways: by composing ó with a dot, or by composing ọ with an acute, or by composing o with both an acute and a dot. And for that last one, the two diacritics can be in either order! So the following should not assert:

```
let chars: [Character] = [
    "\u{1ECD}\u{300}",
    "\u{F2}\u{323}",
    "\u{6F}\u{323}\u{300}",
    "\u{6F}\u{300}\u{323}",
]

assert(chars.dropFirst().all { $0 == chars.first },
    "All the elements in chars should be equal")
```

(The all method checks if the condition is true for all elements in a sequence and is defined in the chapter on collections.)

In fact, some diacritics can be added ad infinitum:

```
let zalgo = "sǫ̈ọ̈n"
```

In the above, zalgo.characters.count returns 4, while zalgo.utf16.count returns 36. And if your code doesn't work correctly with Internet memes, then what good is it, really?

Strings containing emoji can also be a little surprising. For example, a row of emoji flags is considered a single character:

```
let flags = "🇨🇳🇧🇷"
flags.characters.count // 1
// the scalars are the underlying ISO country codes:
(flags.unicodeScalars.map { String($0) }).joinWithSeparator(",")
// N ,L ,G ,B
```

On the other hand, "👍".characters.count returns 2 (one for the generic character, one for the skin tone) and "👨‍👩‍👧‍👦".characters.count returns 4, as the multi-person groupings are composed from individual member emoji joined with the zero-width joiner:

```
"👨\u{200D}👩\u{200D}👧\u{200D}👦" == "👨‍👩‍👧‍👦"
```

Strings and Collections

Strings in Swift have an Index associated type, startIndex and endIndex properties, and a **subscript** that takes the index to fetch a specific character.

This means that String meets all the criteria needed to qualify as conforming to CollectionType. Yet String is *not* a collection. You cannot use it with **for ... in**, nor does it inherit all the protocol extensions of CollectionType or SequenceType.

In theory, you can change this yourself by extending String:

```
extension String: CollectionType {
    // nothing needed here – it already has the necessary implementations
}
```

In fact, you could go even further:

```
extension String: RangeReplaceableCollectionType { }
```

```
// now you can use it like a collection
var greeting = "Hello, world!"
if let comma = greeting.indexOf(",") {
    print(greeting[greeting.startIndex..<comma])
    greeting.replaceRange(greeting.indices,
        with: "How about some original example strings?")
}
```

However, this is probably not wise. Strings are not collections for a reason — it isn't just because the Swift team forgot. When Swift 2.0 introduced protocol extensions, this had the huge benefit of granting all collections and sequences method-like access to dozens of useful algorithms. But this also led to some concerns that collection-processing algorithms presenting themselves as methods on strings would give the implicit indication that these *methods* are completely safe and Unicode-correct, which wouldn't necessarily be true. Even though Character does its best to present combining character sequences as single values, as seen above, there are still some cases where processing a string character by character can result in incorrect results.

To this end, the collection-of-characters view of strings was moved to a property, characters, which put it on a footing similar to the other collection views: unicodeScalars, utf8, and utf16. Picking a specific view prompts you to acknowledge that you're moving into a "collection-processing" mode and that you should consider the consequences of the algorithm you're about to run.

CharacterView, however, has a special place amongst those views. String.Index is actually just a type alias for CharacterView.Index. This means that once you have found an index into the character view, you can then index directly into the string with it.

But for reasons that should be clear from the examples in the previous section, these are not random-access collections. How could they be, when knowing where the nth character of a particular string is involves evaluating just how many code points precede that character?

For this reason, String.Index conforms only to BidirectionalIndexType. You can start at either end of the string, moving forward or backward, and the code will look at the composition of the adjacent characters and skip over the correct number of bytes. However, you need to iterate up and down one character at a time.

String indices also conform to Comparable. You might not know how many characters lie between two indices, but you do at least know that one lies before the other.

You can automate iterating over multiple characters in one go via the advancedBy method:

```
let s = "abcdef"
// advance 5 from the start
```

```
let idx = s.startIndex.advancedBy(5)
s[idx]    // the character "f"
```

If there's a risk of advancing past the end of the string, you can add a limit to prevent advancedBy from going beyond a given index:

```
let safeIdx = s.startIndex.advancedBy(400, limit: s.endIndex)
assert(safeIdx == s.endIndex)
```

If you've read the chapter on generics, you might wonder why advancedBy returns a value of endIndex instead of an optional, which means you can't tell the difference between advance *hitting* the end value and going beyond it. It's not just you — we wonder the same thing.

Now, you might look at this and think, "I know! I can use this to give strings integer subscripting!" So you might do something like this:

```
extension String {
    subscript(idx: Int) -> Character {
        let strIdx = self.startIndex.advancedBy(idx, limit: endIndex)
        guard strIdx != endIndex
            else { fatalError("String index out of bounds") }
        return self[strIdx]
    }
}
```

```
s[5]   // returns "f"
```

However, just as with extending String to make it a collection, this kind of extension is best avoided. You might otherwise be tempted to start writing code like this:

```
for i in 0..<5 {
    print(s[i])
}
```

But as simple as this code looks, it's horribly inefficient. Every time s is accessed with an integer, an $O(n)$ function to advance its starting index is run. Running a linear loop inside another linear loop means this for loop is accidentally $O(n^2)$ — as the length of the string increases, the time this loop takes increases quadratically.

To someone used to dealing with fixed-width characters, this seems challenging at first — how will you navigate without integer indices? But thankfully, String providing access to characters via a collection also means you have several helpful techniques at your disposal. Many of the functions that operate on Array also work on String.characters.

Starting simply, iterating over characters in a string is easy without integer indices. If you want to number each character in turn, you just need a **for ... in** loop:

```
for (i, c) in "hello".characters.enumerate() {
    print("\(i): \(c)")
}
```

```
0: h
1: e
2: l
3: l
4: o
```

Or say you want to find a specific character. In that case, you can use indexOf:

```
var greeting = "Hello!"
if let idx = greeting.characters.indexOf("!") {
    greeting.insertContentsOf(", world".characters, at: idx)
}
```

Just like Array, String supports all the methods of RangeReplaceableCollectionType — but again, it doesn't conform to it. The insertContentsOf function inserts another collection of the same element type (e.g. Character for strings) after a given index. Note that this doesn't have to be another String; you could insert an array of characters into a string just as easily.

One collection-like feature strings do *not* provide is that of MutableCollectionType. This protocol adds one feature to a collection — that of the single-element subscript **set** — in addition to **get**. This is not to say strings aren't mutable — they have several mutating methods. But what you can't do is replace a single character using the subscript operator. The reason comes back to variable-length characters. Most people probably can intuit that a single-element subscript update would happen in constant time, as it does for Array. But since a character in a string may be of variable width, updating a single character could take linear time in proportion to the length of the string, because changing the width of a single element might require shuffling all the later elements up or down in memory. For this reason, you have to use replaceRange, even if that range is only a single element.

Strings and slicing

A good sign that a collection function will work well with strings is if the result is a SubSlice of the input. Performing slicing operations on arrays is a bit awkward, as the value you get back is not an Array, but rather an ArraySlice. This makes writing recursive functions that slice up their input especially painful.

String's collection views have no such trouble. They define their SubSlice to be an instance of **Self**, so the generic functions that take a sliceable type and return a subslice work very well with strings. For example, world here will be of type String.CharacterView:

```
let world = "Hello, world!".characters.suffix(6).dropLast()
```

split, which returns an array of subslices, is also useful for string processing. It's defined like so:

```
extension CollectionType {
    public func split(maxSplit: Int = default,
        allowEmptySlices: Bool = default,
        @noescape isSeparator: (Self.Generator.Element) -> Bool)
        -> [Self.SubSequence]
}
```

You can use its simplest form like this:

```
let commaSeparatedArray = "a,b,c".characters.split { $0 == "," }
```

This can serve a similar function to the NSString method componentsSeparatedByCharactersInSet, but with added configurations for whether or not to drop empty components. But since it takes a closure, it can do more than just compare characters. Here is an example of a primitive word wrap, where the closure captures a count of the length of the line thus far:

```
extension String {
    func wrap(after: Int = 70) -> String {
        var i = 0
        let lines = self.characters.split(allowEmptySlices: true) { character in
            switch character {
```

```
            case "\n", " "  where i >= after:
                i = 0
                return true
            default:
                i += 1
                return false
            }
        }. map(String.init)
        return lines.joinWithSeparator("\n")
    }
}
```

That said, chances are that you'll want to split things by character most of the time, so you might find it convenient to use the variant of split that takes a single separator:

```
extension CollectionType where Generator.Element : Equatable {
    public func split(separator: Self.Generator.Element,
        maxSplit: Int = default,
        allowEmptySlices: Bool = default)
        -> [Self.SubSequence]
}
```

In doing so, you can write "1,2,3".characters.split(","). map(String.init). Or, consider writing a version that takes a sequence of multiple separators:

```
extension CollectionType where Generator.Element: Equatable {
    func split
        <S: SequenceType where Generator.Element == S.Generator.Element>
        (separators: S) -> [SubSequence]
    {
        return split { separators.contains($0) }
    }
}
```

This way, you can write the following:

```
"Hello, world!".characters.split(",! ".characters).map(String.init)
```

A Simple Regular Expression Matcher

To demonstrate how useful it is that string slices are also strings, we'll implement a simple regular expression matcher based on a similar matcher written in C in Brian W. Kernighan and Rob Pike's *The Practice of Programming*. The original code, while beautifully compact, made extensive use of C pointers, so it often doesn't translate well to other languages. But with Swift, through use of optionals and slicing, you can almost match the C version in simplicity.

First, let's define a basic regular expression type:

```
/// A simple regular expression type, supporting ^ and $ anchors,
/// and matching with . and *
public struct Regex {
    private let regexp: String
    /// Construct from a regular expression String
    public init (_ regexp: String) {
        self.regexp = regexp
    }
}
```

Since this regular expression's functionality is going to be so simple, it's not really possible to create an "invalid" regular expression with its initializer. If the expression support were more complex (for example, supporting multi-character matching with []), you'd possibly want to give it a failable initializer.

Next, we extend Regex to support a match function, which takes a string and returns true if it matches the expression:

```
extension Regex {
    /// Returns true if the string argument matches the expression
    public func match(text: String) -> Bool {

        // if the regex starts with ^, then it can only match the
        // start of the input
        if regexp.characters.first == "^" {
            return Regex.matchHere(regexp.characters.dropFirst(),
                text.characters)
        }

        // otherwise, search for a match at every point in the input
        // until one is found
        var idx = text.startIndex
        while true {
            if Regex.matchHere(regexp.characters,
                text.characters.suffixFrom(idx))
```

```
        {
            return true
        }
        guard idx != text.endIndex else { break }
        idx = idx.successor()
    }

    return false
    }
}
```

The matching function doesn't do much except iterate over every possible substring of the input, from the start to the end, checking if it matches the regular expression from that point on. But if the regular expression starts with a ^, then it need only match from the start of the text.

matchHere is where most of the regular expression processing logic lies:

```
extension Regex {
    /// Match a regular expression string at the beginning of text.
    private static func matchHere(
        regexp: String.CharacterView, _ text: String.CharacterView) -> Bool
    {
        // empty regexprs match everything
        if regexp.isEmpty {
            return true
        }

        // any character followed by * requires a call to matchStar
        if let c = regexp.first where regexp.dropFirst().first == "*" {
            return matchStar(c, regexp.dropFirst(2), text)
        }

        // if this is the last regex character and it's $, then it's a match iff the
        // remaining text is also empty
        if regexp.first == "$" && regexp.dropFirst().isEmpty {
            return text.isEmpty
        }

        // if one character matches, drop one from the input and the regex
        // and keep matching
        if let tc = text.first, rc = regexp.first where rc == "." || tc == rc {
            return matchHere(regexp.dropFirst(), text.dropFirst())
        }
```

```
    // if none of the above, no match
    return false
}


/// Search for zero or more `c`'s at beginning of text, followed by the
/// remainder of the regular expression.
private static func matchStar
    (c: Character, _ regexp: String.CharacterView,
        _ text: String.CharacterView)
    -> Bool
{
    var idx = text.startIndex
    while true {   // a * matches zero or more instances
        if matchHere(regexp, text.suffixFrom(idx)) {
            return true
        }
        if idx == text.endIndex || (text[idx] != c && c != ".") {
            return false
        }
        idx = idx.successor()
    }
}
}
```

The matcher is very simple to use:

```
Regex("^h..lo*!$").match("hellooooo!")
```

true

This code makes extensive use of slicing (both with range-based subscripts
and with the dropFirst function) and optionals — especially the ability to
equate an optional with a non-optional value. So, for example,
`if regexp.first == "^"` will work, even with an empty string, because "". first
returns **nil**. However, you can still equate that to the non-optional "^", and
when **nil**, it will return false.

Elsewhere, expressions like these guard against calling dropFirst on an empty
string (which would crash) because they only execute if regexp.first is non-**nil**:

```
if let c = regexp.first where regexp.dropFirst().first == "*" { }

if regexp.first == "$" && regexp.dropFirst().isEmpty
```

The ugliest part of the code is probably the **while true** loop. The requirement is that this loops over every possible substring, *including* an empty string at the end. This is to ensure that expressions like Regex("$").match("abc") return true. If strings worked similarly to arrays, with an integer index, we could write something like this:

```
// ... means up to _and including_ the endIndex
for idx in text.startIndex...text.endIndex {
    // slice string between idx and the end
    if Regex.matchHere(_regexp, text[idx..<text.endIndex]) {
        return true
    }
}
```

The final time around the **for**, idx would equal text.endIndex, so text[idx..<text.endIndex] would be an empty string.

So why doesn't this work? Although you can create index ranges with either the half-open operator ..< (which means "up to *but not* including"), or closed ranges with the ... (which means "up to *and* including"), there is really only one Range type, and it's the half-open version. When you call a ... b, what happens is the ... returns you Range(start: a, end: b.successor()), thus converting your end marker from the one to stop *at* to the one to stop *before*.

This works fine with arrays, because they're integer indexed — if you increment the end index of an array, who cares? But string indices are more complicated. They actually track where in the underlying storage they're pointing. They have to, as we've seen, because only by looking at the string can you know how many bytes to advance.

So if you execute "hello".endIndex.successor(), you'll get a runtime error, which reads "fatal error: can not increment endIndex." Hence, when ... tries to do its trick of turning the end index into a closed interval, you get the same error. As a result, we are stuck with using the C-style loop with a **break**.

StringLiteralConvertible

Throughout this chapter, we've been using String("blah") and "blah" pretty much interchangeably, but they are different. "" is a string literal, just like the array literals covered in the collections chapter.

String literals are slightly more work to implement than array literals because they are part of a hierarchy of three protocols: StringLiteralConvertible, ExtendedGraphemeClusterLiteralConvertible, and UnicodeScalarLiteralConvertible. Each defines an **init** for creating a type from each kind of literal, so you have to implement all three. But unless you really need fine-grained logic based on whether or not the value is being created from a single scalar/cluster, it's probably easiest to implement them all in terms of the string version, like so:

```
extension Regex: StringLiteralConvertible {
    public init ( stringLiteral  value: String) {
        regexp = value
    }
    public init (extendedGraphemeClusterLiteral value: String) {
        self  = Regex(stringLiteral: value)

    }
    public init (unicodeScalarLiteral value: String) {
        self  = Regex(stringLiteral: value)
    }
}
```

Once defined, you can begin using string literals to create the regex matcher by explicitly naming the type:

```
let  r:  Regex = "^h..lo*!$"
```

Or even better is when the type is already named for you:

```
func findMatches(strings: [String], regex: Regex) -> [String]  {
    return strings. filter  { regex.match($0) }
}

findMatches(["foo","bar","baz"], regex: "^b..")
```

By default, string literals create the String type because of this **typealias** in the standard library:

```
typealias StringLiteralType = String
```

But if you wanted to change this default specifically for your application (say you had a different kind of string that was faster for your particular use case — say it implemented a small-string optimization where a couple of characters were held directly in the string itself), you could change this by re-aliasing the value:

typealias StringLiteralType = StaticString

let what = "hello"
what **is** StaticString // *true*

Internal Structure of String

(Note: this section describes the internal organization of Swift.String. While it's correct as of Swift 2.0, it should never be relied on for production use, as it could change at any time. It's presented more to help understand the performance characteristics of Swift strings.)

As of Swift 2.0, if you call sizeof(String), you'll get back a size of 24. At least, this happens on 64-bit platforms – on 32-bit platforms it will be 12. A string's internal storage is made up of something that looks like this:

```
struct String {
    var _core: _StringCore
}

struct _StringCore {
    var _baseAddress: COpaquePointer
    var _countAndFlags: UInt
    var _owner: AnyObject?
}
```

The _core property is currently public and therefore easily accessible. But even if that were to change in a future release, you'd still be able to bitcast any string to _StringCore:

```
let hello = "hello"
let bits = unsafeBitCast(hello, _StringCore.self)
```

(While strings really aggregate an internal type, because they are structs and thus have no overhead other than their members, you can just bitcast the outer container without a problem.)

That's enough to print out the contents using print(bits), but you'll notice that you cannot access the individual fields, such as _countAndFlags, because they're private. To work around this, we can duplicate the _StringCore struct in our own code and do another bitcast:

```
/// A clone of Swift._StringCore to work around access control
struct StringCoreClone {
    var _baseAddress: COpaquePointer
    var _countAndFlags: UInt
    var _owner: AnyObject?
}
```

```
let clone = unsafeBitCast(bits, StringCoreClone.self)
```

Then if you call print(clone._countAndFlags), you'll see that it prints out 5, the length of the string. The base address is a pointer to memory holding the sequence of ASCII characters, so you can also print out this buffer using the C puts function:

```
// extra UnsafePointer init to convert from pointed-to-type of Void to Int8:
puts(UnsafePointer(clone._baseAddress))
```

```
hello
10
```

In doing the above, it will print out hello. Or it might print out hello, followed by a bunch of garbage, because the buffer is not necessarily null-terminated like a regular C string.

So, does this mean Swift uses a UTF-8 representation to store strings internally? You can find out by storing a non-ASCII string instead:

```
let emoji = "Hello, 🌑"
let emojiBits = unsafeBitCast(emoji, StringCoreClone.self)
```

If you do this, you'll see two differences from before. One is that the _countAndFlags property is now a huge number. This is because it isn't just holding the length. The high-order bits are used to store a flag indicating that this string includes non-ASCII values (there's also another flag indicating the string points to the buffer of an NSString). Conveniently, _StringCore has a public count property that returns the length in code units:

```
emoji._core.count
```

9

If count were not available, we could replicate it in our clone struct by masking off the flag bits:

```
extension StringCoreClone {
    var count: Int {
        let mask = 0b11 << UInt(sizeof(UInt)*8 - 2)
        return Int(_countAndFlags & ~mask)
    }
}
```

The second change is that the _baseAddress now points to 16-bit characters. Now that one or more of the characters is no longer ASCII, it triggers String to start storing the buffer as UTF-16. It does this no matter what non-ASCII characters you store in the string — even if they require 32 bits to store, there isn't a third mode where UTF-32 is used.

To prove the buffer is UTF-16 even when the string contains a 4-byte emoji, we can use the UTF16.decode method to decode the buffer:

```
let buf = UnsafeBufferPointer(
    start: UnsafePointer<UInt16>(emojiBits._baseAddress),
    count: emojiBits.count)

var gen = buf.generate()
var utf16 = UTF16()
while case let .Result(scalar) = utf16.decode(&gen) {
    print(scalar, terminator: "")
}
```

This will print out "Hello, 🌑" .

The last _StringCore property, _owner, will be a null pointer. This is because all the strings thus far have been initialized via a string literal, so the buffer points to a constant string in memory in the read-only data part of the binary. Instead, create a non-constant string:

```
var greeting = "hello"
greeting.appendContentsOf(" world")
let greetingBits = unsafeBitCast(greeting, StringCoreClone.self)
```

This string's _owner field will contain a value. This will be a pointer to an ARC-managed class reference, used in conjunction with a function like isUniquelyReferenced to give strings value semantics with copy-on-write behavior.

This _owner manages the memory allocated to hold the string. The picture we've built up so far looks something like this:

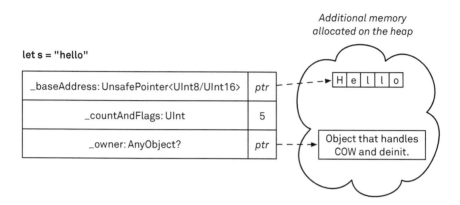

Figure 7.1: Memory of a String value

Since the owner is a class, this means it can have a **deinit** method, which, when triggered, frees the memory:

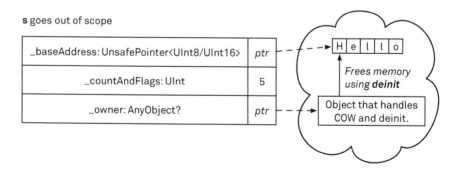

Figure 7.2: When a String goes out of scope

Strings, like arrays and other standard library collection types, are copy-on-write. When you assign a string to a second string variable, the string buffer isn't copied immediately. Instead, as with any copy assignment of a struct, a shallow copy of only the immediate fields takes place, and they initially share that storage:

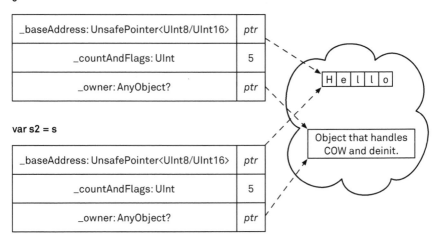

Figure 7.3: Two Strings share the same memory

Then, when one of the strings mutates its contents, the code detects this sharing by checking whether or not the _owner is uniquely referenced. If it isn't, it first copies the shared buffer before mutating it, at which point the buffer is no longer shared:

s2.append("!")

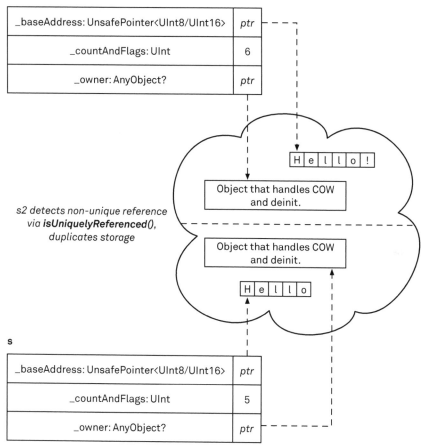

Figure 7.4: String Mutation

For more on copy-on-write, see the chapter on structs and classes.

One final benefit of this structure returns us to slicing. If you take a string and create slices from it, the internals of these slices look like this:

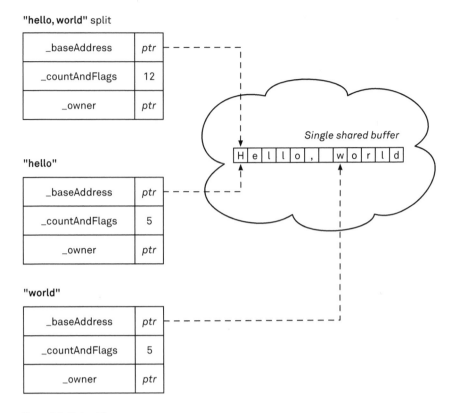

Figure 7.5: String Slices

This means that when calling split on a string, what you are essentially creating is an array of starting/ending pointers to within the original string buffer, as opposed to making numerous copies. This comes at a cost, though — a single slice of a string keeps the whole string in memory. Even if that slice is just a few characters, it could be keeping a string of several megabytes alive.

If you create a String from an NSString, then another optimization means the _owner reference used will actually be a reference to the original NSString, and the buffer will point to that NSString's storage. This can be shown by extracting the owner reference *as* an NSString, so long as the string was originally an NSString:

```
let ns = "hello" as NSString
let s = ns as String
let (_, _, owner) = unsafeBitCast(s, (UInt, UInt, NSString).self)
print(owner) // ref will be a reference,
```

```
owner === ns // equal to the original NSString
```

Internal Organization of Character

As we've seen, Swift.Character represents a sequence of code points that might be arbitrarily long. How does Character manage this? If you run sizeof(Character), you'll see it's nine bytes long. An odd number of bytes is often a sign of an enum — one byte for the enum case, and the rest for the associated value(s).

So characters internally look a little like this:

```
enum Character {
    case Large(Buffer)
    case Small(Int64)
}
```

This technique — holding a small number of elements internally and switching to a heap-based buffer — is sometimes called the "small string optimization." Since characters are almost always just a handful of bytes, it works particularly well here.

Of course, characters aren't enums; they're structs, so the enum will be an internal private representation. In fact, you can see it in the Swift 2.0 REPL. Just type the following into a command line:

```
$ echo ":type lookup Character" | swift | less
```

Then watch as the internal guts of the Character type scroll across your screen. You can use this technique to explore any type in the standard library in order to understand more about its internal implementation (again, this is only for better understanding — never make assumptions about these implementation details; you should only ever rely on the public interfaces).

Code Unit Views

Sometimes it's necessary to drop down to a lower level of abstraction and operate directly on Unicode code points instead of characters. There are a few common reasons for this.

Firstly, maybe you actually need the code units, perhaps for rendering into a UTF-8-encoded webpage, or for interoperating with a non-Swift API that takes them.

For an example of an API that requires code units, let's look at using NSCharacterSet in combination with Swift strings. NSString and its friends operate on UTF-16 code points. So if you wanted to use NSCharacterSet to split up a string, you could do it via the utf16 view:

```
extension String {
    func words (splitBy: NSCharacterSet = .alphanumericCharacterSet()) -> [String] {
        return self.utf16.split {
            !splitBy.characterIsMember($0)
        }.flatMap(String.init)
    }
}
```

```
let s = "Wow! This contains _all_ kinds of things like 123 and \"quotes\"?"
s.words()
```

```
["Wow", "This", "contains", "all", "kinds", "of", "things", "like", "123", "and", "quotes
```

This will break the string apart at every non-alphanumeric character, giving you an array of String.UTF16View slices. Those can be turned back into strings via map with the String initializer that takes a UTF16View. This is a failable initializer (in case an index falls on an intra-character boundary), hence the use of flatMap (as described in the optionals chapter) to filter out any **nil** elements.

The good news is, even after going through this fairly extensive pipeline, the string slices in words will *still* just be views onto the original string; this property isn't lost by going via the UTF16View and back again.

A second reason for using these views is that operating on code units rather than fully composed characters can be much faster. This is because to compose grapheme clusters, you must look ahead of every character to see if it's followed by combining characters. To see just how much faster these views can be, take a look at the performance section later on.

Finally, the UTF-16 view has one benefit the other views do not have: it could be random access. This is possible for just this view type because, as we've seen, this is how strings are held internally within the String type. What this means is the nth UTF-16 code unit is always at the nth position in the buffer (even if the string is in "ASCII buffer mode" – it's just a question of the width of the entries to advance over).

String.UTF16View.Index used to be extended to conform to RandomAccessIndexType inside the Foundation framework, but ceased to be with the 2.0 release. But since it possesses all the necessary implementations to conform to it, you can add this yourself:

```
extension String.UTF16Index: RandomAccessIndexType {
    /* no implementation needed */
}
```

That said, it's probably rarer than you think to need random access. Most practical string use cases just need serial access. But some processing algorithms rely on random access for efficiency. For example, the Boyer-Moore search algorithm relies on the ability to skip along the text in jumps of multiple characters.

If the UTF-16 view were random access, you could use it with algorithms that require such a characteristic. So you could, for example, use the search algorithm that we define in the generics chapter with it:

```
let helloWorld = "Hello, world!"
if let idx = helloWorld.utf16.search("world".utf16)?
    .samePositionIn(helloWorld)
{
    print(helloWorld[idx..<helloWorld.endIndex])
}
```

```
world!
```

But beware! These convenience or efficiency benefits come at a price, which is that your code may no longer be completely Unicode-correct. So unfortunately, the following assertion will hold:

```
let text = "Look up your Pok\u{0065}\u{0301}mon in a Pokédex."
assert(text.utf16.search("Pokémon".utf16) == nil)
```

Unicode defines diacritics that are used to combine with alphabetic characters as being alphanumeric, so this fares a little better:

```
let nonAlphas = NSCharacterSet.alphanumericCharacterSet().invertedSet
text.utf16.split(isSeparator: nonAlphas.characterIsMember)
```

```
[StringUTF16("Look"), StringUTF16("up"), StringUTF16("your"),
StringUTF16("Pokémon"), StringUTF16("in"), StringUTF16("a"),
StringUTF16("Pokédex")]
```

CustomStringConvertible and CustomDebugStringConvertible

Functions like print, String.init, and string interpolation are written to take any type, no matter what. Even without any customization, the results you get back might be acceptable:

```
print(Regex("colou?r"))
// prints out Regex("colou?r")
```

Then again, you might want something a little prettier, especially if your type contains private variables you don't want displayed. But never fear! It only takes a minute to give your custom class a nicely formatted output when it's passed to print:

```
extension Regex: CustomStringConvertible {
    public var description: String {
        return "/\(regexp)/"
    }
}
```

Now, if someone converts your custom type to a string through various means — using it with a streaming function like print, passing it to String.init, or using it in some string interpolation — it will print out as /expression/.

There's also CustomDebugStringConvertible, which you can implement when someone calls String(reflecting:), in order to provide more debugging output than the pretty printed version:

```
extension Regex: CustomDebugStringConvertible {
    public var debugDescription: String {
        return "{expression: \(regexp)}"
    }
}
```

String(reflecting:) falls back to using CustomStringConvertible if CustomDebugStringConvertible isn't implemented. So often it isn't worth implementing if your type is simple. However, if your custom type is a container, it's probably polite to conform to CustomDebugStringConvertible in order to print the debug versions of the elements the type contains. So we can extend the Queue example from the collections chapter:

```
extension Queue: CustomStringConvertible, CustomDebugStringConvertible {
    var description: String {
        // print contained elements using String.init, which favors
        // CustomStringConvertible
        let elements = map { String($0) }.joinWithSeparator(", ")
        return " [\(elements)]"
    }

    var debugDescription: String {
        // print contained elements using String.init(reflecting :), which favors
        // CustomDebugStringConvertible
        let elements = map { String(reflecting: $0) }.joinWithSeparator(", ")
        return " [\(elements)]"
    }
}
```

Given that conforming to CustomStringConvertible implies that a type has a pretty print output, you may be tempted to write something like the following generic function:

```
func doSomethingAttractive<T: CustomStringConvertible>(with value: T) {
    // print out something incorporating value, safe in the knowledge
    // it will print out sensibly
}
```

If you do this, though, you'll soon come to the distressing discovery that String does not conform to CustomStringConvertible! But why? Surely strings are the most printable thing of all! This is the Swift team's way of telling you not to use CustomStringConvertible in this manner. Instead of poking at types to establish whether or not they have a description property, you should use String. init regardless and live with the ugly output if a type doesn't conform to printable. And it's a good reason to implement CustomStringConvertible whenever you write more than a very simple type. It only takes a handful of lines.

Streamable and OutputStreamType

If your type is more complex, it might be easier to implement the Streamable protocol instead. This requires a generic method, writeTo, which accepts any type that conforms to OutputStreamType, and writes **self** to it. The easiest way to do this is with print, which has an overload that takes an output stream. It is very easy to make a mistake here by accidentally forgetting the output stream parameter. Unless you test with a target that is not the standard output, you might not even notice:

```
extension Queue: Streamable {
    func writeTo<Target: OutputStreamType>(inout target: Target) {
        print("[", terminator: "", toStream: &target)
        print(self.map { String($0) }.joinWithSeparator(","),
            terminator: "", toStream: &target)
        print("]", terminator: "", toStream: &target)
    }
}
```

So if you implement Streamable, what can you stream to? Well, strings are output streams:

```
var s = ""
let q: Queue = [1,2,3]
q.writeTo(&s)

print(s)

[1,2,3]
```

String is the only type in the standard library that is an output stream (i.e. that conforms to OutputStreamType). However, we can make our own output streams. For example, one that just buffers writes to an array:

```
struct ArrayStream: OutputStreamType {
    var buf: [String] = []
    mutating func write(string: String) {
        buf.append(string)
    }
}
```

Or, extend NSMutableData so that it takes a stream, writing it as UTF-8-encoded output:

```
extension NSMutableData: OutputStreamType {
    public func write(string: String) {
        string.nulTerminatedUTF8.dropLast().withUnsafeBufferPointer {
            self.appendBytes($0.baseAddress, length: $0.count)
        }
    }
}
```

While String is the only type that conforms to OutputStreamType, other functions like print also make use of streamable types. You can see this if you write the following rather silly sample:

```
struct SlowStreamer: Streamable, ArrayLiteralConvertible {
    let contents: [String]
    init (arrayLiteral elements: String...) {
        contents = elements
    }
    func writeTo<Target: OutputStreamType>(inout target: Target) {
        for x in contents {
            print(x, toStream: &target)
            sleep(1)
        }
    }
}
```

```
let slow: SlowStreamer = [
    "You'll see that this gets",
    "written slowly line by line",
    "to the standard output",
]
```

```
print(slow)
```

As new lines are printed to target, the output appears; it doesn't wait for the call to complete. Internally, presumably print is using some OutputStreamType-conforming wrapper on the standard output. You could write something similar for standard error, like this:

```
struct StdErr: OutputStreamType {
    mutating func write(string: String) {
        // strings can be passed directly into C functions that take a
        // const char* - see the interoperability chapter for more!
        fputs(string, stderr)
    }
}
```

```
var standarderror = StdErr()

print("oops!", &standarderror)
```

Streams can also hold state and potentially transform their output. Additionally, you can chain them together:

```
struct ReplacingStream<T: OutputStreamType>: OutputStreamType {
    var outputStream: T
    let toReplace: DictionaryLiteral<String, String>
    init (replacing: DictionaryLiteral<String, String>, output: T) {
        outputStream = output
        toReplace = replacing
    }
    mutating func write(string: String) {
        let toWrite = toReplace.reduce(string) {
            $0.stringByReplacingOccurrencesOfString($1.0, withString: $1.1)
        }
        print(toWrite, &outputStream, appendNewline: false)
    }
}

var replacer = ReplacingStream(
    replacing: ["in the cloud": "on someone else's computer"],
    output: standarderror)

let source = "More and more people are finding it convenient " +
    "to store their data in the cloud."

print(source, &replacer)
```

DictionaryLiteral is used in the above code instead of a regular dictionary. This is useful when you want to be able to use the [key:value] literal syntax, but you don't want the two side effects you'd get from using a Dictionary: elimination of duplicate keys and reordering of the keys. If this isn't what you want, then DictionaryLiteral is a nice alternative to an array of pairs (i.e. [(key, value)]) while allowing the caller to use the more convenient [:] syntax.

String Performance

There's no denying that coalescing multiple variable-length UTF-16 values into extended grapheme clusters is going to be more expensive than just ripping through a buffer of 16-bit values. But what is that cost? One way to test performance would be to adapt the regular expression matcher above to work against all of the different collection views.

But this presents a problem. Ideally, you would write a generic regex matcher with a placeholder for the view. But this doesn't work — the four different views don't all implement a common "string view" protocol. Also, in our regex matcher, we need to represent specific character constants like * and ^ to compare against the regex. In the UTF16View, these would need to be UInt16, but with the character view, they'd need to be characters. Finally, we want the regex matcher initializer itself to still take a String. How would it know which method to call to get the appropriate view out?

One technique is to bundle up all the variable logic into a single type and then parameterize the regex matcher on that type. First, we define a protocol that has all the necessary information:

```
protocol StringViewSelector {
    associatedtype ViewType: CollectionType

    static var caret: ViewType.Generator.Element { get }
    static var asterisk: ViewType.Generator.Element { get }
    static var period: ViewType.Generator.Element { get }
    static var dollar: ViewType.Generator.Element { get }

    static func viewFrom(s: String) -> ViewType
}
```

This information includes an associated type for the view we're going to use, getters for the four constants needed, and a function to extract the relevant view from a string.

Given this, you can implement concrete versions like so:

```
struct UTF8ViewSelector: StringViewSelector {
    static var caret: UInt8 { return UInt8(ascii: "^") }
    static var asterisk: UInt8 { return UInt8(ascii: "*") }
    static var period: UInt8 { return UInt8(ascii: ".") }
    static var dollar: UInt8 { return UInt8(ascii: "$") }

    static func viewFrom(s: String) -> String.UTF8View { return s.utf8 }
}
```

```
struct CharacterViewSelector: StringViewSelector {
    static var caret: Character { return "^" }
    static var asterisk: Character { return "*" }
    static var period: Character { return "." }
    static var dollar: Character { return "$" }

    static func viewFrom(s: String) -> String.CharacterView { return s.characters }
}
```

You can probably guess what UTF16ViewSelector and
UnicodeScalarViewSelector look like.

These are what some people call "phantom types" — types that only exist at
compile time and that don't actually hold any data. Try calling
sizeof(CharacterViewSelector) — it'll return zero. It contains no data. All we're
using these types for is to parameterize behavior of another type: the regex
matcher. It will use them like so:

```
struct Regex<V: StringViewSelector
    where V.ViewType.Generator.Element: Equatable,
        V.ViewType.SubSequence == V.ViewType>
{
    let regexp: String
    /// Construct from a regular expression String
    init (_ regexp: String) {
        self.regexp = regexp
    }

    /// Returns true if the string argument matches the expression
    func match(text: String) -> Bool {
        let text = V.viewFrom(text)
        let regexp = V.viewFrom(self.regexp)

        // if the regex starts with ^, then it can only match the start
        // of the input
        if regexp.first == V.caret {
            return Regex.matchHere(regexp.dropFirst(), text)
        }

        // otherwise, search for a match at every point in the input until
        // one is found
        var idx = text.startIndex
        while true {
            if Regex.matchHere(regexp, text.suffixFrom(idx)) {
                return true
```

```
        }
        guard idx != text.endIndex else { break }
        idx = idx.successor()
    }
    return false
}


/// Match a regular expression string at the beginning of text.
static func matchHere(regexp: V.ViewType, _ text: V.ViewType) -> Bool {
    // more matching code
    return true
}
// etc.
}
```

Once the code is rewritten like this, it's easy to write some benchmarking code that measures the time taken to process some arbitrary regular expression across very large input:

```
func benchmark
    <V: StringViewSelector where V.ViewType.Generator.Element: Equatable,
        V.ViewType.SubSequence == V.ViewType>
    (_: V.Type) {
    let r = Regex<V>("h..a*")
    var count = 0

    let startTime = CFAbsoluteTimeGetCurrent()
    while let line = readLine() {
        if r.match(line) { count = count &+ 1 }
    }
    let totalTime = CFAbsoluteTimeGetCurrent() - startTime
    print("\(V.self): \(totalTime)")
}

func ~=<T: Equatable>(lhs: T, rhs: T?) -> Bool {
    return lhs == rhs
}


switch Process.arguments.last {
case "ch": benchmark(CharacterViewSelector.self)
case "8": benchmark(UTF8ViewSelector.self)
case "16": benchmark(UTF16ViewSelector.self)
case "sc": benchmark(UnicodeScalarViewSelector.self)
default: print("unrecognized view type")
```

}

The results show the following speeds for the different views in processing the regex on a large corpus of English text (128,000 lines, 1 million words):

View	Time
UTF16	0.5 seconds
UnicodeScalar	0.8 seconds
UTF8	1.1 seconds
Characters	9.1 seconds

Only you can know if your use case justifies choosing your view type based on performance. It's almost certainly the case that these performance characteristics only matter when you are doing extremely heavy string manipulation, but if you are certain that what you are doing would be correct when operating on the UTF-16 data, then this can give you a decent speedup.

Error Handling

8

Swift provides multiple ways for dealing with errors and even allows us to build our own mechanisms. In the chapter on optionals, we looked at optionals and assertions. An optional indicates that a value may or may not be there; we have to inspect the optional and unwrap the value before we can use it. An assertion validates that a condition is true; if the condition doesn't hold, the program crashes.

If we look at the interfaces of existing Swift types, we can get a good feeling for when to use an optional and when not to. Optionals are there for safety. For example, when you look up a key in a dictionary, it's often expected that the key might not be present. Therefore, a dictionary lookup returns an optional result.

Compare this to arrays: when looking up an element at a specific index, the element is returned directly and not wrapped in an optional. This is because the programmer is expected to know if an array index is valid. Accessing an array with an index that is out of bounds is considered a programmer error, and consequently, this will crash your application. If you're unsure whether or not an index is within bounds, you need to check beforehand.

Assertions are a great tool for identifying bugs in your code. Used correctly, they show you at the earliest possible moment when your program is in a state you did not expect. They should never be used to signal *expected errors* such as a network error.

An alternative to returning an optional from a function that can fail is to mark the function as **throws**. Besides a different syntax for how the caller must handle the success and failure cases, the key difference to returning an optional is that throwing functions can return a rich error value that carries information about the error that occurred.

This difference is a good guideline for when to use one approach over the other. Consider the first and last methods on CollectionType again. They have exactly one error condition (the collection is empty) — returning a rich error would not give the caller more information than what is already present in the optional value. Compare this to a function that executes a network request: many things can fail, from the network being down to being unable to parse the server's response. Rich error information is necessary to allow the caller to react differently to different errors (or just to show the user what exactly went wrong).

The Result Type

Before we look at Swift's built-in error handling in more detail, let's discuss the Result type, which will help clarify how Swift's error handling works when you take away the syntactic sugar. A Result type is very similar to an optional. Recall that an optional is just an enumeration with two cases: a None or **nil** case, with no associated value; and a Some case, which has an associated value. The Result type is an **enum** with two cases as well: a failure case, which carries an associated error value; and a success case, also with an associated value. Just like optionals, Result has one generic parameter:

```
enum Result<A> {
    case Failure(ErrorType)
    case Success(A)
}
```

Let's suppose we are writing a function to read a file from disk. As a first try, we could define the interface using an optional. Because reading a file might fail, we want to be able to return **nil**:

```
func contentsOfFile1(filename: String) -> String?
```

The interface above is very simple, but it does not tell us anything about why reading the file failed. Does the file not exist? Or do we not have the right permissions? This is another example where the failure reason matters. Let's define an **enum** for the possible error cases:

```
enum FileError: ErrorType {
    case FileDoesNotExist
    case NoPermission
}
```

Now we can change the type of our function to return either an error or a valid result:

```
func contentsOfFile(filename: String) -> Result<String>
```

Now the caller of the function can look at the result cases and react differently based on the error. In the code below, we try to read the file, and in case reading succeeds, we print the contents. If the file does not exist, we print that, and we handle any remaining errors in a different way:

```
let result = contentsOfFile("input.txt")
```

```
switch result {
    case let .Success(contents):
        print(contents)
    case let .Failure(error):
        if let fileError = error as? FileError
            where fileError == .FileDoesNotExist
        {
            print("Empty file")
        } else {
            // Handle error
        }
}
```

Swift's built-in error handling is implemented almost like this, only with a different syntax. Instead of giving a function a Result return type to indicate that it can fail, we mark it as **throws**. Note that Result applies to types, whereas **throws** applies to functions. We will come back to this difference later in this chapter. For every throwing function, the compiler will verify that the caller either catches the error or propagates it to its caller. In the case of contentsOfFile, the type including **throws** looks like this:

```
func contentsOfFile(filename: String) throws -> String
```

From now on, our code will not compile unless we mark every call to contentsOfFile with **try**. The **try** keyword serves two purposes: first, it signals to the compiler that we know we're calling a function that can throw an error. More importantly, it immediately makes clear to readers of the code which functions can throw.

Calling a throwing function also requires us to make a decision about how we want to deal with possible errors. We can either handle an error by using **do/catch**, or we can have it propagate up the call stack by marking the calling function as **throws**. We can use pattern matching to catch specific errors or catch all errors. In the example below, we explicitly catch a FileDoesNotExist case and then handle all other errors in a catch-all case. Within this catch-all case, a variable error is automatically available:

```
do {
    let result = try contentsOfFile("input.txt")
    print(result)
} catch FileError.FileDoesNotExist {
    print("File does not exist")
} catch {
    print(error)
```

```
    // Handle any other error
}
```

> The error handling syntax in Swift probably looks familiar to you. Many other languages use the same **try**, **catch**, and **throw** keywords for exception handling. Despite the resemblance, error handling in Swift does not incur the runtime cost that is often associated with exceptions. The compiler treats **throw** like a regular return, making both code paths very fast.

If we want to expose more information in our errors, we can use an enum with associated values. (We could have also used a struct or class instead; any type that conforms to the ErrorType protocol can be used as an error in a throwing function.) For example, if we want to write a file parser, we can choose to model the possible errors like this:

```
enum ParseError: ErrorType {
    case WrongEncoding
    case Warning(line: Int, message: String)
}
```

Now, if we want to parse a file, we can again use pattern matching to distinguish between the cases. In the case of .Warning, we can bind the line number and warning message to a variable:

```
do {
    let contents = try parseFile(contents)
    print(contents)
} catch ParseError.WrongEncoding {
    print("This file uses the wrong encoding")
} catch let ParseError.Warning(line, message) {
    print("Warning at line \(line): \(message)")
} catch {
}
```

There is an issue with the code above. Even if we are absolutely sure that the only error that could happen is of type ParseError (from which we handled all cases), we still need to write a final **catch** case to convince the compiler that we exhaustively handled all possible errors. In a future version, the compiler might be able to check exhaustiveness within a module, but across modules, this problem cannot be solved. The reason is that Swift errors are untyped: we can only mark a function as **throws**, but we cannot specify *which* errors it will throw. This was a conscious design decision: most of the time, you only care about whether or not an error was present. If we would need to specify the types of all errors, this might get out of hand quickly: it would make functions' type signatures quite complicated, especially for functions that call several other throwing functions and propagate their errors.

In a future release, Swift will probably have typed errors; this is actively discussed on the mailing lists.

Because errors in Swift are untyped, it is important to document the types of errors your functions can throw. Xcode supports a **throws** keyword in documentation markup for this purpose. Here's an example:

```
/// Opens a text file  and returns its  contents.
///
/// - parameter filename: The name of the file to read.
/// - returns: The file  contents, interpreted as UTF-8.
/// - throws: `FileError` if  the  file  does not exist or
///             the process doesn't have read permissions.
func contentsOfFile(filename: String) throws -> String
```

The Quick Help popover that appears when you Option-click on the function name will now include an extra section for the thrown errors.

However, sometimes it can be useful to use the type system to specify the errors a function can throw. If we care about this, we can come up with a slightly altered Result type, which has an additional generic parameter for the error type:

```
enum Result<A, Error> {
    case Failure(Error)
    case Success(A)
}
```

This way, we can declare functions using an explicit error type. The following parseFile function will return either an array of strings or a ParseError. We do not have to handle any other cases when calling it, and the compiler knows this:

```
func parseFile(contents: String) -> Result<[String], ParseError>
```

In code where your errors have a significant semantic meaning, you can choose to use a typed Result type instead of Swift's built-in error handling. This way, you can let the compiler verify that you catch all possible errors. However, in most applications, using **throws** and **do/try/catch** will lead to simpler code. There is another big benefit to using the built-in error handling: the compiler will make sure you cannot ignore the error case when calling a function that might throw. With the definition of parseFile above, we could write the following code:

```
let _ = parseFile(contents)
```

If the function were marked as **throws**, the compiler would force us to call it using **try**. The compiler would also force us to either wrap that call in a **do/catch** block or propagate the error.

In the example above, it might not be too important when you ignore the error. But especially when dealing with functions that do not return a normal result, it can really help you not forget to catch the error. For example, consider the following function:

```
func setupServerConnection() throws {
    // Implementation
}
```

Because the function is marked as **throws**, we need to call it with **try**. If the server connection fails, we probably want to switch to a different code path or display an error. By having to use **try**, we are forced to think about this case. However, if we would have chosen to return a Result<()> instead, it would be all too easy to ignore the result.

Errors and Objective-C Interfaces

In Objective-C, there is no mechanism that's similar to **throws** and **try**. Instead, the common pattern in Cocoa is that a method returns NO or **nil** when an error occurs. Additionally, a pointer to an error object is passed as an argument. The method can use this variable to pass information about the error to the caller. For example, the contentsOfFile would look like this in Objective-C:

```
- (NSString *)contentsOfFile(NSString *)fileName error:(NSError **)error;
```

Swift automatically translates methods that follow this pattern to the **throws** syntax. The error parameter gets removed since it is no longer needed, and

BOOL return types are changed to Void. This is a great help when dealing with existing frameworks in Objective-C. The method above gets imported like this:

```
func contentsOfFile(fileName: String) throws
```

Errors and Function Parameters

In the following example, we will write a function that checks a list of files for validity. The checkFile function can return three possible values. If it returns **true**, the file is valid. If it returns **false**, the file is invalid. If it throws an error, something went wrong when checking the file:

```
func checkFile(contents: String) throws -> Bool
```

As a first step, we can write a simple function that loops over a list of filenames and makes sure that checkFile returns **true** for every file. If checkFile returns **false**, we want to make sure to exit early, avoiding any unnecessary work. Since we don't catch any errors that checkFile throws, the first error would propagate to the caller and likewise exit early:

```
func checkAllFiles(filenames: [String]) throws -> Bool {
    for  filename in filenames {
        guard try checkFile(filename) else { return false }
    }
    return true
}
```

Checking whether all the elements in an array conform to a certain condition is something that might happen more often in our app. For example, consider the function checkPrimes, which checks whether all numbers in a given list are prime numbers. It works in exactly the same way as checkAllFiles. It loops over the array and checks all elements for a condition (isPrime), exiting early when one of the numbers is not prime:

```
func checkPrimes(numbers: [Int]) -> Bool {
    for  number in numbers {
        guard isPrime(number) else { return false }
    }
    return true
}
```

Both functions mix the process of iterating over a sequence (the **for** loops) with the actual logic that decides if an element meets the condition. This is a good opportunity to create an abstraction for this pattern, similar to map or filter . To do that, we can add a function named all to CollectionType. Like filter , all takes a function that performs the condition check as an argument. The difference to filter is the return type. all returns **true** if all elements in the sequence satisfy the condition, whereas filter returns the elements themselves:

```
extension SequenceType {
    func all(@noescape check: Generator.Element -> Bool) -> Bool {
        for el in self {
            guard check(el) else { return false }
        }
        return true
    }
}
```

This allows us to rewrite checkPrimes in a single line, which makes it easier to read once you know what all does. It helps us focus on the essential parts:

```
func checkPrimes(numbers: [Int]) -> Bool {
    return numbers.all(isPrime)
}
```

However, we cannot rewrite checkAllFiles to use all, because checkFile is marked as **throws**. We could easily rewrite all to accept a **throws** function, but then we would have to change checkPrimes too, either by marking checkPrimes as **throws**, using **try**!, or by wrapping the call to all in a **do/catch** block. Alternatively, we could define two versions of all: one that **throws** and one that doesn't. Except for the **try** call, their implementations would be identical.

Fortunately, there is a better way. By marking all as **rethrows**, we can write both variants in one go. **rethrows** tells the compiler that this function will only throw an error when its function parameter throws an error. This allows the compiler to waive the requirement that call must be called with **try** when the caller passes in a non-throwing check function:

```
extension SequenceType {
    func all(@noescape check: Generator.Element throws -> Bool) rethrows
        -> Bool
    {
```

```
        for el in self {
            guard try check(el) else { return false }
        }
        return true
    }
}
```

The implementation of checkAllFiles is now very similar to checkPrimes, but because the call to all can now throw an error, we need to insert an additional **try**:

```
func checkAllFiles(filenames: [String]) throws -> Bool {
    return try filenames.all(checkFile)
}
```

Almost all sequence and collection functions in the standard library that take a function argument are marked as **rethrows**. For example, the map function is marked as **rethrows**, only throwing when the transformation function is marked as **throws** as well.

Cleaning Up Using defer

Let's go back to the contentsOfFile function from the beginning of this chapter for a minute and have a look at the implementation. In many languages, it is common to have a **try**/finally construct, where the block marked with finally is always executed when the function returns, regardless of whether or not an error was thrown. The **defer** keyword in Swift has a similar purpose but works a bit differently. Like finally, a **defer** block is always executed when a scope is exited, regardless of the reason of exiting — whether it's because a value is successfully returned, because an error happened, or any other reason. Unlike finally, a **defer** block does not require a leading **try** or **do** block, and it is more flexible in terms of where you place it in your code:

```
let file = open("test.txt", O_RDONLY)
defer { close(file) }
let string = try processFile(file)
```

While **defer** is often used together with error handling, it can be useful in other contexts too, for example when you want to keep the code for initialization and cleanup of a resource close together. Putting related parts of the code close to each other can make your code significantly more readable, especially in longer functions.

If there are multiple **defer** blocks in the same scope, they are executed in reverse order: you can think of them as a stack. At first, it might feel strange that the **defer** blocks run in reverse order. However, if we look at an example, it should quickly make sense:

```
guard let database = openDatabase(...) else { return }
defer { closeDatabase(database) }
guard let connection = openConnection(database) else { return }
defer { closeConnection(connection) }
guard let result  = runQuery(connection, ...) else { return }
```

If an error happens, for example during the runQuery call, we want to close the connection first and the database second. Because the **defer** is executed in reverse order, this happens automatically. The runQuery depends on openConnection, which in turn depends on openDatabase. Therefore, cleaning these resources up needs to happen in reverse order.

There are some cases in which **defer** blocks do not get executed: when your program segfaults or raises a fatal error (e.g. using fatalError or by force unwrapping a **nil**), all execution halts immediately.

Errors and Optionals

Errors and optionals are both very common ways for functions to signal that something went wrong. Earlier in this chapter, we gave you some advice on how to decide which pattern you should use for your own functions. You will end up working a lot with both, and passing results to other APIs will often make it necessary to convert back and forth between functions marked as **throws** and optional values. For example, the **try**? keyword allows us to ignore the error of a **throws** function and convert the return value into an optional that tells us if the function succeeded or not:

```
if  let contents = try? parseFile(filename) {
    print(contents)
}
```

If we use the **try**? keyword, we have strictly less information than before: we only know if the function returned a successful value or if it returned some error — any specific information about that error gets thrown away. If we go the other way, from an optional to a function that throws, we have to provide the error value that gets used in case the optional is nil:

```
func optional<A>(value: A?, orError e: ErrorType) throws -> A {
    guard let x = value else { throw e }
    return x
}
```

This can be useful in conjunction with multiple **try** statements or when you are working inside a function that's already marked as **throws:**

```
let int = try optional(Int("42"), orError: ReadIntError.CouldNotRead)
print(int)
```

The existence of the **try**? keyword may appear contradictory to Swift's philosophy that ignoring errors should not be allowed. However, we still have to explicitly write **try**?. In cases where you are not interested in the error message, this can be very helpful.

It's also possible to write equivalent functions for converting between Result and **throws**, or between **throws** and Result, or between optionals and Result.

Chaining Errors

Chaining multiple calls to functions that can throw errors becomes trivial with Swift's built-in error handling — there is no need for nested **if** statements or similar constructs. We simply place these calls into a single **do/catch** block (or a common wrapper function that is also marked as **throws**). The first error that occurs breaks the chain and switches control to the **catch** block (or propagates the error to the caller):

```
func checkFilesAndFetchProcessID(filenames: [String]) -> Int {
    do {
        try filenames.all(checkFile)
        let contents = try contentsOfFile("Pidfile")
        return try optional(Int(contents),
            orError: ReadIntError.CouldNotRead)
    } catch {
        return 42 // Default value
    }
}
```

If we'd rather work with Result, it isn't hard to implement a variant of all that returns a Result. Chaining multiple calls that return a Result is essentially a sequence of flatMap operations. A variant of flatMap for Result would work like the existing overload for optionals: if the input value is the success case, unwrap it and apply the passed-in transformation function to it. If the input value is the failure case, return it unchanged and don't call the transformation function at all. It is quite elegant too:

```
func checkFilesAndFetchProcessID(filenames: [String]) -> Result<Int> {
    return filenames
        . all (checkFile)
        .flatMap { _ in contentsOfFile("Pidfile") }
        .flatMap { contents in
            Int(contents).map(Result.Success)
                ?? .Failure(ReadIntError.CouldNotRead)
        }
}
```

Higher-Order Functions and Errors

At the moment of writing, Swift errors do not play too nicely with callback functions. Let's look at a function that asynchronously computes a large number and calls back our code when the computation has finished:

```
func compute(callback: Int -> ())
```

We can call it by providing a callback function. The callback receives the result as the only parameter:

```
compute { result in
    print(result)
}
```

If the computation can fail, we could specify that the callback receives an optional integer — which would be nil — in case of a failure:

```
func compute(callback: Int? -> ())
```

Now, in our callback, we must check whether the optional is non-nil, e.g. by using the ?? operator:

```
compute { result in
    print(result ?? -1)
}
```

But what if we want to report specific errors to the callback rather than just an optional? We might first try the type signature below. Perhaps surprisingly, this type has a totally different meaning. Instead of saying that the computation might fail, it expresses that the callback itself could throw an error:

```
func compute(callback: Int throws -> ())
```

This highlights the key difference that we mentioned earlier: optionals and Result work on types, whereas **throws** works only on function types. Annotating a function with **throws** means that the *function* might fail. It becomes a bit clearer when we try to rewrite the above (wrong) attempt using Result:

```
func compute(callback: Int -> Result<()>)
```

We really wanted to have the Result wrapper around the Int parameter, as opposed to having the callback's return type:

```
func compute(callback: Result<Int> -> ())
```

Unfortunately, there is currently no clear way to write the variant above with **throws**. The best we can do is wrap the Int inside another throwing function. This makes the type more complicated:

```
func compute(f: (() throws -> Int) -> ())
```

And using this variant becomes more complicated for the caller too. In order to get the integer out, the callback now has to call the throwing function. However, instead of returning an integer, the function could also throw an error:

```
compute { (theResult: () throws -> Int) in
    do {
        let result = try theResult()
        print(result)
    } catch {
        print("An error happened: \(error)")
    }
}
```

So Result might be the better choice for asynchronous error handling. However, if you have been using **throws** for synchronous functions, switching to Result for asynchronous functions introduces a discrepancy between the two kinds of interfaces and probably makes your API harder to use. When you have a lot of asynchronous functions, the tradeoff of using Result might be worth it, but if you only have a single callback, the nested function technique shown above may be the better choice.

Conclusion

When Apple introduced error handling in Swift 2.0, a lot of eyebrows were raised. In the Swift 1.x days, people had been rolling their own Result types, mostly with a typed error case. The fact that **throws** uses untyped errors is a mixed blessing. There is the advantage that the type signature stays a lot simpler. For example, if more than one type of error could happen, a type signature might quickly look like this:

```
func checkFilesAndFetchProcessID(filenames: [String])
    throws ReadFileError, CheckFileError, MiscellaneousError -> Int
```

However, the downside in Swift is also big: there is no way to signal that only one type of error could occur, leading to extra boilerplate. Furthermore, the fact that **throws** only works on functions and not on other types also makes things unnecessarily complex (as we have seen with the asynchronous callback example). This is another case where Swift is very pragmatic and optimizes for the 80 percent case. The downside is that when you deviate from the simple behavior, things quickly become awkward: wrapping results in an extra function just to be able to use the built-in error handling makes things unnecessarily complex. And mind you, we're not talking about an obscure edge case here — asynchronous failable APIs are commonplace.

If you want to be able to specify error types, you can use Result, with a generic parameter for the error type. However, this introduces another construct to your code base. Depending on what you are building, the added complexity might be worth it.

In the meantime, we now have many possible choices for handling the unexpected in our code. When we cannot possibly continue, we can use fatalError or an assertion. When we are not interested in the kind of error, or if there's only one kind of error, we can use optionals. When we need more than one kind of error, or want to provide additional information, we can use Swift's built-in errors or write our own Result type. When we want to write functions that take a function as a parameter, we can use **rethrows** to allow for both throwing and non-throwing function parameters. Finally, the **defer** statement is very useful when using the built-in errors. By using **defer** statements, we can clean up everything once the scope exits, regardless of whether or not it's a normal scope exit, because of a **throws**, or because of an early **return**.

Generics

Like most modern languages, Swift has a number of features that can all be grouped under *generic programming*. For example, we can write generic data types. We have seen types such as Array and Set, which are generic over their elements. We can also write generic functions, which are generic over their input or output types. The definition **func** identity<A>(input: A) -> A defines a function that works on any type A. We can also write functions with the same name but different types. In a way, we can even think of protocols with an associated type as "generic protocols." The associated type allows us to abstract over specific implementations. The GeneratorType is an example of such a protocol: it is generic over the Element type it generates. In this chapter, we will look at how to write generic code.

The goal of generic programming is to express algorithms with minimal assumptions. For example, consider the findElement function from the collections chapter. We could have written it as an extension on Array, which is a big assumption. Instead, we extended SequenceType, which is a small assumption. SequenceType only assumes iteration, but it doesn't make any further assumptions.

In this chapter, we will use generic programming to write an algorithm for subtracting two sequences. We will provide multiple implementations of the algorithm, each relying on a different set of assumptions. Finally, we will look at how we can use generic data types to factor out common code. We will refactor networking code, which is usually complex and asynchronous. After refactoring, we will end up with a single asynchronous part and many simple parts that rely on generics. If you're interested in the theoretical details behind generic programming, there is a paper you can read, entitled "An Extended Comparative Study of Language Support for Generic Programming."

Library Code

Suppose you find yourself in need of identifying all the entries in one array that aren't in another. Say you're given an updated set of data, and you want to highlight the new or changed rows. The Set type gives you a really easy way to do this:

```
let old = [1, 2, 3]
let new = [1, 2, 4, 5]

Set(new).subtract(old)
```

[5, 4]

This might be all you need. However, there are some shortcomings. The first is that Set will collapse multiple entries into one. So if your use case allows duplicates in old, this is no good. And since Set is an unordered collection, those entries won't be in the same order as they appeared in old. If you're using this code to update a table view, you'll need to solve both problems.

Keeping the entries in order is easily solved with a bit more code, using filter on new:

```
let oldSet = Set(old)
new.filter { !oldSet.contains($0) }
```

[4, 5]

The second problem is harder to work around. To be used in a set, a type has to conform to the Hashable protocol. If you wanted to wrap the above code into a generic function, you would have to write it something like this:

```
extension CollectionType where Generator.Element: Hashable {
    /// Return a new array with elements in `self` that do not
    // occur in `toRemove`.
    func subtract(toRemove: [Generator.Element]) -> [Generator.Element] {
        let removeSet = Set(toRemove)
        return self.filter {
            !removeSet.contains($0)
        }
    }
}
```

You'd then pass the two arrays into this function to do the same subtraction operation:

```
new.subtract(old)
```

[4, 5]

subtract is defined as an extension on the SequenceType protocol, where the elements of the sequence areHashable. It takes an array of the same type to remove, and it returns a new array with the elements removed. subtract doesn't care about what the elements are, just so long as they conform to Hashable, because only hashable types can be used with Set. The element type can be an Int, a String, or your own custom user-defined class, just so long as it's hashable.

But what if your type isn't hashable? Not all types are — especially not user-defined types. How about we lower the bar and instead just require conformance to Equatable? In doing so, we can't use Set, but we could use the standard function, contains:

```
extension SequenceType where Generator.Element: Equatable {
    func subtract(toRemove: [Generator.Element]) -> [Generator.Element] {
        return self. filter  {
            !toRemove.contains($0)
        }
    }
}
```

Now, you can call subtract on any type, so long as it conforms to Equatable. For example, the Range type conforms, but it isn't Hashable:

```
let ranges1 = [0..<1, 1..<4]
let ranges2 = [0..<1, 1..<4, 5..<10]

ranges2.subtract(ranges1)

[Range(5..<10)]
```

This is great in that it's more general, so it works with a wider range of types. However, it comes with a big downside: this generality has cost us in performance. The algorithm has performance characteristics of $O(n^2)$ — that is, as the input sizes grow, the worst-case time it takes to run grows quadratically. This is because contains runs in linear time on arrays — $O(n)$. This makes sense if you think about what it needs to do: loop over the contents of the source sequence, checking if they match a given element. But our subtract algorithm calls contains inside another loop — the one inside filter — which *also* runs in linear time in a similar fashion. And running an $O(n)$ loop inside an $O(n)$ loop results in an $O(n^2)$ function.

This is fine for small inputs, and perhaps you're only ever going to call this with arrays with entries in the hundreds. But call it with arrays with thousands or millions of elements and you'll be sorry. The Set-based version doesn't have this problem because hash-based lookups can be done in constant time; the filter in that version runs in $O(n)$.

But the good news is: you do *not* have to pick one of these options. You can implement *both* versions of subtract using a technique called overloading. You may be familiar with overloading to allow functions to be written to take two different kinds of arguments, such as the overload on String.**init** that takes either another String or an Int. Swift is very flexible about overloading — you can overload not just by input type, but by return type too. And you can overload based on different constraints on a generic placeholder, as seen above.

Swift has a complex set of rules for which overloaded function to pick, based on whether or not a function is generic and what kind of type is being passed in. While they're too long to go into here, they can be summarized as "pick the most specific one." For example, non-generic functions are picked over generic ones.

Here, there are two versions of subtract, and both are generic. But the version that requires the elements to be Hashable is more specific, because Hashable extends Equatable, and thus it imposes more constraints. Given that these constraints are probably there to make the algorithm more efficient — as they are in the case of subtract — the more specific function is probably the better choice.

There's another way in which subtract can be made more general. Up until now, it has only taken an array of elements to subtract. But Array is a specific type. Really, subtract doesn't need to be this specific. Across the two versions, there are only three function calls: filter in both, Set.**init** in the hashable version, and contains in the equatable version. In all three cases, these functions only require an input type that conforms to the protocol SequenceType:

```
extension SequenceType {
    /// Return an `Array` containing the elements of `self`, in order,
    /// that satisfy the predicate `includeElement`.
    func filter (includeElement: (Self.Generator.Element) throws -> Bool)
        rethrows -> [Self.Generator.Element]
}

extension SequenceType where Generator.Element: Equatable {
    /// Return `true` iff `x` is in `self`.
    func contains(element: Self.Generator.Element) -> Bool
}

// And inside `Set`:
```

```
struct Set<Element: Hashable>:
    Hashable, Equatable, CollectionType, Indexable, SequenceType,
    ArrayLiteralConvertible
{
    // ...
    /// Create a `Set` from a finite  sequence of items.
    init<S : SequenceType where S.Generator.Element == Element>
        (_ sequence: S)
}
```

Given this, the only thing subtract needs is for toRemove to be of some type
that also conforms to SequenceType. What's more is that those two sequence
types *don't have to be the same.* They just need to be sequences of the same
element. So here's the hashable version, rewritten to operate on any two kinds
of sequence:

```
extension SequenceType where Generator.Element: Hashable {
    func subtract
        // Define a placeholder for the toRemove sequence type, requiring
        // it 's the same type as the Self sequence
        <S: SequenceType where S.Generator.Element == Generator.Element>
        (toRemove: S) -> [Generator.Element]
    {
        let removeSet = Set(toRemove)
        return self. filter  { !removeSet.contains($0) }
    }
}
```

Now that the two sequences don't have to be the same type, this opens up a lot
more possibilities. For example, you could pass in a Range of numbers to
remove:

```
[2, 4, 8].subtract(0..<3)
```

```
[4, 8]
```

A similar change can be made to the version that requires the elements to be
equatable.

Parameterizing Behavior with Closures

But this still leaves us with a question. What about sequences of things that
aren't even equatable?

Arrays, for example, are not equatable. They do have an == operator, defined like this:

```
/// Returns true if  these arrays contain the same elements.
func ==<T : Equatable>(lhs: [T], rhs: [T]) -> Bool
```

But that doesn't mean you can use them with subtract:

```
// error:  cannot invoke 'subtract' with an argument list of type  '([ Int ])
[[1,  2],  [3],  [4]]. subtract([3])
```

This is because Array does not conform to Equatable. It can't, because the type the array contains might not, itself, be equatable. So it can provide an implementation of == for when the contained type *is* equatable, but it can't conform to the protocol.

So how to make subtract work with non-equatable types? We can do this by giving control of what equality means to the caller, requiring them to supply a function to determine equality. For example, there is a second version of contains that does this:

```
extension SequenceType where Generator.Element : Equatable {
    /// Return `true` iff  an element in `self` satisfies `predicate`.
    func contains
        (@noescape predicate: (Self.Generator.Element) throws -> Bool)
        rethrows -> Bool
}
```

That is, it takes a function that takes an element of the sequence and performs some check. It runs the check on each element, returning **true** as soon as the check returns **true**.

This version of contains is much more powerful. For example, you can use it to check for any condition inside a sequence:

```
let  isEven = { $0 % 2 == 0 }
print ((0..<5). contains(isEven))
print ([1,3,99]. contains(isEven))
```

true
false

We can leverage this more flexible version of contains to write a similarly flexible version of subtract:

```
extension SequenceType {
    func subtract<S: SequenceType>
        (toRemove: S,
            predicate: (Generator.Element, S.Generator.Element) -> Bool)
        -> [Generator.Element]
    {
        return self. filter  { sourceElement in
            !toRemove.contains { removeElement in
                predicate(sourceElement, removeElement)
            }
        }
    }
}
```

Now, we can subtract one sequence of arrays from another by supplying a
closure expression that compares the arrays using ==:

```
[[1,  2],  [3],  [4]]. subtract([[1,  2],  [3]])  { $0 == $1 } as [[ Int ]]
```

```
[[4]]
```

The two sequences' elements don't even have to be of the same type, so long as
the supplied closure handles the comparison:

```
let ints  = [1,  2,  3]
let strings = ["1",  "2"]
```

```
ints.subtract(strings) { $0 == Int($1) }
```

```
[3]
```

Operating Generically on Collections

Suppose you find yourself in need of an algorithm that operates on collections.
You reach for your nearest favorite reference[1], which happens to be written in
Java, and port the code to Swift.

For example, here is a binary search — albeit a boringly iterative, rather than
recursive, one:

---

1 http://algs4.cs.princeton.edu/home/

```
extension Array {
    /// Returns the first index where `value` appears in `self`, or `nil`,
    /// if `value` is not found.
    ///
    /// - Requires: `isOrderedBefore` is a strict weak ordering over the
    /// elements in `self`, and the elements in the array are already
    /// ordered by it.
    /// - Complexity: O(log `count`)
    func binarySearch
        (value: Element, isOrderedBefore: (Element, Element) -> Bool)
        -> Int?
    {
        var left  = 0
        var right  = count - 1

        while left <= right {
            let mid = (left + right) / 2
            let candidate = self[mid]

            if isOrderedBefore(candidate,value) {
                left = mid + 1
            } else if isOrderedBefore(value,candidate) {
                right = mid - 1
            } else {
                // If neither element comes before the other, they _must_ be
                // equal, per the strict ordering requirement of isOrderedBefore
                return mid
            }
        }
        // Not found
        return nil
    }
}

extension Array where Element: Comparable {
    func binarySearch(value: Element) -> Int? {
        return self.binarySearch(value, isOrderedBefore: <)
    }
}
```

For such a famous and seemingly simple algorithm, a binary search
is notoriously hard to get right[a]. This one contains a bug that also

existed in the Java implementation for two decades — one we'll fix in the generic version. But we also don't guarantee that it's the only bug!

a http://googleresearch.blogspot.com/2006/06/extra-extra-read-all-about-it-nearly.html

It's worth noting some of the conventions from the Swift standard library that this follows:

→ Similar to indexOf, it returns an optional index, with **nil** representing "not found."

→ It is defined twice — once with a user-supplied parameter to perform the comparison, and once relying on conformance to supply that parameter as a convenience to callers.

→ The ordering must be a strict weak ordering. This means that when comparing two elements, if neither is ordered before the other, they *must* be equal.

This works for arrays, but if you wanted to binary search a ContiguousArray or an ArraySlice, you are out of luck. It should really be an extension to CollectionType **where** Index: RandomAccessIndexType — the **where** clause being necessary to preserve the logarithmic complexity, as you need to be able to locate the midpoint in constant time and also check the ordering of the indices using <=.

A shortcut might be to require the collection to have an Int index. This will cover almost every random-access collection in the standard library, and it means you can cut and paste the entire Array version as is:

```
extension CollectionType where Index == Int {
    public func binarySearch(value: Generator.Element,
        isOrderedBefore: (Generator.Element, Generator.Element) -> Bool)
        -> Index?
    {
        // identical implementation to that of Array...
    }
}
```

Warning: if you do this, you will introduce an *even worse* bug, which we will come to shortly.

But this is still restricted to integer-indexed collections, and collections don't always have an integer index. Dictionary, Set, and the various String collection views have custom index types. The most notable random-access example in the standard library is ReverseRandomAccessCollection, which, as we saw in the collections chapter, has an opaque index type that wraps the original index, converting it to the equivalent position in the reversed collection.

If you lift the requirement for an Int index, you'll hit several compiler errors. The code needs some rewrites in order to be fully generic. So here is a fully generic version:

```
extension CollectionType where Index: RandomAccessIndexType {
    public func binarySearch(value: Generator.Element,
        isOrderedBefore: (Generator.Element, Generator.Element) -> Bool)
        -> Index?
    {
        guard !isEmpty else { return nil }
        var left  = startIndex
        var right  = endIndex - 1

        while left <= right {
            let mid = left.advancedBy(left.distanceTo(right)/2)
            let candidate = self[mid]

            if isOrderedBefore(candidate, value) {
                left = mid + 1
            } else if isOrderedBefore(value, candidate) {
                right = mid - 1
            } else {
                // If neither element comes before the other, they _must_ be
                // equal, per the strict ordering requirement of isOrderedBefore
                return mid
            }
        }
        // Not found
        return nil
    }
}

extension CollectionType
    where Index: RandomAccessIndexType, Generator.Element: Comparable
{
    func binarySearch(value: Generator.Element) -> Index? {
        return binarySearch(value, isOrderedBefore: <)
    }
}
```

The changes are small but significant. First, the **left** and **right** variables have changed type to no longer be integers. Instead, we are using the start and end index values. These might be integers, but they might also be opaque types like String's index type (or Dictionary's or Set's, not that these are random access).

But secondly, the simple statement (**left** + **right**) / 2 has been replaced by the slightly uglier **left**.advancedBy(**left**.distanceTo(**right**)/2). How come?

The key concept here is that there are actually two types involved in this calculation: Index and Index.Distance. These are *not necessarily the same thing*. When using integer indices, we happen to be able to use them interchangeably. But loosening that requirement breaks this.

The distance is the number of times you would need to call successor to get from one point in the collection to another. The end index must be "reachable" from the start index — there are always a finite integer number of times you need to call successor to get to it. This means it must be an integer (though not necessarily an Int). So this is a constraint in the definition of ForwardIndexType:

```
public protocol ForwardIndexType : _Incrementable {
    associatedtype Distance : _SignedIntegerType = Int
}
```

_SignedIntegerType requires the type to conform to IntegerLiteralConvertible, which is why we can write endIndex - 1 (it could also be written as endIndex.predecessor()). This is also why we need an extra **guard** to ensure the collection isn't empty. When you're just doing integer arithmetic, there's no harm in generating a **right** value of -1 and then checking that it's less than zero. But when dealing with any kind of index, you need to make sure you don't move back through the start of the collection, which might be an invalid operation. (For example, what would happen if you tried to go back one from the start of a doubly linked list?)

_SignedIntegerType also conforms to IntegerArithmeticType, so you can add distances together or find the remainder of dividing one by another. _SignedIntegerType also belongs to SignedNumberType, so you can find absolute distances between indices.

What we *cannot* do is add two indices of any kind together, because what would that mean? If you had the linked list from the collections chapter, you obviously couldn't "add" the pointers to two nodes together. Instead, we must think only in terms of adding distances to indices by using advancedBy(distance:).

This way of thinking takes some getting used to if you're used to thinking in terms of arrays. But think of many array index expressions as a kind of shorthand. For example, when we wrote **let right** = count - 1, really what we meant was **right** = startIndex.advancedBy(count - 1). It's just that when the index is an Int and startIndex is zero, this reduces to 0 + count - 1, which in turn reduces to count - 1.

This leads us to the serious bug in the implementation that took our Array code and just applied it to CollectionType: collections with integer indices don't necessarily start with an index of zero, the most common example being ArraySlice. A slice created via myArray[3..<5] will have a startIndex of three. Try and use our simplistic generic binary search on it, and it will crash *at runtime*. While we were able to require that the index be an integer, the Swift type system has no good way of requiring that the collection be zero-based. And even if it did, in this case, it'd be a silly requirement to impose, since we know a better way. Instead of adding together the left and right indices and halving the result, we find half the distance between the two, and then we advance the left index by that amount to reach the midpoint.

> This version also fixes the bug in our initial implementation. If you didn't spot it, it's that if the array is extremely large, then adding two integer indices together might overflow before being halved (suppose count was approaching Int.max and the searched-for element was the last one in the array). Adding half the distance between the two indices, on the other hand, doesn't happen. Of course, the chances of anyone ever hitting this bug is very low, which is why the bug in the Java standard library took so long to be discovered.

Now, we can use our binary search algorithm to search ReverseRandomAccessCollection:

```
let a = ["a", "b", "c", "d", "e", "f", "g"]
let r = a.reverse()

assert(r.binarySearch("g", isOrderedBefore: >) == r.startIndex)
```

And we can also search slices, which are not zero-based:

```
let s = a[2..<5]
assert(s.startIndex != 0)
assert(s.binarySearch("c") == s.startIndex)
```

To help cement this concept, here is another example, this time an implementation of the Fisher-Yates[2] shuffling algorithm:

```
extension Array {
    mutating func shuffleInPlace() {
        for i in 0..<(count - 1) {
            let j = Int(arc4random_uniform(UInt32(count - i))) + i

            // Guard against the (slightly pedantic) requirement of swap that you
            // not try to swap an element with itself.
            guard i != j else { continue }

            swap(&self[i], &self[j])
        }
    }

    func shuffle() -> [Element] {
        var clone = self
        clone.shuffleInPlace()
        return clone
    }
}
```

Again, we've followed a standard library practice: providing an in-place version, since this can be done more efficiently, and then a non-mutating version that generates a shuffled copy of the array, which can be implemented in terms of the in-place version.

So how can we write a generic version of this that doesn't mandate integer indices? Just like with binary search, we still need random access, but we also have a new requirement that the collection be mutable, since we want to be able to provide an in-place version. The use of count - 1 will definitely need to change in a way similar to the binary search.

Before we get to the generic implementation, there's an extra complication. We want to use arc4random_uniform to generate random numbers, but we

2 https://en.wikipedia.org/wiki/Fisher–Yates_shuffle

don't know exactly what type of integer Index.Distance will be. We know it's an integer, but not necessarily that it's an Int.

To handle this, we need to use numericCast, which is a function for converting generically between different integer types. Using this, we can write a version of arc4random_uniform that works on any signed integer type (we could write a version for unsigned integer types too, but since index distances are always signed, we don't need to):

```
extension _SignedIntegerType {
    static func arc4random_uniform(upper_bound: Self) -> Self {
        precondition(
            upper_bound > 0 &&
                upper_bound.toIntMax() < UInt32.max.toIntMax(),
            "arc4random_uniform only callable up to \(UInt32.max)")
        return numericCast(
            Darwin.arc4random_uniform(numericCast(upper_bound)))
    }
}
```

> You could write a version of arc4random that operates on ranges spanning negative numbers, or above the max of UInt32, if you wanted to. But to do so would take quite a lot more code. If you're interested, the definition of arc4random_uniform is actually open source and quite well commented, and it gives several clues as to how you might do this.

Now that we have this, we can write generic code that generates random numbers within any range of indices:

```
extension Range {
    var arc4random: Element {
        return startIndex.advancedBy(
            Index.Distance.arc4random_uniform(count)
        )
    }
}
```

And finally, we use this in our generic shuffle implementation:

```
extension MutableCollectionType where Index: RandomAccessIndexType {
    mutating func shuffleInPlace() {
```

```
        for i in indices.dropLast() {
            let j = (i ..< endIndex).arc4random
            guard i != j else { continue }
            swap(&self[i], &self[j])
        }
    }
}

extension SequenceType {
    func shuffle() -> [Generator.Element] {
        var clone = Array(self)
        clone.shuffleInPlace()
        return clone
    }
}
```

You'll see that to replace the use of count - 1, instead of using the range
operator to define the values to loop over with i, we used the .indices operator,
which gives us the full range, and then we just dropped the last one, using
dropLast.

Then, we use our new range-based arc4random to get the random index to
swap with, and the rest remains the same.

You might wonder why we didn't extend MutableCollectionType when
implementing the non-modifying shuffle. Again, this is a pattern you see often
in the standard library — for example, when you sort a ContiguousArray, you
get back an Array, and not a ContiguousArray.

In this case, the reason is that our immutable version relies on the ability to
clone the collection and then shuffle it in place. This, in turn, relies on the
collection having value semantics. But not all collections are guaranteed to
have value semantics. If NSMutableArray conformed to MutableCollectionType
(which it doesn't — probably because it's bad form for Swift collections to not
have value semantics — but could), then shuffle and shuffleInPlace would
have the same effect, since NSMutableArray has reference semantics.
var clone = self just makes a copy of the reference, so a subsequent
clone.shuffleInPlace would shuffle self — probably not what the user would
expect. Instead, we take a full copy of the elements into an array and shuffle
and return that.

There is a compromise approach. You could write a version of shuffle to return the same type of collection as the one being shuffled, so long as that type also supported RangeReplaceableCollectionType:

```
extension MutableCollectionType
    where Self: RangeReplaceableCollectionType,
        Index: RandomAccessIndexType
{
    func shuffle() -> Self {
        var clone = Self()
        clone.appendContentsOf(self)
        clone.shuffleInPlace()
        return clone
    }
}
```

This relies on the two abilities of RangeReplaceableCollectionType: to create a fresh empty version of the collection, and to then append any sequence (in this case, **self**) to that empty collection, thus guaranteeing a full clone takes place. The standard library doesn't take this approach — probably because the consistency of always creating an array for any kind of non-in-place operation is preferred — but it's an option if you want it. However, remember to create the sequence version as well, so that you offer shuffling for non-mutable range-replaceable collections and sequences.

SubSequence and Generic Algorithms

Here's one final example to demonstrate a problem you will encounter if you try and use slicing generically.

Say you want to write an algorithm that searches for a given subsequence — so similar to indexOf, but searching for a subsequence rather than an individual element. In theory, a naive solution to this is simple: iterate over every index in the collection, checking to see if the slice from that index starts with the pattern. However, if you try it, you will find you get a compiler error:

```
extension CollectionType
    where Generator.Element: Equatable,
        SubSequence.Generator.Element == Generator.Element
{
    func search
        <Other: SequenceType
            where Other.Generator.Element == Generator.Element>
```

```
        (pattern: Other) -> Index?
    {
        for idx in self.indices {
            // error: cannot convert value of type 'Other'
            // to expected argument type
            if suffixFrom(idx).startsWith(pattern) {
                return idx
            }
        }
        return nil
    }
}
```

This seems odd. We've constrained the elements of Other to be the same as our own elements (via Other.Generator.Element == Generator.Element). Unfortunately, though, there is one thing that isn't guaranteed, which is that SubSequence.Generator.Element — that is, the type of an element in a slice — is equal to the type of an element in the collection. Of course; it should be! But as of Swift 2.0, the language is not powerful enough to write this constraint. To do so would require a declaration of the SubSequence associated type that looks something like this:

```
protocol CollectionType {
    associatedtype SubSequence: Indexable, SequenceType
        // this won't compile! since you can't
        // put where clauses on associatedtypes...
        where SubSequence.Generator.Element == Generator.Element
}
```

Instead, to fix this, you must constrain your protocol extension to ensure that any slices you use contain the same element as the collection. A first attempt might be to require the subsequence be the same as the collection:

```
extension CollectionType
where Generator.Element: Equatable, SubSequence == Self {
    // implementation of search same as before
}
```

This would work when a subsequence has the same type as its collection, such as is the case with strings:

```
// this now compiles, and returns true:
"hello".characters.search("ell".characters)
```

But as we saw in the collections chapter, the slice type for arrays is ArraySlice, so you could not search arrays. Therefore, we need to constrain a little less and instead require that the subsequences' elements match:

```
extension CollectionType
    where Generator.Element: Equatable,
        SubSequence.Generator.Element == Generator.Element
{
    // implementation of search same as before
}
```

Overrides and Optimizations

Finally, it's often the case that you can provide a more efficient generic algorithm if you tighten the constraints slightly. For example, you could improve the speed of the search algorithm above if you knew that both the searched collection and the pattern had random-access indices. That way, you could avoid searching for the pattern in the part of the collection that was too short to match it, and when the pattern was longer than the collection, you could avoid searching completely.

For this to work, you need to guarantee that both **Self**.Index and Other.Index conform to RandomAccessIndexType. We then find ourselves with an algorithm that is about as much constraint as it is code:

```
extension CollectionType
    where Generator.Element: Equatable, Index: RandomAccessIndexType,
        SubSequence.Generator.Element == Generator.Element
{
    func search
        <Other: CollectionType where
            Other.Index: RandomAccessIndexType,
            Other.Index.Distance == Index.Distance,
            Other.Generator.Element == Generator.Element>
        (pat: Other) -> Index?
    {
        // if pattern is longer, this cannot match, exit early
        guard !isEmpty && pat.count <= count else { return nil }

        // otherwise, from the start up to the end
        // less space for the pattern
        for i in startIndex...endIndex.advancedBy(-pat.count) {
            // check if a slice from this point
```

```
            // starts with the pattern
            if self.suffixFrom(i).startsWith(pat) {
                // if it does, we've found it
                return i
            }
        }
        // otherwise, not found
        return nil
    }
}
```

We've added one other constraint here: the distance types of the two collections are the same. This keeps the code simple, though it does rule out the possibility that they might differ. This is pretty rare though — even Bit, the index for CollectionOfOne, uses Int for its Distance. The alternative would be a light sprinkling of numericCasts — for example,
guard numericCast(pat.count) <= count **else** { **return nil** }.

Since Range is also a collection, you could also rewrite the inner **for** loop as a call to indexOf, with the closure defining the comparison operation as matching the pattern. Because indexOf returns an optional already, with **nil** for not found, you can just return the result of calling indexOf directly. This can make the intent of the code clearer:

```
    return (startIndex...endIndex.advancedBy(-pat.count))
            .indexOf { self.suffixFrom($0).startsWith(pat) }
```

One thing to be conscious of is that the compiler does *not* force you into specifying that the indices be random access. If you comment out the two random-access index constraints, the code will still run and compile. However, you would have overloaded search with a potentially *less* efficient algorithm when the indices *weren't* random access, because even ForwardIndexType supports an .advancedBy member function. Whether or not the overload is faster would vary, depending on the relative lengths of both the searched collection and the pattern. This is because calculating their lengths and advancing them would happen in linear rather than constant time, by repeatedly calling successor the given number of times. In this case, since we only call that function once, it might still be an optimization, but not necessarily.

But imagine calling advancedBy multiple times in a loop. For example, suppose with the binary search we defined above, you left off the RandomAccessIndexType qualifier. The code would still compile, but this would give you a linear time call inside your loop, turning the algorithm accidentally quadratic — much slower than the time it takes to perform a linear search through a collection.

Designing with Generics

As we have seen, generics can be used to provide multiple implementations of the same functionality. We can write generic functions but provide specific implementations for certain types. Also, by using protocol extensions, we can write generic algorithms that operate on many types.

Generics can also be very helpful during the design of your program, in order to factor out shared functionality and reduce boilerplate. In this section, we'll refactor a normal piece of code, pulling out the common functionality by using generics. Not only can we make generic functions, but we can also make generic data types.

Let's write some functions to interact with a web service. For example, consider fetching a list of users and parsing it into the User datatype. We write a function, loadUsers, which loads the users from the network asynchronously and then calls the callback with the list of fetched users.

We implement it in a naive way. First, we create the URL. Then, we load the data synchronously (this is just for the sake of the example; in production code, you should always load your data asynchronously). Next, we parse the JSON, which will give us arrays of dictionaries. Finally, we transform the plain JSON objects into User structs. In case the URL loading fails, data will be **nil**, and the callback will be called with **nil**. In case the JSON deserialization fails, json will be **nil**. And finally, in case the user parsing fails, users will be **nil**:

```
func loadUsers(callback: [User]? -> ()) {
    let usersURL = webserviceURL.URLByAppendingPathComponent("/users")
    let data = NSData(contentsOfURL: usersURL)
    let json = data.flatMap {
        try? NSJSONSerialization.JSONObjectWithData($0,
            options: NSJSONReadingOptions())
    }
    let users = (json as? [AnyObject]).flatMap { jsonObject in
        jsonObject.flatMap(User.init)
    }
    callback(users)
}
```

Now, if we want to write the same function to load other resources, we would need to copy most of the code. For example, if we consider a function to load blog posts, it could look like this:

```
func loadBlogPosts(callback: [BlogPost] -> ())
```

And the implementation would be almost the same. Both functions are hard to test: we need to make sure the web service is accessible from the tests, or else find some way to fake the requests. Because the functions take a callback, we need to make sure we can test them asynchronously.

Instead of copy-pasting, however, we can extract the User-specific parts and reuse the other parts. For example, we could add the path component and the conversion function as parameters. Because we want to be able to pass in different types for the conversion function, we make our loadResource function generic over A:

```
func loadResource<A>(pathComponent: String,
    parse: AnyObject -> A?,
    callback: A? -> ()) {
    let resourceURL = webserviceURL
        .URLByAppendingPathComponent(pathComponent)
    let data = NSData(contentsOfURL: resourceURL)
    let json = data.flatMap {
        try? NSJSONSerialization.JSONObjectWithData($0,
            options: NSJSONReadingOptions())
    }
    callback(json.flatMap(parse))
}
```

Now, we can rewrite our loadUsers function as follows:

```
func loadUsers2(callback: [User]? -> ()) {
    loadResource("/users", parse: jsonArray(User.init), callback: callback)
}
```

We use the helper function, jsonArray, which first tries to convert an AnyObject to an array of AnyObjects, and then tries to parse each element using the supplied function:

```
func jsonArray<A>(f: AnyObject -> A?) -> AnyObject -> [A]? {
    return { arr in
        (arr as? [AnyObject]).map { $0.flatMap(f) }
    }
```

```
}
```

And to load the blog posts, we just change the path component and the parsing function:

```
func loadBlogPosts(callback: [BlogPost]? -> ()) {
    loadResource("/posts", parse: jsonArray(BlogPost.init), callback: callback)
}
```

This saves us from a lot of duplication. Now we can take the time to refactor our synchronous URL handling into asynchronous loading, and we don't need to update either loadUsers or loadBlogPosts. Even though loadBlogPosts is now very short, it is still hard to test: it is callback based, and it depends on the web service being accessible.

Before we add asynchronous loading, we take this a step further. In the loadResource function, the parameters pathComponent and parse are very tightly coupled. Instead of passing them in separately, we can bundle them up in a struct. Just like functions, structs can be generic too:

```
struct Resource<A> {
    let  pathComponent: String
    let  parse: AnyObject -> A?
}
```

Now, we can write an alternative definition of loadResource, which uses a Resource as a description of what to load:

```
extension Resource {
    func loadSynchronous(callback: A? -> ()) {
        let  resourceURL = webserviceURL
            .URLByAppendingPathComponent(self.pathComponent)
        let  data = NSData(contentsOfURL: resourceURL)
        let  json = data.flatMap {
            try? NSJSONSerialization.JSONObjectWithData($0,
                options: NSJSONReadingOptions())
        }
        callback(json.flatMap(self.parse))
    }
}
```

Instead of defining top-level functions for our resources, we can now just define values of the Resource struct. This makes it very easy to add new resources without having to create new functions:

```
let usersResource: Resource<[User]> =
    Resource(pathComponent: "/users", parse: jsonArray(User.init))
let postsResource: Resource<[BlogPost]> =
    Resource(pathComponent: "/posts", parse: jsonArray(BlogPost.init))
```

Now, adding an asynchronous variant is very simple, and we don't need to change any of our existing code describing the endpoints. This means we have completely decoupled our endpoints from the network calls. We boiled down usersResource and postResource to their absolute minimums so that they only describe where the resource is located and how to parse it:

```
extension Resource {
    func loadAsynchronous(callback: A? -> ()) {
        let session = NSURLSession.sharedSession()
        let resourceURL = webserviceURL
            .URLByAppendingPathComponent(pathComponent)

        session.dataTaskWithURL(resourceURL) { data, response, error in
            let json = data.flatMap {
                try? NSJSONSerialization.JSONObjectWithData($0,
                    options: NSJSONReadingOptions())
            }
            callback(json.flatMap(self.parse))
        }.resume()
    }
}
```

We can now also test things easily. Testing whether a Resource is configured correctly is much simpler than having to (asynchronously) test the loadUsers function. Usually, networking code is hard to test, because everything is asynchronous, and because the web service needs to be available. In our current approach, we only need to asynchronously test the loadAsynchronous method; all the other parts are simple and do not involve asynchronous code. Of course, the Resource data type can be extended to have more configuration options, such as the HTTP method, a way to add POST data, and so on.

In this section, we started with a non-generic variant of loading some data from the network. Next, we created a generic function with multiple arguments, which allowed us to write our examples in a much shorter way. Finally, we bundled up the arguments into a separate Resource data type, which makes the code even more decoupled. It allows us to write a completely different function for loading resources without changing the resources themselves.

Conclusion

In the beginning of the chapter, we defined generic programming as writing algorithms with minimal assumptions. Looking back, we expressed our subtract method with minimal assumptions about data abstractions, without losing efficiency. We added both specific and generic variants. For example, there is one version for elements that are Hashable, one version for elements that are Equatable, and a version that takes a closure. We relied on the compiler to automatically select the most specific form for our problem.

In the asynchronous networking example, we have removed many assumptions about the network stack from our Resource struct. There is no assumption about the root domain and no assumption about how to load data. Instead, we only have a declarative description of API endpoints. Here, generic programming makes our resources simpler and less coupled. This also makes testing simple.

In the next chapter, we will look at protocols, which are key building blocks when programming with generics. They help constrain our generic types and make any assumptions about the types explicit.

Protocols

10

At WWDC 2015, there was an influential session called Protocol-Oriented Programming. In this section, we will look at an example of protocol-oriented programming and see why it is useful.

Let's suppose we need to write a calendar app. The requirements are simple: we need to display all the calendar events in a list, ordered by date. When the user taps an event, we show the event's details. To list the events, we create a custom view for displaying the list. (Note that we only cover the important parts, in order to keep the explanation brief.)

A list of events always displays only a subset of the events (those that fit on screen). In our app, we want to be able to show all events in a certain date range. Therefore, we define a struct that can store a date range:

```
struct DateRange {
    var startDate: NSDate
    var endDate: NSDate
}
```

We also write a custom initializer that takes a date and creates a range. We use the date as the start date and calculate the end date:

```
extension DateRange {
    init (startDate: NSDate = NSDate(), durationInDays days: Int = 1) {
```

Also, we define a simple struct, Event. This structs holds the event's title and date. Later on, we can replace this with a more complicated struct or an object that comes from the database:

```
struct Event {
    let title : String
    let date: NSDate
}
```

We're ready to write our CalendarView. Because we're writing an iOS app, we create a UIView subclass with three properties:

→ displayRange to get and set the date range.

→ delegate for the delegate, so that we can respond to changes initiated by the user.

→ events, which stores the events in an array. In a real app, this would probably be a data source object that can load the events on demand.

```
class MyCalendarView: UIView {
    var displayRange: DateRange = DateRange()
    var delegate: CalendarViewDelegate?
    var events: [Event] = []
}
```

To add the views for the individual events, we just loop over all the events in our source array. We only include the events that are in the range we want to display. For each event, we add a view:

```
func setupViews() {
    let displayedEvents = events.filter {
        displayRange.contains($0.date)
    }
    for event in displayedEvents {
        addEventView(event)
    }
}
```

Sharing Code among Classes

Now suppose we are presented with a new requirement: we want a second kind of view. Perhaps it's a monthly view, or an agenda view just listing upcoming appointments. How can we reuse the code we've already written?

The first reaction for many programmers used to Objective-C might be to subclass. They would create an abstract class — AbstractCalendarView — with subclasses like WeekView or AgendaView. But before we look at a solution, we will first look at some general problems with subclassing.

Sharing code through subclasses is inflexible. Classes can only have one superclass, and this can become a problem. For example, what if your WeekView wants to be a subclass of AbstractCalendarView and UICollectionView? There are more examples in Cocoa — e.g. with NSMutableAttributedString, the designers had to choose between NSAttributedString and NSMutableString as a base class.

Some languages have multiple inheritance — the most famous being C++. But this leads to something called the "diamond problem." For example, if multiple inheritance were possible, we could envision an NSMutableAttributedString that inherits from both NSMutableString and NSAttributedString. But what happens if both of those classes override a method of NSString? You could deal with it by just picking one of the methods. But what if that method is isEqual:? Providing good behavior for multiple inheritance is really hard.

Because multiple inheritance is so complicated, most languages do not support it. Yet many languages do support conforming to multiple protocols. This does not have the same problems. In Swift, the compiler warns us when the use of a method is ambiguous.

Protocol extensions are a way of sharing code without sharing base classes. Protocols define a minimal viable set of methods for a type to implement. Extensions can then build on these minimal methods to implement more complex features.

For example, to implement a generic algorithm that sorts any sequence, you need two things. First, you need a way to iterate over the elements. And second, you need to be able to compare the elements. That's it. There are no demands as to how the elements are held. They could be in a linked list, an array, or any iterable container. What they are does not matter — they could be strings, integers, dates, or people. As long as you write down the two aforementioned constraints in the type system, you can implement sort:

```
extension SequenceType where Generator.Element: Comparable {
    public func sort() -> [Self.Generator.Element]
}
```

To implement sortInPlace, you need more building blocks. You need random access to the elements, rather than just linear iteration. CollectionType captures this. MutableCollectionType adds mutation to it. Finally, you need to compare and offset indices in constant time. RandomAccessIndexType allows for that. This may sound complex, but it captures exactly the prerequisites needed to perform an in-place sort:

```
extension MutableCollectionType
    where Index: RandomAccessIndexType, Generator.Element: Comparable
{
    public mutating func sortInPlace()
}
```

Minimal capabilities described by protocols compose well. You can add different capabilities of different protocols to a type, bit by bit. We saw this in the collections chapter when we first built a List type by giving it a single method, cons. Without changing the original List struct, we made it conform to SequenceType. In fact, we could have done this even if we weren't the original authors of this type. By adding conformance to SequenceType, we get all the extension methods of SequenceType for free.

Adding new shared features via a common superclass is not this flexible; you can't just decide later to add a new common base class to many different classes. When you do, you risk major refactoring. And if you aren't the owner of these subclasses, you can't do it at all!

Subclasses have to know which methods they can override without breaking the superclass. For example, when a method is overridden, a subclass might need to call the superclass method at the right point: either at the beginning, somewhere in the middle, or at the end of the method. This moment is often unspecified. Also, by overriding the wrong method, a subclass might break the superclass without a warning.

Let's go back to our CalendarView example. Instead of a shared superclass, we can define a protocol that both views conform to. This has some advantages:

→ We are not forced to use a specific superclass. MyCalendarView can subclass from UIStackView or UITableView. MonthCalendarView can subclass from UICollectionView. The subclasses — not a CalendarView superclass — make this decision.

→ The views do not have to be careful of overriding methods of CalendarView. They still need to be careful when they override UIView methods, but this is inevitable.

→ We do not need empty methods in our protocol. As we will see, we can use protocol extensions for default implementations.

As a first step, let's create a CalendarView protocol. This contains three properties: displayRange, delegate, and events. In protocols, we need to be explicit about what these properties can do, so we mark all three as both **get** and **set:**

```
protocol CalendarView {
    var displayRange: DateRange { get set }
    var delegate: CalendarViewDelegate? { get set }
    var events: [Event] { get set }
}
```

This makes it easy to let both views conform to our protocol. In MyCalendarView, we already have these properties. Thus, we can make

MyCalendarView conform with a single line. This is quite powerful, as we can retroactively add a protocol to a type. Even with a different interface, we could make MyCalendarView conform to CalendarView. We only need to write an extension and implement the required methods:

```
extension MyCalendarView: CalendarView { }
```

In the implementation of MyCalendarView, we filtered the events array. We made sure to only include events that are in the displayRange. Rather than duplicating this code, we move it to the protocol. We write an extension that uses both events and displayRange to do this:

```
extension CalendarView {
    var eventsInRange: [Event] {
        return events.filter { displayRange.contains($0.date) }
    }
}
```

Every type that conforms to CalendarView gets this capability for free. We have seen this technique before. For example, if a type conforms to SequenceType, it gets a lot of extra functionality for free. All this functionality is built on top of a few required methods.

With our protocol in place, we can also think of completely different implementations. For example, we could build a command-line calendar app that just prints out all the events in a range:

```
struct TextCalendarView: CalendarView {
    var displayRange: DateRange
    var delegate: CalendarViewDelegate?
    var events: [Event] = []

    func display() {
        let formatter = NSDateFormatter()
        formatter.dateStyle = .ShortStyle
        formatter.timeStyle = .ShortStyle
        for event in eventsInRange {
            print("\(formatter.stringFromDate(event.date)): \(event.title)")
        }
    }
}
```

This code sharing wouldn't be so easy if CalendarView were a subclass of UIView.

Overriding Protocol Methods

Before we continue with our CalenderView, let's consider some protocol extension subtleties. Let's say we get the task to make our calendar items shareable on social media. We immediately start with a protocol, Shareable. Conforming types must provide a socialMediaDescription property:

```
protocol Shareable {
    var socialMediaDescription: String { get }
}
```

We can add a share method in a protocol extension. This prints the social media description to the standard output. We also add a second method that formats the output:

```
extension Shareable {
    func share() {
        print("Sharing: \(self.socialMediaDescription)")
    }

    func linesAndShare() {
        print("----------")
        share()
        print("----------")
    }
}
```

All we need to do to make any type conform to Shareable is implement socialMediaDescription. When we do that, we get the share method from the protocol extension for free. Yet, if we choose to, we can also create a custom variant of the share method in a conforming type. For example, if we make String conform to Shareable, we could do it like this:

```
extension String: Shareable {
    var socialMediaDescription: String { return self }

    func share() {
        print("Special String Sharing: \(self.socialMediaDescription)")
    }
}
```

Now, if we create a string and call share on it, it will use our custom implementation:

```
"hello".share()
// Prints "Special String Sharing: hello"
```

Yet we get a different result if we use "hello" as a Shareable value:

```
let hello: Shareable = "hello"
hello.share()
// Prints: "Sharing: hello"
```

Things get even more interesting. What happens if we call linesAndShare directly on a String?

```
"hello".linesAndShare()
// Prints:
//
// ----------
// Sharing: hello
// ----------
```

The output of the last two examples might surprise you. Even though we defined share on String, it did not override our default implementation; it merely shadowed it. Which of the two share implementations gets called depends on the type information the compiler sees at the call site. The method invocation is statically dispatched, as opposed to dynamically dispatched, which would take the receiver's type at runtime into account.

We get a different behavior if we make the share method a *protocol requirement*, i.e. we add it to the protocol:

```
protocol Shareable {
    var socialMediaDescription: String { get }
    func share()
}
```

Now calls to share will be dynamically dispatched:

```
let hello: Shareable = "hello"
hello.share()
// Prints "Special String Sharing: hello"
```

This distinction between static and dynamic dispatch in protocol extensions can be confusing. If you ever wonder why your custom implementation of an extension method is not getting called, the reason is probably that the method is not listed in the protocol's requirements.

It also means that protocol extensions can contain two things with different semantics, depending on whether or not they are backed by the protocol's requirements. Every protocol requirement creates a *customization point* that conforming types are required to implement. An implementation of the requirement in the protocol extension provides a default behavior for types that don't want to provide a customization, but those that do can be sure that their implementation will always be called, because calls are dynamically dispatched.

On the other hand, implementations in protocol extensions that are not backed by a requirement are always statically dispatched. You should use these to provide shared functionality to all conforming types that are not intended as customization points.

Aside from performance benefits, static dispatch also solves a common problem in languages with dynamic dispatch. If we were writing Objective-C, the share method on String would override the method in the protocol. Thus, we always prefixed custom extensions to types (e.g. oci_share()). That way, it was not possible to override a method by mistake. In Swift, this isn't necessary anymore.

Adding Associated Types

Just before getting our calendar app ready, we might decide to use a different way of storing events. Rather than having them in the Event struct, we store events in a database using Core Data. A simple solution would be to just replace all occurences of Event with CoreDataEvent. Yet we might want to keep using the Event structs in our tests, because these structs are easier to create.

Rather than replacing, we can make our protocol generic over the type of events by using an associated type inside the protocol. The updated definition of our CalendarView looks like this:

```
protocol CalendarView {
    associatedtype EventType

    var displayRange: DateRange { get set }
    var delegate: CalendarViewDelegate? { get set }
    var events: [EventType] { get set }
}
```

Before Swift 2.2, the **associatedtype** keyword for associated types was called **typealias**. In code that was written before Swift 2.2, you will see **typealias** used for both associated types and type aliases.

Here, we immediately run into a problem. Our extension that adds the eventsInRange method doesn't compile anymore. The issue is event.date. The code still assumes that the events stored in the events array are of type Event. We can make this assumption explicit. In the extension, we state that it only works when the associated type, EventType, is an Event:

```
extension CalendarView where EventType == Event {
    var eventsInRange: [EventType] {
        return events.filter { displayRange.contains($0.date) }
    }
}
```

Now the eventsInRange method is only available when the associated type is Event. Yet our CoreDataEvent also has a date property. Of course, we could add another extension specifically for CoreDataEvent. Instead, we create a new protocol, HasDate, which states that a type has a date property:

```
protocol HasDate {
    var date: NSDate { get }
}
```

Both Event and CoreDataEvent can conform to this protocol with a single line, as they both already have the date property. We change the extension above to only implement eventsInRange when EventType conforms to HasDate. This way, the extension works for both Event and CoreDataEvent. If we choose to add a different event type later on, we only have to make it conform to HasDate:

```
extension CalendarView where EventType: HasDate {
    var eventsInRange: [EventType] {
        return events.filter { displayRange.contains($0.date) }
    }
}
```

We can use our TextCalendarView without changing it. The events property is an array of Event values, so the compiler will infer that the associated type is Event, and there is no need to specify it. If we want to make our TextCalendarView generic, we can add a generic parameter, E. As long as a type

E conforms to HasDate, we can display the events on the command line. The changed variant looks like this:

```
struct TextCalendarView<E: HasDate>: CalendarView {
    var displayRange: DateRange
    var delegate: CalendarViewDelegate?
    var events: [E] = []

    func display() {
        for event in eventsInRange {
            let formatter = NSDateFormatter()
            formatter.dateStyle = .ShortStyle
            formatter.timeStyle = .ShortStyle
            print("\(formatter.stringFromDate(event.date)): \(event)")
        }
    }
}
```

The current solution is more complicated than the class we started with, MyCalendarView. Yet pulling out shared functionality into a protocol made it possible to share code without subclassing. The current solution is a lot more generic. We are able to change how we display the data by using a different view that conforms to the CalendarView protocol. Also, we can change the source of the data: we can display any event type as long as there's a date property.

In your own applications, you can decide to take some of the steps above if your code needs to be more flexible. Yet, as with any technique, you need to be mindful of the tradeoffs. Making your code more generic can also make it more complicated. Is that a price you want to pay? It is often a good idea to start with a non-generic version and refactor it step by step.

If we take a step back, we can analyze why the protocol-based version is more flexible. When we are dealing with a protocol, we only know something about the *interface* of a type. We know that there are certain methods and/or variables available. We do not know about the implementation details of a type conforming to a protocol. Yet some protocols state implementation requirements, such as asymptotic complexity.

When we deal with classes, the interface and implementation are tightly coupled. A class exposes certain methods of its implementation as being callable. A subclass needs to take great care to override those methods in the correct order. In other words, a subclass needs to know a lot about the implementation details of a superclass. This tight coupling makes subclassing more complicated than working with protocols.

Protocols with Self Requirements

Often, we can use protocol types just like normal types. For example, let's say we create a protocol that states that an event has to have a date and a title:

```
protocol EventLike {
    var date: NSDate { get }
    var title : String { get }
}
```

With an empty extension, we can make the Event struct above conform to EventLike.

We can use EventLike just like any other type. For example, we could define a variable with the explicit type EventLike. This discards the type information that it contains an Event. From that moment on, we can only access the date and title properties in a read-only way. The interface is limited to the protocol. Even though there is an Event underneath, we cannot access it as such:

```
let sampleEvent: EventLike = Event(title: "My event", date: NSDate())
```

We can also put different types that conform to the same protocol in a collection. For example, we can create an array of EventLike objects:

```
let sampleCDEvent = CoreDataEvent(title: "My CD event", date: NSDate())
var events: [EventLike] = [sampleEvent, sampleCDEvent]
```

The array above allows us, for example, to map over it and fetch all the dates. Because date is in the protocol, we can access the property on the EventLike values in the array:

```
let dates = events.map { $0.date }
```

Now, we add some more functionality to the EventLike protocol. For example, we can add a method, overlapsWith, which checks whether or not two events overlap:

```
protocol EventLike {
    var date: NSDate { get }
```

```
    var title : String { get }
    func overlapsWith(other: Self) -> Bool
}
```

We can add a durationInSeconds property to the Event struct. This allows us to conform to the new EventLike protocol again:

```
struct Event {
    let title : String
    let date: NSDate
    let durationInSeconds: NSTimeInterval
}

extension Event: EventLike {
    func overlapsWith(other: Event) -> Bool {
        return date.timeIntervalSinceDate(other.date) < durationInSeconds ||
            other.date.timeIntervalSinceDate(date) < other.durationInSeconds
    }
}
```

This change made the new EventLike protocol a completely different thing than the old version. It cannot be a standalone type anymore, because we added a method that refers to **Self**. For example, the following code no longer compiles:

```
let test: EventLike = Event(title: "Chris", date: NSDate(),
    durationInSeconds: 100)
```

There is a good reason why we cannot use protocols as standalone types when they have a **Self** requirement. For example, let's consider the overlapsWith method. When we use an Event, we can only expect a reasonable result if we call overlapsWith with another Event as the parameter. By trying to say that the test value is of type EventLike, we throw away that information. Without this limitation on **Self** protocols, we would be able to call overlapsWith with a different type.

As we now know, we cannot use the new version of EventLike as a standalone type. This also means that we cannot use it as a generic parameter. For example, we cannot define an array with EventLike as the element type:

```
let array: [EventLike] = [] // This does not compile
```

By including **Self** in the protocol, we have limited our flexibility. This is a good thing, because of the way we implemented overlapsWith: calling it with a different type would make no sense. Yet, all is not lost. We can still store EventLike elements in a collection. We do need to add one constraint: all elements need to have the same type. For example, we can create a new **struct** that stores an array of values that have the same generic type. We do this by making the struct generic. However, we constrain the generic type by saying that it needs to conform to the EventLike protocol. Now we have a homogeneous array (i.e. all elements have the same type):

```
struct EventStorage<E: EventLike> {
    let events: [E]
}
```

Our type is still generic; we can put it to use with other event types, as long as they conform to EventLike. We cannot mix different event types into a single array. Yet we can still write useful functions. For example, we can write an extension to check whether or not an event overlaps with any of the existing events:

```
extension EventStorage {
    func containsOverlappingEvent(event: E) -> Bool {
        return !events.lazy. filter (event.overlapsWith).isEmpty
    }
}
```

We cannot pass just any EventType into the method above. Again, the parameter needs to have the same type as the elements in the array.

Associated Types

Protocols with associated types are similar to protocols with **Self** requirements. You cannot declare them as standalone variable types. To think about why, consider the following scenario. Suppose you declare a protocol for storing some arbitrary type and then fetching it back:

```
protocol StoringType {
    associatedtype Stored

    init (_ value: Stored)
    func getStored() -> Stored
}

// An implementation that stores Ints
struct IntStorer: StoringType {
```

```
    private let stored: Int
    init (_ value: Int) { stored = value }
    func getStored() -> Int { return stored }
}

// An implementation that stores Strings
struct StringStorer: StoringType {
    private let stored: String
    init (_ value: String) { stored = value }
    func getStored() -> String { return stored }
}

let intStorer = IntStorer(5)
intStorer.getStored() // returns 5

let stringStorer = StringStorer("five")
stringStorer.getStored() // returns "five"
```

So far, so good.

The main reason to have a variable with a protocol type is to get dynamic behavior. You can assign values with different types to the variable. This gives you polymorphic behavior at runtime, depending on the underlying type.

But you can't do this if the protocol has an associated type. How would the following code work in practice?

```
// as you've seen, this won't compile because
// StoringType has an associated type.

// randomly assign either a string or int storer to someStorer:
var someStorer: StoringType = arc4random()%2 == 0 ? intStorer : stringStorer
let x = someStorer.getStored()
```

In the above code, what would the type of x be? An Int? A String? In Swift, all types must be fixed at compile time. A function cannot change types at runtime.

Just like with protocols that have a **Self** reference, you can only use StoringType as a generic constraint. Suppose you wanted to print out any kind of stored type. You could write a function like this:

```
func printStoredValue<S: StoringType>(storer: S) {
    let x = storer.getStored()
```

```
    print(x)
}
```

```
printStoredValue(intStorer)
printStoredValue(stringStorer)
```

This is okay, because at compile time, it's as if the compiler writes out two versions of printStoredValue: one for Ints, and one for Strings. Within those two versions, x has a specific type.

When you compare protocols in Swift with protocols in Objective-C, you can also see the difference between regular protocols and protocols with associated types or a **Self** requirement. We can use regular protocols in the same places where we would have used protocols in Objective-C. However, protocols with associated types or a **Self** requirement are completely different: we cannot express them in Objective-C at all.

Even when you are not comparing to Objective-C, it is helpful to think of protocols with associated types or **Self** requirements as completely different from regular protocols. They are not standalone types; we can only use them as generic constraints.

Protocol Internals

Protocols and Generics

Given a protocol with no **Self** or associated type requirements, such as CustomStringConvertible (one of the few like this in the standard library), how are the following different from one another?

This:

func f(x: CustomStringConvertible) { }

Versus this:

func g<T: CustomStringConvertible>(x: T) { }

Let's examine the differences. Warning: some of the behavior below is undocumented and subject to change. We tested all the code using the latest

Swift version at time of writing, but the behavior might change in future versions. Also, all size numbers assume a 64-bit platform.

Functional Differences

What is the difference between the two examples above? In the first case, the function takes an argument with the protocol type, CustomStringConvertible, and it can then access the argument value via any of the methods that protocol provides.

In the second case, g takes an argument of any type T that conforms to CustomStringConvertible. This means T is the type of whatever was passed in as the argument. If you pass in an Int, then T is an Int. If you pass in an array of integers, then T is an [Int].

For most purposes, this distinction doesn't matter when implementing the body of the function. Even though T might be an Int or an [Int], you can only use any properties guaranteed by CustomStringConvertible, because the function needs to work on *any* type that conforms to CustomStringConvertible. So you can't call x.successor() or x.count — only x.description.

The most important functional difference between the two forms comes when the function returns a value. Suppose you wanted to write your own version of the standard library's abs function. It could look something like this:

```
func myAbs<T: SignedNumberType>(x: T) -> T {
    if x < 0 {
        return -x
    } else {
        return x
    }
}

// myAbs works for any kind of signed number
// (e.g. Int, Int64, Float, Double, etc.)
let i: Int8 = -4
let j = myAbs(i)
// j will be of type Int8, with value 4
```

This function relies on three things provided by SignedNumberType: a negation operator, a less-than operator (via SignedNumberType conforming to Comparable), and the ability to create a zero of the same type for comparison (via IntegerLiteralConvertible). It compares to zero and then returns the original value or its negation. It also returns the same type as the input. If you pass in an Int8, you get back an Int8. If you pass in a Double, you get back a Double. If we would write this function using protocols, you'd get back the type of the protocol. Not only would that be inconvenient for type inference purposes, but you might also need to cast the result back to the type you wanted, using **as**! to make use of it. This loss of specific type information is referred to as *type erasure*.

As of Swift 2.0, you are also able to write this function as a protocol extension. But this is still a generic function, much like the free function above. Instead, **Self** takes the place of T, and the implicit variable **self** takes the place of the argument x. Extending a protocol also gives us the benefit of being able to write abs as a computed property. This feels more natural to use:

```
extension SignedNumberType {
    var myAbs: Self {
        if self < 0 {
            return -self
        } else {
            return self
        }
    }
}
let k = i.myAbs
// j will be of type `Int8`, with value 4
```

Protocols Internals

Aside from that, how else do the two functions differ? Well, there are still some ways you can tell the difference between the protocol and the T placeholder. For example, you can look at the size of the value:

```
func takesProtocol(x: CustomStringConvertible) {
    // this will print "40" every time:
    print(sizeofValue(x))
}
```

```
func takesPlaceholder<T: CustomStringConvertible>(x: T) {
    // this will print whatever the size of
    // the argument type is (for example, Int64
    // is 8, Int8 is 1, class references are 8)
    print(sizeofValue(x))
```

```
}
```

```
takesProtocol(1 as Int16)     // prints 40
takesPlaceholder(1 as Int16)  // prints 2
```

```
class MyClass: CustomStringConvertible {
    var description: String { return "MyClass" }
}
```

```
takesProtocol(MyClass())     // prints 40
takesPlaceholder(MyClass()) // prints 8
```

So it looks like CustomStringConvertible is some kind of fixed-sized box that holds any kind of value that is printable. This kind of boxing is a common feature in other languages like Java and C#. But in the code above, Swift even puts references to classes inside this 40-byte box. This might surprise you if you're used to thinking of protocols as references to pure virtual base classes. This Swift box is geared up to hold both value *and* reference types. Class-only protocols are smaller, at 16 bytes, as they never need to hold a larger-sized payload.

We can again rewrite the generic function as a protocol extension:

```
extension CustomStringConvertible {
    func asExtension() {
        print(sizeofValue(self))
    }
}
```

We then observe that it behaves identically to the generic placeholder:

```
(1 as Int16).asExtension()
MyClass().asExtension()
```

```
()
```

So when a type is boxed up into a protocol reference, what's inside those 40 bytes? We can write some bitcasting code in Swift that gives us some insight:

```
// function to dump out the contents of a protocol variable
func dumpCustomStringConvertible(c: CustomStringConvertible) {
    var p = c
    // you could also do this with unsafeBitCast
    withUnsafePointer(&p) { ptr -> Void in
```

```
        let intPtr = UnsafePointer<Int>(ptr)
        for i in 0.stride(to: sizeof(CustomStringConvertible)/8, by: 1) {
            print("\(i):\t 0x\(String(intPtr[i], radix: 16))")
        }
    }
}

let i = Int(0xb1ab1ab1a)
dumpCustomStringConvertible(i)

// prints out:
// 0:      0xb1ab1ab1a
// 1:      0x7fff5ad10f48
// 2:      0x2000000000
// 3:      0x10507bfa8
// 4:      0x105074780
```

With a single 8-byte integer, the protocol appears to pack the value into the protocol value itself. The next two words look like uninitialized memory (their contents vary on each run) used for padding. The last two words are pointers to metadata[1] about the underlying type.

If we create a custom struct of size 16 or 24, this is also held within the first three words of the protocol. Once we go above this, it switches over to holding a pointer to the referenced value:

```
struct FourInts: CustomStringConvertible {
    var a = 0xaaaa
    var b = 0xbbbb
    var c = 0xcccc
    var d = 0xdddd
    var description: String { return String(a,b,c,d) }
}

dumpCustomStringConvertible(FourInts())

// prints out:
// 0:      0x7f8b5840fb90 // this is a pointer to a FourInts value
// 1:      0xaaaa         // uninitialized  garbage (?)
// 2:      0xbbbb         // ditto
// 3:      0x10dde52a8    // metadata
// 4:      0x10dde51b8    // metadata
```

---

1 https://www.mikeash.com/pyblog/friday-qa-2014-08-01-exploring-swift-memory-layout-part-ii.html

How can we tell that the first part is a pointer to a FourInts type? Well, we can dereference it and see! We need to add a parameter to dumpCustomStringConvertible, which tells the function the real type of the underlying value:

```
func dumpCustomStringConvertible
    <T>(var p: CustomStringConvertible, type: T.Type)
{
    withUnsafePointer(&p) { ptr -> Void in
        let intPtr = UnsafePointer<Int>(ptr)
        for i in 0.stride(to: (sizeof(CustomStringConvertible)/8), by: 1) {
            print("\(i):\t 0x\(String(intPtr[i], radix: 16))")
        }
        // if the pointed-to value is too big to fit :
        if sizeof(T) > 24 {
            // we have an integer, and we want to turn it into a pointer,
            // so we use the bitPattern: constructor of UnsafePointer<T>
            let valPtr = UnsafePointer<T>(bitPattern: Int(intPtr.memory))
            // and now we can look at the value at that location in memory
            print("value at pointer: \(valPtr.memory)")
        }
    }
}
```

```
dumpCustomStringConvertible(FourInts(), type: FourInts.self)
```

```
// prints out:
// 0:       0x7f8b5840fb90
// 1:       0x7fff909c5395
// 2:       0xaaaa
// 3:       0x10dde52a8
// 4:       0x10dde51b8
// value at pointer: (43690, 48059, 52428, 56797)
```

Bingo! Those are the values of the four integers.

One final point before we move on. When you refer to a value type using a protocol, this does *not* turn it into a reference type:

```
protocol Incrementable {
    var x: Int { get }
    mutating func inc()
}
```

```
struct S: Incrementable {
```

```
    var x = 0
    mutating func inc() {
        x += 1
    }
}

var p1: Incrementable = S()
var p2 = p1
p1.inc()
p1.x  // now 1
p2.x  // still  0
```

Performance Implications

Protocols used like this seem to add some level of indirection. Does that cost us anything compared to using the generic placeholder approach? To test this out, we can construct some trivial structs that perform a basic operation, and then we can run that operation via both a protocol and a generic placeholder.

First, here's the protocol:

```
protocol NumberGeneratorType {
    mutating func generateNumber() -> Int
}
```

We're pretty restricted in what can be done without resorting to associated types, so all it does is print a number. Here are three implementations that do different things — along with two harnesses that iterate multiple times, totaling the returned numbers:

```
struct RandomGenerator: NumberGeneratorType {
    func generateNumber() -> Int {
        return Int(arc4random_uniform(10))
    }
}

struct IncrementingGenerator: NumberGeneratorType {
    var n: Int
    init(start: Int) { n = start }
    mutating func generateNumber() -> Int {
        n += 1
        return n
    }
}
```

```
struct ConstantGenerator: NumberGeneratorType {
    let n: Int
    init (constant: Int) { n = constant }
    func generateNumber() -> Int {
        return n
    }
}


func generateUsingProtocol(g: NumberGeneratorType, count: Int) -> Int {
    var generator = g
    return 0.stride(to: count, by: 1).reduce(0) { total, _ in
        total &+ generator.generateNumber()
    }
}


func generateUsingGeneric<T: NumberGeneratorType>(g: T, count: Int) -> Int {
    var generator = g
    return 0.stride(to: count, by: 1).reduce(0) { total, _ in
        total &+ generator.generateNumber()
    }
}
```

If we compile the code above with -O and set count to 10,000, we get the following timings when we run the program:

Method	Time
Generic rand	261,829µs
Protocol rand	286,625µs
Generic incr	5,481µs
Protocol incr	45,094µs
Generic const	0µs
Protocol const	43,666µs

So what does this tell us? Calling arc4random is quite expensive, so the marginal difference made by the protocol is negligible but noticeable. But in the case of the incrementing generator, it's a lot more in proportion to the actual operation being performed.

And in the case of the constant generator, the compiler has managed to optimize away all the code of the generic version and turn it into a single multiply operation (number of iterations times the constant)! As such, it takes a constant amount of time. The protocol indirection acted as a barrier to this same optimization.

In fact, if you recompile with -Ounchecked, the same happens with the incrementing generator too. Only the check for overflow on the increment prevented the compiler from optimizing. The protocol versions remain the same.

For the most part, this can be put in the "premature optimization" camp. The big wins are about the expressiveness generics give you and how they avoid type erasure, as shown in the earlier section. But if you're in the habit of writing generic functions, the performance gains are nice too. When writing reusable library functions like sort or reduce, which are called a lot and perform tight loops, they're critical.

Of course, all this is subject to change. Given that the protocols are not being used to get any kind of dynamic behavior, perhaps the compiler *could* have optimized them too. But it doesn't appear to at the moment.

Dynamic Dispatch

Dynamic behavior might be one occasion when you'd prefer to use protocols rather than generics. Protocols can give you dynamic dispatch, even on structs. Let's look at a simple example.

Structs, Protocols, and Dynamic Dispatch

Consider the following code:

```
func f(p: CustomStringConvertible) {
    print(p)
}

func g<T: CustomStringConvertible>(t: T) {
    print(t)
}

let a = [1,2,3]
let i = 1

// this will work fine: either can be converted to CustomStringConvertible
// and passed in, then the appropriate version of `description` is called
```

```
// at runtime
f(arc4random()%2 == 0 ? a : i)
```

The function f takes a boxed value as its argument. Thus, we can call it with different types, based on a runtime value. The protocol type gives us dynamic behavior, even when we use structs.

The following snippet will *not* compile. T needs to be fixed as either an array of Ints or an Int at compile time; it can't be both:

```
g(arc4random()%2 == 0 ? a : i)
```

This is a contrived example, but it shows how even structs in Swift can get dynamic behavior at runtime via protocols. In the section above, we have seen how this can decrease performance. More importantly, the function f is less flexible; it cannot return the input type directly. Instead, it can only return the input type inside a protocol box that erases the type.

Array Covariance

If you try to pass [String] (or any other type) into a function that takes [Any] (or any other array of a protocol rather than a specific type), you will get an error ('String' is not identical to 'Any').

While every type conforms to Any, this is not the same as Any being a universal implicit superclass that all types inherit from.

As we saw above, when you cast a type to a protocol, you create a new value with a different structure. So for a string to be of type Any, it needs to be physically transformed from the String representation:

```
sizeof(String) // 24 bytes (on 64-bit, anyway) to the Any representation:
sizeof(Any) // 32 bytes, which includes some metadata about what the type really is
```

Since value types are held directly in the array, the array would be a very different shape. So under the hood, the compiler would have to do the equivalent of this:

```
names.map { $0 as Any } // create a new array with the Any versions
```

Swift could perhaps automate this process for you (it does if you pass a single variable into a function that takes Any). But we're glad it doesn't. Suppose your array was huge — this would be a lot of processing happening implicitly under the hood.

This is different from when you have an array of reference types, all of which are pointers to the actual data, and so all the same size, and which need no transformation when upcasting:

```
class C  { }
class D: C { }

let  d = D()
let  c:  C = d
// These values will be the same:
unsafeBitCast(d, UnsafePointer<Void>.self)
unsafeBitCast(c, UnsafePointer<Void>.self)
```

So saying "this array of [D] is really an array of [C]" is just a matter of the compiler agreeing the types can be substituted and that no data transformation needs to take place:

```
// This works fine; no runtime transformation needed:
func f(cs: [C]) { }
let  ds = [D(),D()]
f(ds)
```

But protocols still are different from superclass references when used with classes:

```
protocol P { }
extension C: P { }

sizeofValue(C())        // 8 bytes (just a pointer)
sizeofValue(C() as P)  // 40 bytes

func g(ps: [P]) { }
g(ds)  // 'wont compile, needs transformation
```

Conclusion

Protocols in Swift are important building blocks. They allow us to write flexible code that decouples the interface and implementation. For example, we saw a CalendarView protocol that was implemented by different types. We wrote extensions on protocols to add functionality in a generic way. We distinguished between two different types of protocols: first, the "simple" protocols, which are like Objective-C protocols; and second, the protocols with associated types (or a **Self** requirement), which are more powerful. This power comes at a price: we cannot use them as standalone types anymore. We also looked at the implementation details of protocols. There are functional differences between using them as standalone types and using them as generic constraints. Using protocols as generic constraints allows us to have a more flexible output type, whereas using them as standalone types gives us dynamic runtime behavior.

We expect that protocols will have a big impact in the Swift community and in the long term as well. Yet we also want to warn against overusing them. Sometimes, using a simple concrete type like a struct or a class is much easier to understand than a protocol, and this increases the readability of your code. There are also times when using a protocol can increase readability of your code a lot — especially when you deal with legacy APIs, it could be interesting to wrap the types in those APIs in a protocol.

One of the big upsides of using protocols is that they provide a *minimal viable interface*. They specify exactly what the interface looks like. This lets us create multiple types that conform to the interface, making it easier to write test code. Rather than having to set up a complicated tree of dependencies, we can just create a simple test type that conforms to the protocol.

Hands-On: Wrapping CommonMark

In this chapter, we'll create a wrapper around the CommonMark library. CommonMark is a formal specification for Markdown, a popular syntax for formatting plain text. If you have ever written a post on GitHub or Stack Overflow, you've probably used Markdown.

CommonMark provides a reference implementation written in C that is both fast and well tested. Swift's ability to call into C code allows us to take advantage of the abundance of existing C libraries. Writing a wrapper around the library's interface in Swift is often much easier and involves less work than having to reinvent the wheel; meanwhile, users of our wrapper will see no difference in terms of type safety or ease of use compared to a fully native solution. All we need to start is the dynamic library and its header files.

We'll take a layered approach. First, we will create a very thin Swift class around the opaque types the library exposes. In a second step, we will then wrap this class with Swift enums.

Wrapping the C Library

Let's begin by wrapping a single function, which takes in Markdown-formatted text and returns the resulting HTML code in a string. The C interface looks like this:

```
/** Convert 'text' (assumed to be a UTF-8 encoded string with length
 * 'len') from CommonMark Markdown to HTML, returning a null-terminated,
 * UTF-8-encoded string.
 */
char *cmark_markdown_to_html(const char *text, int len, int options);
```

Swift presents the C string in the first parameter as an UnsafePointer to a bunch of Int8 values (we know from the documentation that these are expected to be UTF-8 code units). We also need to pass in the length, and we can just pass in 0 for the options:

```
func cmark_markdown_to_html
    (text: UnsafePointer<Int8>, len: Int, options: Int32)
    -> UnsafeMutablePointer<Int8>
```

We want our wrapper function to work with Swift strings, of course, so you might think that we need to convert the Swift string into an Int8 pointer. However, bridging between native and C strings is such a common operation that Swift will do this automatically for us. We do have to be careful with the length parameter, as the function expects the length of the UTF-8-encoded string in bytes, and not the number of characters. We get the correct value from the string's utf8 view:

```
extension String {
    public func markdownToHTML() -> String {
        let outString = cmark_markdown_to_html(self, self.utf8.count, 0)
        return String(UTF8String: outString)!
    }
}
```

In the implementation above, we force-unwrap the initialized string. We can safely do this because we know that cmark_markdown_to_html always returns a valid string. By force-unwrapping inside the method, the library user can call the markdownToHTML method without having to worry about optionals — the result would never be **nil** anyway.

> Note that the automatic bridging of native Swift strings to C strings assumes that the C function you want to call expects the string to be UTF-8 encoded. This is the right choice in most cases, but if the C API assumes a different encoding, you cannot use the automatic bridging. However, it is often still easy. For example, if you need an array of UTF-16 code points, you can use Array(string.utf16).

Wrapping the cmark_node Type

In addition to the straight HTML output, the cmark library also provides a way to parse a Markdown text into a structured tree of elements. For example, a simple text could be transformed into a list of block-level nodes such as paragraphs, quotes, lists, code blocks, headers, and so on. Some block-level elements contain other block-level elements (for example, quotes can contain multiple paragraphs), whereas others contain only inline elements (for example, a header can contain a part that's emphasized). No element can contain both (for example, the inline elements of a list item are always wrapped in a paragraph element).

The C library uses a single data type, cmark_node, to represent the nodes. It is opaque, meaning that the authors of the library chose to hide its definition. All we see in the headers are functions that operate on or return pointers to cmark_node. Swift imports these pointers as COpaquePointers.

Let's wrap a node in a native Swift type to make it easier to work with. As we have seen in the chapter on structs and classes, we need to think about value semantics whenever we create a custom type: is the type a value, or does it make sense for instances to have identity? In the former case, we should favor a struct or enum, whereas the latter requires a class. Our case is interesting: on one hand, the node of a Markdown document is a value — two nodes that have the same element type and contents should be indistinguishable, hence they shouldn't have identity. On the other hand, since we don't know the internals of cmark_node, there is no straightforward way to make a copy of a node, so we can't guarantee value semantics. For this reason, we start with a class. Later on, we will write another layer on top of this class to provide an interface with value semantics.

Our class simply stores the opaque pointer and frees the memory cmark_node uses on **deinit** when there are no references left to an instance of this class. We only free memory at the document level, because otherwise we might free nodes that are still in use. Freeing the document will also automatically free all the children recursively. Wrapping the opaque pointer in this way will give us automatic reference counting for free:

```
public class Node: CustomStringConvertible {
    let node: COpaquePointer

    init (node: COpaquePointer) {
        self.node = node
    }

    deinit {
        guard type == CMARK_NODE_DOCUMENT else { return }
        cmark_node_free(node)
    }
}
```

The next step is to wrap the cmark_parse_document function, which parses a Markdown text and returns the document's root node. It takes the same arguments as cmark_markdown_to_html: the string, its length, and an integer describing parse options. The return type of that function in Swift is COpaquePointer, which represents the node:

```
func cmark_parse_document
    (buffer: UnsafePointer<Int8>, len: Int, options: Int32)
    -> COpaquePointer
```

We turn the function into a convenience initializer for our class. Note that the function can return **nil** if parsing fails. In this context, **nil** does *not* represent an optional value, but rather the C null pointer. Our initializer should be failable and return **nil** (the optional value) in this case:

```
public convenience init?(markdown: String) {
    let node = cmark_parse_document(markdown, markdown.utf8.count, 0)
    guard node != nil else { return nil }
    self. init (node: node)
}
```

As mentioned above, there are a couple of interesting functions that operate on nodes. For example, there's one that returns the type of a node, such as paragraph or header:

```
cmark_node_type cmark_node_get_type(cmark_node *node);
```

In Swift, it looks like this:

```
func cmark_node_get_type(node: COpaquePointer) -> cmark_node_type
```

cmark_node_type is a C enum that has cases for the various block-level and inline elements that are defined in Markdown, as well as one case to signify errors:

```
typedef enum {
    /* Error status */
    CMARK_NODE_NONE,

    /* Block */
    CMARK_NODE_DOCUMENT,
    CMARK_NODE_BLOCK_QUOTE,
    ...

    /* Inline */
    CMARK_NODE_TEXT,
    CMARK_NODE_EMPH,
    ...
} cmark_node_type;
```

Swift imports plain C enums as structs containing only an Int32. Additionally, for every case in an enum, a top-level variable is generated. Only enums marked with the NS_ENUM macro, used by Apple in its Objective-C frameworks, are imported as native Swift enumerations:

```
struct cmark_node_type : RawRepresentable, Equatable {
    public init (_ rawValue: UInt32)
    public init (rawValue: UInt32)
    public var rawValue: UInt32
}
```

```
var CMARK_NODE_NONE: cmark_node_type { get }
var CMARK_NODE_DOCUMENT: cmark_node_type { get }
```

In Swift, the type of a node should be a property of the Node data type, so we turn the cmark_node_get_type function into a computed property of our class:

```
var type: cmark_node_type {
    return cmark_node_get_type(node)
}
```

Now we can just write node.type to get an element's type.

There are a couple more node properties we can access. For example, if a node is a list, it can have one of two list types: bulleted or ordered. All other nodes have the list type "no list." Again, Swift represents the corresponding C enum as a struct, with a top-level variable for each case, and we can write a similar wrapper property. In this case, we also provide a setter, which will come in handy later in this chapter:

```
var listType: cmark_list_type {
    get { return cmark_node_get_list_type(node) }
    set { cmark_node_set_list_type(node, newValue) }
}
```

There are similar functions for all the other node properties, such as header level, fenced code block info, and link URLs and titles. These properties often only make sense for specific types of nodes, and we can choose to provide an interface either with an optional (e.g. for the link URL) or with a default value (e.g. the default header level is 0). This illustrates a major weakness of the library's C API that we can model much better in Swift. We will talk more about this below.

Some nodes can also have children. For iterating over them, the CommonMark library provides the functions cmark_node_first_child and cmark_node_next. We want our Node class to provide an array of its children. To generate this array, we start with the first child and keep adding children until either cmark_node_first_child or cmark_node_next returns nil, signaling the end of the list. Note again that this **nil** is not an optional **nil**; it is a C null pointer. Because of this, we can't use the optional binding syntax using **while let**, and we need to check manually for **nil** inside the loop:

```
var children: [Node] {
    var result: [Node] = []
    var child = cmark_node_first_child(node)
    while child != nil {
        result.append(Node(node: child))
        child = cmark_node_next(child)
    }
    return result
}
```

We could also have chosen to return a sequence rather than an array, as shown below. However, there is a problem with this. The elements are returned lazily, and the node structure might change between production and consumption of the sequence. In that case, the code below will return wrong values, or even worse, crash. Depending on your use case, returning a lazily constructed sequence might be exactly what you want, but if your data structure can change, returning an array is a much safer choice:

```
var childrenS: AnySequence<Node> {
    return AnySequence { () -> AnyGenerator<Node> in
        var child = cmark_node_first_child(self.node)
        return AnyGenerator {
            let result: Node? = child == nil ? nil : Node(node: child)
            child = cmark_node_next(child)
            return result
        }
    }
}
```

With this simple wrapper class for nodes, accessing the abstract syntax tree produced by the CommonMark library from Swift becomes a lot easier. Instead of having to call functions like cmark_node_get_list_type, we can just write node.listType and get autocompletion and type safety. However, we are not done yet. Even though the Node class feels much more native than the C functions, Swift allows us to express a node in an even more natural and safer way, using enums with associated values.

A Safer Interface

As we mentioned above, there are many node properties that only apply in certain contexts. For example, it doesn't make any sense to access the headerLevel of a list or the listType of a code block. Enumerations with associated values allow us to specify only the metadata that makes sense for each specific case. We will create one enum for all allowed inline elements, and another one for block-level items. That way, we can enforce the structure of a CommonMark document. For example, a plain text element just stores a String, whereas emphasis nodes contain an array of other inline elements. These enumerations will be the public interface to our library, and the Node class can stay internal to our library:

```
public enum InlineElement {
    case Text(text: String)
    case SoftBreak
    case LineBreak
    case Code(text: String)
    case InlineHtml(text: String)
    case Emphasis(children: [InlineElement])
    case Strong(children: [InlineElement])
    case Link(children: [InlineElement], title : String?, url: String?)
    case Image(children: [InlineElement], title: String?, url: String?)
}
```

Similarly, paragraphs and headers can only contain inline elements, whereas block quotations always contain other block-level elements. A list is defined as an array of Block elements that represent the list items:

```
public enum Block {
    case List(items: [[Block]], type: ListType)
    case BlockQuote(items: [Block])
    case CodeBlock(text: String, language: String?)
    case Html(text: String)
    case Paragraph(text: [InlineElement])
    case Header(text: [InlineElement], level: Int)
    case HorizontalRule
}
```

The ListType is just a simple enum that states whether a list is ordered or unordered:

```
public enum ListType {
```

```
    case Unordered
    case Ordered
}
```

Since enums are value types, this also lets us treat nodes as values by converting them to their enum representations. We write a pair of functions: one function that creates Block and InlineElement values from the Node type, and another function that reconstructs a Node from these enums. This allows us to write functions that transform either InlineElement or Block values and reconstruct a CommonMark document, which can then be rendered into HTML, into man pages, or back into Markdown text.

Let's start by writing a function that converts a Node into an InlineElement. We switch on the node's type and construct the corresponding InlineElement value. For example, for a text node, we take the node's string contents, named literal in the cmark library. We can safely force-unwrap literal because we know that text nodes always have this value, whereas other node types might have **nil** values for literal. For example, emphasis and strong nodes only have child nodes, and no literal value. To parse the latter, we map over the node's children and call inlineElement recursively. Instead of duplicating that code, we create an inline function, parseChildren, that only gets called when needed. The **default** case should never get reached, so we choose to trap the program if it does. This follows the convention that returning an optional or using **throws** should generally only be used for expected errors, and not to signify programmer errors:

```
extension Node {
    func inlineElement() -> InlineElement {
        let parseChildren = { self.children.map { $0.inlineElement() } }
        switch type {
        case CMARK_NODE_TEXT:
            return .Text(text: literal !)
        case CMARK_NODE_SOFTBREAK:
            return .SoftBreak
        case CMARK_NODE_LINEBREAK:
            return .LineBreak
        case CMARK_NODE_CODE:
            return .Code(text: literal !)
        case CMARK_NODE_INLINE_HTML:
            return .InlineHtml(text: literal !)
        case CMARK_NODE_EMPH:
            return .Emphasis(children: parseChildren())
        case CMARK_NODE_STRONG:
            return .Strong(children: parseChildren())
```

```
case CMARK_NODE_LINK:
    return .Link(children: parseChildren(), title :  title ,
        url: urlString)
case CMARK_NODE_IMAGE:
    return .Image(children: parseChildren(), title:  title ,
        url: urlString)
default:
    fatalError("Expected inline element, got \(typeString)")
    }
  }
}
```

Converting block-level elements follows the same pattern. Note that
block-level elements can have either inline elements, list items, or other
block-level elements as children, depending on the node type. In the
cmark_node syntax tree, list items get wrapped with an extra node. In the
parseListItem function, we remove that layer and directly return an array of
block-level elements:

```
extension Node {
  public func block() -> Block {
      let parseInlineChildren = { self.children.map { $0.inlineElement() } }
      let parseBlockChildren = { self.children.map { $0.block() } }
      switch type {
      case CMARK_NODE_PARAGRAPH:
          return .Paragraph(text: parseInlineChildren())
      case CMARK_NODE_BLOCK_QUOTE:
          return .BlockQuote(items: parseBlockChildren())
      case CMARK_NODE_LIST:
          let type = listType == CMARK_BULLET_LIST ?
              ListType.Unordered : ListType.Ordered
          return .List(items: children.map { $0.parseListItem() }, type: type)
      case CMARK_NODE_CODE_BLOCK:
          return .CodeBlock(text: literal !,  language: fenceInfo)
      case CMARK_NODE_HTML:
          return .Html(text: literal !)
      case CMARK_NODE_HEADER:
          return .Header(text: parseInlineChildren(), level: headerLevel)
      case CMARK_NODE_HRULE:
          return .HorizontalRule
      default:
          fatalError("Unrecognized node: \(typeString)")
      }
    }
  }
}
```

Now, given a document-level Node, we can easily convert it into an array of Block elements. The Block elements are values: we can freely copy or change them without having to worry about references. This is very powerful for manipulating nodes. Since values, by definition, do not care how they were created, we can also create a Markdown syntax tree in code, from scratch, without using the CommonMark library at all. The types are much clearer too; you can't accidentally do things that wouldn't make sense — such as accessing the title of a list — as the compiler will not allow it. Aside from making your code safer, this is a very robust form of documentation — by just looking at the types, it is obvious how a CommonMark document is structured. And unlike comments, the compiler will make sure that this form of documentation is never outdated.

It's now very easy to write simple functions that operate on our new data types. For example, if we want to build a list of all the level 1 and 2 headers from a Markdown document for a table of contents, we can just loop over all children and check whether they are headers and have the correct level:

```
func tableOfContents(document: String) -> [Block] {
    let blocks = Node(markdown: document)?.children.map { $0.block() } ?? []
    return blocks.filter {
        switch $0 {
        case .Header(_, let level) where level < 3: return true
        default: return false
        }
    }
}
```

Before we build more operations like this, let's tackle the inverse transformation: converting a Block back into a Node. We need this because we ultimately want to use the CommonMark library to generate HTML or other text formats from the Markdown syntax tree we've built or manipulated, and the library can only deal with cmark_node_type.

Our plan is to create two functions named node: one that converts an InlineElement to a node, and another that handles Block elements. We start by extending Node with a new initializer that creates a new cmark_node from scratch, with the specified type and children. Recall that we wrote a **deinit**, which frees the root node of the tree (and recursively, all its children). This **deinit** will make sure that the node we allocate here gets freed eventually:

```
convenience init(type: cmark_node_type, children: [Node] = []) {
    let node = cmark_node_new(type)
```

```
    for child in children {
        cmark_node_append_child(node, child.node)
    }
    self.init(node: node)
}
```

We'll frequently need to create text-only nodes, or nodes with a number of children, so let's add three convenience initializers to make that easier:

```
extension Node {
    convenience init(type: cmark_node_type, literal: String) {
        self.init(type: type)
        self.literal = literal
    }
    convenience init(type: cmark_node_type, blocks: [Block]) {
        self.init(type: type, children: blocks.map { $0.node() })
    }
    convenience init(type: cmark_node_type, elements: [InlineElement]) {
        self.init(type: type, children: elements.map { $0.node() })
    }
}
```

Now we are ready to write the two conversion functions. Using the initializers we just defined, it becomes very straightforward. We switch on the element and create a node with the correct type. Here's the version for inline elements:

```
extension InlineElement {
    func node() -> Node {
        let node: Node
        switch self {
        case .Text(let text):
            node = Node(type: CMARK_NODE_TEXT, literal: text)
        case .Emphasis(let children):
            node = Node(type: CMARK_NODE_EMPH, elements: children)
        case .Code(let text):
            node = Node(type: CMARK_NODE_CODE, literal: text)
        case .Strong(let children):
            node = Node(type: CMARK_NODE_STRONG, elements: children)
        case .InlineHtml(let text):
            node = Node(type: CMARK_NODE_INLINE_HTML, literal: text)
        case let .Link(children, title, url):
            node = Node(type: CMARK_NODE_LINK, elements: children)
            node.title = title
            node.urlString = url
        case let .Image(children, title, url):
```

```
                node = Node(type: CMARK_NODE_IMAGE, elements: children)
                node.title  = title
                node.urlString = url
        case .SoftBreak: node = Node(type: CMARK_NODE_SOFTBREAK)
        case .LineBreak: node = Node(type: CMARK_NODE_LINEBREAK)
        }
        return node
    }

}
```

Creating a node from a block-level element is very similar. The only slightly
more complicated case is lists. Recall that in the above conversion from Node
to Block, we removed the extra node the CommonMark library uses to
represent lists, so we need to add that back in here:

```
extension Block {
    func node() -> Node {
        let  node: Node
        switch self {
        case .Paragraph(let children):
            node = Node(type: CMARK_NODE_PARAGRAPH, elements: children)
        case let  .List(items, type):
            let  listItems  = items.map {
                Node(type: CMARK_NODE_ITEM, blocks: $0)
            }
            node = Node(type: CMARK_NODE_LIST, children: listItems)
            node.listType = type == .Unordered
                ? CMARK_BULLET_LIST
                : CMARK_ORDERED_LIST
        case .BlockQuote(let items):
            node = Node(type: CMARK_NODE_BLOCK_QUOTE, blocks: items)
        case let  .CodeBlock(text, language):
            node = Node(type: CMARK_NODE_CODE_BLOCK, literal: text)
            node.fenceInfo = language
        case .Html(let text):
            node = Node(type: CMARK_NODE_HTML, literal: text)
        case let  .Header(text, level):
            node = Node(type: CMARK_NODE_HEADER, elements: text)
            node.headerLevel = level
        case .HorizontalRule:
            node = Node(type: CMARK_NODE_HRULE)
        }
        return node
    }
}
```

```
}
```

Finally, to provide a nice interface for the user, we define a public initializer that takes an array of block-level elements and produces a document node, which we can then render into one of the different output formats:

```
extension Node {
    public convenience init(blocks: [Block]) {
        self.init(type: CMARK_NODE_DOCUMENT, blocks: blocks)
    }
}
```

Now we can go in both directions: we can load a document, convert it into [Block] elements, modify those elements, and turn them back into a Node. This allows us to write programs that extract information from Markdown or even change the Markdown dynamically.

Iterating the Nodes

This book is written in Markdown, and during the production, we needed to convert the Markdown into multiple output formats. For example, we made a PDF for reading on devices, where links were clickable. We also produced a PDF for the printer, where all links were replaced with plain text and a footnote showing the URL. To perform this transformation, we can write a function, deepApply, which maps over all inline elements recursively. As a first try, we could define an interface that allows us to apply a function to every inline element:

```
func deepApply(elements: [Block], f: InlineElement -> InlineElement) -> [Block]
```

However, this approach is limited to one-to-one replacements or mutations of elements. This wouldn't work even if all we wanted to do was replace a link by its text. Though this looks like a one-to-one replacement, link elements actually contain an array of other inline elements as children. And since we don't have a generic container node type, there is no element we can replace the link with. Neither can we add new elements (such as a footnote) to the syntax tree or remove any nodes entirely. A more generic interface would be to return an array of InlineElements. That way, we could choose to remove an element (return an empty list), not change it (return a singleton list with just the element), or completely change it (return a different list). The function signature looks like this:

```
public func deepApply(elements: [Block],
    _ f: InlineElement -> [InlineElement]) -> [Block] {
```

You can find the implementation in the sample code[1]. Next, let's write a function that strips a link element by replacing it with the link text. We can switch on the element type, and if it is a link, we return the children (which are inline elements themselves). Otherwise, we just return a one-element array with the original element:

```
func stripLink(element: InlineElement) -> [InlineElement] {
    switch element {
    case let .Link(children, _, _):
        return children
    default:
        return [element]
    }
}
```

We can now strip all the links in an array of block-level elements:

```
deepApply(elements, stripLink)
```

Adding the footnotes is a bit harder, because CommonMark doesn't have built-in support for footnotes or superscripts, so we need to add them manually. We can easily generate inline HTML with a superscript tag. However, in order to generate increasing numbers, we need to keep track of a counter. We do this by adding an **inout** parameter to the addFootnote function. The function can mutate this variable in its body, and the new value gets copied back to the caller when the function returns. Note that we also have to use currying, because deepApply expects us to pass a function of type InlineElement -> [InlineElement] and not
(**inout** Int, InlineElement) -> [InlineElement]. With currying, we can construct a function of the required type when given an **inout** Int:

```
func addFootnote(inout counter: Int) -> InlineElement -> [InlineElement] {
    return { element in
        switch element {
        case let .Link(children, _, _):
            counter += 1
            return children +
                [InlineElement.InlineHtml(text: "<sup>\(counter)</sup>")]
```

1 https://github.com/objcio/commonmark-swift

```
        default:
            return [element]
        }
    }
}
```

To call the function, we first define a variable counter. Because it's an **inout** parameter, we need to add an ampersand to the variable name when we pass it to the function. Swift requires us to be explicit about this so that we won't accidentally make a mistake:

```
var counter = 0
let newElements = deepApply(elements, addFootnote(&counter))
```

There is another way to write the addFootnote function. We can define the counter variable inside the function and return a closure that captures the counter. By moving the burden of creating the counter into the function itself, this improved version is easier to use and also safer — whereas the counter variable in the previous example might be modified from other places in the code, the counter variable below is only shared between all the closures:

```
func addFootnote2() -> InlineElement -> [InlineElement] {
    var counter = 0
    return { element in
        switch element {
        case let .Link(children, _, _):
            counter += 1
            return children +
                [InlineElement.InlineHtml(text: "<sup>\(counter)</sup>")]
        default:
            return [element]
        }
    }
}
```

The last step is to generate the actual footnotes. To do that, we need to extract the links from the document. We use a function, deepCollect, which iterates over all the elements in the document at any level in the hierarchy. It applies a function to each element, and we can return any kind of value from that function. We have to return our values in an array so that they can all be combined when deepCollect finishes. Here is a function that we can use with deepCollect. It checks if an element is a link, and if yes, it returns the link's URL:

```swift
func linkURL(element: InlineElement) -> [String?] {
    switch element {
    case let .Link(_, _, url):
        return [url]
    default:
        return []
    }
}
```

deepCollect has two overloads. One works on Block elements, and one works on InlineElement values:

```swift
public func deepCollect<A>(elements: [Block], f: Block -> [A]) -> [A]
public func deepCollect<A>(elements: [Block], f: InlineElement -> [A]) -> [A]
```

Collecting all the links in a tree of elements works like this:

```swift
let links: [String?] = deepCollect(elements, linkURL)
```

Using deepCollect and deepApply, we can easily extract and manipulate all kinds of information from a Markdown document. We can then turn that back into a Node and render it to HTML, Markdown, or man pages. The native Swift enums we created provide a very nice interface to work with, while the conversion functions between the Swift enums and the C data structure still give us access to the complete feature set of the CommonMark library.

By first creating a thin wrapper around the C library (the Node class), we abstracted the conversion from the underlying C API. This allowed us to focus on providing a Swift-like interface. The entire project is available on GitHub[2].

---

2 https://github.com/objcio/commonmark-swift

Advanced Interoperability

12

One of Swift's greatest strengths is the low friction when interoperating with C and Objective-C. Swift can automatically bridge Objective-C types, and it can even bridge with many C types. This allows us to use existing libraries and provide a nice interface on top, an example of which we've seen in the chapter on wrapping CommonMark. In this chapter, we will build a small TCP server by wrapping parts of a larger library, libuv[1], which is an asynchronous I/O library.

This choice of library may raise some eyebrows. Much of libuv is about asynchronous queueing and thread pooling. Why bother to wrap libuv when Grand Central Dispatch is available?

Well, aside from it being a good demo for some of the trickier problems of Swift/C interaction, libuv is cross-platform. The biggest Swift news announced at WWDC in 2015 wasn't a language feature — it was that Swift was going open source, including a Linux version. This led some to wonder: "Why would anyone use Swift on Linux? They won't have Foundation and all the other benefits of the Apple APIs and ecosystem." Even with large parts of Foundation included in the initial open source release, there are many powerful C libraries out there, and as we saw in the CommonMark chapter, with a little interoperability knowledge, they can be efficiently wrapped in a Swift-like API without too much code.

Function Pointers

Before we start with libuv, let's have a look at wrapping the standard C qsort sorting function. The type as it is imported in Swift's Darwin module (or if you're on Linux, Glibc) is given below (we've added the argument names back in; unfortunately they get lost during the import process):

```
func qsort( base: UnsafeMutablePointer<Void>, nel: Int, width: Int,
    compar: (@convention(c) (UnsafePointer<Void>, UnsafePointer<Void>)
        -> Int32)!)
```

The man page (man qsort) describes how to use the qsort function:

---

1 https://github.com/libuv/libuv

> The qsort() and heapsort() functions sort an array of nel objects, the
> initial member of which is pointed to by base. The size of each object
> is specified by width.
>
> The contents of the array base are sorted in ascending order according
> to a comparison function pointed to by compar, which requires two
> arguments pointing to the objects being compared.

And here is a wrapper function that uses qsort to sort an array of Swift strings:

```
func qsortStrings(inout array: [String]) {
    qsort(&array, array.count, strideof(String)) { a, b in
        let l: String = UnsafePointer(a).memory
        let r: String = UnsafePointer(b).memory
        if r > l { return -1 }
        else if r == l { return 0 }
        else { return 1 }
    }
}
```

Let's look at each of the arguments being passed to qsort:

→ The first argument is a pointer to the base of the array. Swift arrays
  automatically convert to C-style base pointers when you pass them into
  a function that takes an UnsafePointer. We have to use the & prefix
  because it is an UnsafeMutablePointer (a void *base in the C
  declaration). If the function didn't need to mutate its input and were
  declared in C as const void *base, the ampersand wouldn't be needed.
  This matches the difference with **inout** arguments in Swift functions.

→ Second, we have to provide the number of elements. This one is easy; we
  can use the count property of the array.

→ Third, to get the width of each element, we use strideof, *not* sizeof. In
  Swift, sizeof returns the true size of a type, but when locating elements
  in memory, platform alignment rules may lead to gaps between adjacent
  elements. The stride is the size of the type, plus some padding (which
  may be zero) to account for this gap. For strings, size and stride are
  currently the same on Apple's platforms, but this won't be the case for
  all types (specific structs and enums). When translating code from C to
  Swift, you probably want to write strideof in cases where you would have
  written sizeof in C.

→ The last parameter is a pointer to a C function that is used to compare two elements from the array. Swift automatically bridges this to a Swift function type, so we can pass any closure or function that has a matching signature. However, there is one big caveat: C function pointers are just pointers; they can't capture any values. For that reason, the compiler will only allow you to provide closures that don't capture any local variables as the last parameter. It signifies this with the **@convention**(c) attribute.

The function accepts two void pointers. A C void pointer can be a pointer to anything. The first thing we must do is cast it to a pointer of the actual type (we hope) it is. In the case of qsort, we know the pointers reference elements in the array, which are Swift strings in our example. Finally, the function needs to return an Int32: a positive number if the first element is greater than the second, 0 if they're equal, and a negative number if the first is less than the second.

It's easy enough to create another wrapper that works for a different type; we can copy and paste the code, change String to a different type, and we're done. But we would really like to make the code generic. This is where we hit the limit of C function pointers. At the time of writing this book, the Swift compiler segfaulted on the code below. And even if it hadn't, the code is still impossible: it captures things from outside the closure. More specifically, it captures the comparison and equality operators, which are different for each A. There is nothing we can do about this — we simply encountered a hard limitation of the way C works:

```
func qsortWrapper<A: Comparable>(inout array: [A]) {
    qsort(&array, array.count, strideof(A)) { a, b in
        let l: A = UnsafePointer(a).memory
        let r: A = UnsafePointer(b).memory
        if r > l { return -1 }
        else if r == l { return 0 }
        else { return 1 }
    }
}
```

One way to think about this limitation is by thinking like the compiler. A C function pointer is just an address in memory that points to a block of code. In the case of functions that do not have any context, this address will be static and known at compile time. However, in

> case of a generic function, an extra parameter (the generic type) is passed in. Therefore, there are no addresses for specialized generic functions. This is the same for closures. Even if the compiler could rewrite a closure in such a way that it would be possible to pass it as a function pointer, the memory management could not be done automatically — there is no way to know when to release the closure.

In practice, this is a problem for many C programmers as well. On OS X, there is a variant of qsort called qsort_b, which takes a block — instead of a function pointer — as the last parameter. If we replace qsort with qsort_b in the code above, it will compile and run fine.

However, qsort_b is not available on most platforms. And other functions aside from qsort might not have a block-based variant, either. Most C APIs that work with callbacks offer a different solution. They take an extra unsafe void pointer as a parameter and pass that pointer on to the callback function. The user of the API can use this to pass an arbitrary piece of data to each invocation of the callback function. qsort also has a variant, qsort_r, which does exactly this. Its type signature includes an extra parameter, thunk, which is an unsafe mutable void pointer. Note that this parameter has also been added to the type of the comparison function pointer because qsort_r passes the value to that function:

```
func qsort_r(base: UnsafeMutablePointer<Void>, nel: Int, width: Int,
    thunk: UnsafeMutablePointer<Void>,
    compar: (@convention(c)
        (UnsafeMutablePointer<Void>, UnsafePointer<Void>,
            UnsafePointer<Void>)
        -> Int32)!
)
```

If qsort_b is not available on our platform, we can reconstruct it in Swift using qsort_r. We can pass anything we want as the thunk parameter, as long as we cast it to an unsafe mutable void pointer. In our case, we want to pass the comparison closure. We can automatically create an unsafe mutable pointer out of a variable defined with var if we prefix it with an ampersand. So all we need to do is store the comparison closure that is passed as an argument to our qsort_b variant in a variable named thunk. Then we can call qsort_r and pass in the reference to the thunk variable. Inside the callback, we cast the void pointer back to its real type, Block, and then simply call the closure:

```
typealias Block = (UnsafePointer<Void>, UnsafePointer<Void>) -> Int32
```

```
func qsort_block(array: UnsafeMutablePointer<Void>, _ count: Int,
    _ sz: Int, f: Block)
{
    var thunk = f
    qsort_r(array, count, sz, &thunk) { (ctx, p1, p2) -> Int32 in
        return UnsafePointer<Block>(ctx).memory(p1,p2)
    }
}
```

Using qsort_block, we can redefine our qsortWrapper function and provide a nice generic interface to the qsort algorithm from the C standard library:

```
func qsortWrapper<A: Comparable>(inout array: [A]) {
    qsort_block(&array, array.count, strideof(A)) { a, b in
        let l: A = UnsafePointer(a).memory
        let r: A = UnsafePointer(b).memory
        if r > l { return -1 }
        else if r == l { return 0 }
        else { return 1 }
    }
}
```

It might seem like a lot of work to use a sorting algorithm from the C standard library. After all, Swift's built-in sort function is much easier to use, and it's faster in most cases. However, there are many other interesting C APIs out there that we can wrap with a type-safe and generic interface using the same technique.

Wrapping libuv

libuv is a cross-platform library for asynchronous and event-driven programming, and it's written in C. On Apple's platforms, the aforementioned tasks are usually handled by NSRunLoop and Grand Central Dispatch, but if we want to write cross-platform Swift, we could use libuv. It is the library behind Node.js and a number of other projects. An Introduction to libuv, a book by Nikhil Marathe, is a good resource if you want to learn more about libuv.

A Simple Example

A good way to start developing Swift bindings is to translate some sample code to Swift. Here's an example from the book mentioned above that shows a libuv version of Hello World in C:

```c
int main() {
    uv_loop_t *loop = malloc(sizeof(uv_loop_t));
    uv_loop_init(loop);

    printf("Now quitting.\n");
    uv_run(loop, UV_RUN_DEFAULT);

    uv_loop_close(loop);
    free(loop);
    return 0;
}
```

In Swift, we can change the order of the code a bit by using the **defer** statement, which allows us to group together alloc and dealloc, as well as **init** and close. All **defer** blocks will be executed in reverse order just before the scope is left. We allocate a single uv_loop_t by passing 1 to UnsafeMutablePointer.alloc:

```swift
func loopAndQuit() {
    let loop = UnsafeMutablePointer<uv_loop_t>.alloc(1)
    defer { loop.dealloc(1) }

    uv_loop_init(loop)
    defer { uv_loop_close(loop) }

    print("Now quitting")
    uv_run(loop, UV_RUN_DEFAULT)
}
```

To illustrate the way we are going to build up our abstractions, we will wrap the loop in a class. Because we're dealing with mutable pointers, a struct would not be the right choice here since it signals value semantics, whereas we can only provide reference semantics. The implementation of our class is very straightforward: we move the allocation and initialization to the **init** phase and the closing and deallocation to the **deinit** phase, and then we only need to provide a method to run the loop:

```swift
typealias LoopRef = UnsafeMutablePointer<uv_loop_t>
```

```swift
class Loop {
    let loop: LoopRef

    init (loop: LoopRef = LoopRef.alloc(1)) {
        self.loop = loop
        uv_loop_init(loop)
    }

    func run(mode: uv_run_mode) {
        uv_run(loop, mode)
    }

    deinit {
        uv_loop_close(loop)
        loop.dealloc(1)
    }

    static var defaultLoop = Loop(loop: uv_default_loop())
}
```

We can rewrite our program in three lines now. We've moved all the details of dealing with a loop into the class. Note that as long as the loop is in scope, the pointer will be valid. However, once it goes out of scope, **deinit** will get called and free the memory:

```swift
func main() {
    let loop = Loop()
    print("Now quitting")
    loop.run(UV_RUN_DEFAULT)
}
```

Just like with the CommonMark wrapper, it is preferable to wrap existing libraries by creating very thin classes around the library's main data types. This makes the wrapper very easy to understand. Higher-level abstractions can be added as a second step.

A TCP Server

Let's write a simple TCP server next. This takes several steps:

1. Initialize a new TCP socket.
2. Bind the socket to an address.

3. Listen for new connections and handle them in a C callback.

In the callback, we need to do the following things:

1. Create a socket for the client.

2. Accept the incoming connection from the server using the newly created socket.

3. Start reading data on the client socket.

4. Write back a response to the client.

5. Free up any resources.

Some of the details of this are rather mundane, so we will only focus on the interesting parts in this chapter. The full source code is available on GitHub[2].

Wrapping Streams

Streams are one of the essential data types in libuv. A stream is a two-way communication channel, and it has operations for opening, reading, writing, and closing. There are three types of streams implemented by libuv: TCP sockets, pipes, and console streams (such as standard input and standard output). The terminology used by libuv is sometimes confusing. For example, the listen function works on sockets but is implemented on streams. Yet we follow libuv and also implement it on our stream wrapper.

We will start by writing a simple wrapper around the stream data type. In libuv, a stream "object" is represented by a pointer to a uv_stream_t. Again, we wrap it in a class:

```
typealias StreamRef = UnsafeMutablePointer<uv_stream_t>

class Stream {
    var stream: StreamRef

    init (_ stream: StreamRef) {
        self.stream = stream
    }
}
```

To start listening, we can wrap the uv_listen function. It will start listening and calls the callback we passed in when a new connection is received. Note that the callback is a C function pointer — we will look at how to deal with these later in the chapter. In the callback, we need to accept the socket, so we write another wrapper around the uv_accept function:

```
func listen(backlog numConnections: Int, callback: uv_connection_cb)
    throws -> ()
{
    let result = uv_listen(stream, Int32(numConnections), callback)
    if result < 0 { throw UVError.Error(code: result) }
}

func accept(client: Stream) throws -> () {
    let result = uv_accept(stream, client.stream)
    if result < 0 { throw UVError.Error(code: result) }
}
```

Finally, another basic function is closing a socket. In our use case, we do not reuse the socket handle after it is closed, so instead of just closing, we'll also free the memory. In the Stream class above, we could perform the free in **deinit**. In this case, however, we cannot do that. Because we will be working with asynchronous callback functions, the wrapper class might go out of scope while an asynchronous function is still being run. Freeing the memory for the stream pointer at that moment would crash our code:

```
func closeAndFree() {
    uv_close(UnsafeMutablePointer(stream)) { handle in
        free(handle)
    }
}
```

Wrapping TCP Sockets

The next entity we'll wrap is a TCP socket. Sockets are represented by the uv_tcp_t type, and in our wrapper class, we again want to store a pointer to it. The documentation of libuv tells us that uv_tcp_t is a "subclass" of uv_stream_t. This means that in C, we can safely downcast:

```
uv_tcp_t *tcp = ...;
uv_stream_t *stream = (uv_stream_t*) tcp;
```

This is reflected in our TCP socket class. We create a socket instance variable, and in the **init** function, we call the superclass's **init** function and do the same unsafe cast:

```
class TCP: Stream {
    let socket = UnsafeMutablePointer<uv_tcp_t>.alloc(1)

    init (loop: Loop = Loop.defaultLoop) {
        super.init(UnsafeMutablePointer(self.socket))
        uv_tcp_init(loop.loop, socket)
    }
}
```

Now, if we want to start a TCP server, we add a method to the TCP class that binds the socket to an address. The Address class is another simple wrapper (it's not shown here, but it is available in the full source code):

```
func bind(address: Address) {
    uv_tcp_bind(socket, address.address, 0)
}
```

Now we have all the parts ready to build a simple TCP server. As a first try, we could do something like the code below. We create a new socket, bind it to port 8888, and start listening for incoming connections. When a connection comes in, we don't process any data and just close it immediately:

```
func TCPServer(handleRequest: (Stream, NSData, () -> ()) -> ()) throws {
    let server = TCP()
    let addr = Address(host: "0.0.0.0", port: 8888)
    server.bind(addr)
    try server.listen (backlog: numConnections, callback: { stream, status in
        let client = TCP()
        try! server.accept(client)
        client.closeAndFree()
    })
    Loop.defaultLoop.run(UV_RUN_DEFAULT)
}
```

However, when compiling the code above, we immediately run into a problem. The callback that the C library expects needs to be a C function pointer. The server variable is captured from the surrounding context, and as such, the closure cannot be converted into a C function pointer. To work around this, we use the stream parameter in the callback (which has the type

UnsafeMutablePointer<uv_stream_t>). We then reconstruct the server socket from this:

```
func TCPServer(handleRequest: (Stream, NSData, () -> ()) -> ()) throws {
    let server = TCP()
    let addr = Address(host: "0.0.0.0", port: 8888)
    server.bind(addr)
    try server.listen(backlog: numConnections, callback: { stream, status in
        let server = Stream(stream)
        let client = TCP()
        try! server.accept(client)
        client.closeAndFree()
    })
    Loop.defaultLoop.run(UV_RUN_DEFAULT)
}
```

However, when we try to do anything more advanced, we run into the same problem as before: we cannot capture any variables outside of the callback blocks, otherwise our blocks cannot be used as C function pointers any longer. In the case of qsort, we used a variant of the function that took a void pointer and passed that on to the callback. libuv uses a similar technique. Instead of functions taking a void pointer, many of the data types have a field called data, which is there for exactly the same reason.

For example, any data we read from the client socket is delivered to us in chunks, so the data reading callback will be invoked multiple times. We could use the stream's data field to store the buffered data and thus pass it to the surrounding scope, but that approach would be rather inflexible and hard to use. Instead, we will write versions of listen and read that directly take native Swift closures as callbacks. That way, users of our API will get the interface they expect without having to worry about the hoops we had to jump through.

Ultimately, we still need a way to pass the Swift closures to the C callback. To do this, we store an object containing both the read and the listen callbacks in a property named context of the Stream class. The Stream class is then responsible for the conversion of the object to and from a void pointer, which we will show in a bit:

```
typealias ReadBlock = ReadResult -> ()
typealias ListenBlock = (status: Int) -> ()

class StreamContext {
    var readBlock: ReadBlock?
    var listenBlock: ListenBlock?
```

```
}
```

We add a new listen method to the stream object, which takes a Swift closure and stores it in the context. Then, when the callback is called, we recreate a Stream object from the serverStream (which has type uv_stream_t), grab the Swift closure from the context, and call it. Note that in the C variant, the callback is passed a pointer to the server stream, which holds the context. We don't need that parameter in the Swift callback because we can use variable capture to refer to the two sockets inside the closure:

```swift
func listen(numConnections: Int, theCallback: ListenBlock) throws -> () {
    context.listenBlock = theCallback
    try listen(backlog: numConnections) { serverStream, status in
        let stream = Stream(serverStream)
        stream.context.listenBlock?(status: Int(status))
    }
}
```

We do the same for read. The read callback takes a stream, the number of bytes read, and a buffer object. The callback gets called multiple times — once for each chunk of data. There are three different cases that can occur within the callback. These are communicated through the value of bytesRead: if bytesRead is positive, a chunk of data is available. If it is UV_EOF, all data has been read. And if it is any other negative value, an error occurred. To distinguish between these cases, we create an enum:

```swift
enum ReadResult {
    case Chunk(NSData)
    case EOF
    case Error(UVError)
}
```

We can add an extra initializer to construct a ReadResult from both the number of bytes read and a pointer to a uv_buf_t. In case we get EOF, we set self to EOF; in case we get an error, we set self to the error case; and finally, in case we read some bytes, we initialize an NSData value with the chunk that we just read:

```swift
extension ReadResult {
    init(bytesRead: Int, buffer: UnsafePointer<uv_buf_t>) {
        if bytesRead == Int(UV_EOF.rawValue) {
            self = .EOF
        } else if bytesRead < 0 {
            self = .Error(.Error(code: Int32(bytesRead)))
```

```
    } else {
      self = .Chunk(NSData(bytes: buffer.memory.base, length: bytesRead))
    }
  }
}
```

We now have all the parts in place to implement read. First, we store the Swift callback in our context. Then, inside the read callback, we reconstruct our Stream object from the serverStream. We then use bytesRead and buf to construct a ReadResult, and finally call the Swift callback with the read result:

```
func read(callback: ReadBlock) throws {
    context.readBlock = callback
    uv_read_start(stream, alloc_buffer) { serverStream, bytesRead, buf in
        defer { free_buffer(buf) }
        let stream = Stream(serverStream)
        let data = ReadResult(bytesRead: bytesRead, buffer: buf)
        stream.context.readBlock?(data)
    }
}
```

Storing Void Pointers

To store the context object in the stream's void pointer, we need to take a slightly different approach than what we have seen before. Thus far, we have used the ampersand prefix to create an unsafe mutable pointer. This just creates a pointer to the memory of a variable, but it does not retain the value. However, since libuv is an asynchronous library, the callback that uses our unsafe pointer will almost certainly outlive the variable. The solution is to manually retain the variable and then release it once we're done. Therefore, we create a function, retainedVoidPointer, which retains the pointer (or returns a null pointer in case the value is **nil**). The manual retain means we need to be careful about the lifetime and release it again once we're done with the object. For that, we have releaseVoidPointer. Because we cannot retain structs, we need to wrap the struct in a Box. Then, using Unmanaged, we can convert it into an unsafe mutable pointer via an opaque pointer:

```
// Retains the value A if it's non-nil
func retainedVoidPointer<A>(x: A?) -> UnsafeMutablePointer<Void> {
    guard let value = x else { return nil }
    let unmanaged = Unmanaged.passRetained(Box(value))
    return UnsafeMutablePointer(unmanaged.toOpaque())
}
```

```swift
// Releases the value inside the pointer and returns it
func releaseVoidPointer<A>(x: UnsafeMutablePointer<Void>) -> A? {
    guard x != nil else { return nil }
    return Unmanaged<Box<A>>.fromOpaque(COpaquePointer(x))
        .takeRetainedValue().unbox
}
```

Finally, we'll need an unsafeFromVoidPointer function that does not release the pointer. This function just returns the value stored in the pointer (unless it was a nil pointer):

```swift
// Returns the value inside the pointer without releasing
func unsafeFromVoidPointer<A>(x: UnsafeMutablePointer<Void>) -> A? {
    guard x != nil else { return nil }
    return Unmanaged<Box<A>>.fromOpaque(COpaquePointer(x))
        .takeUnretainedValue().unbox
}
```

Now we can extend our Stream class with a property, _context, which stores an optional StreamContext object in the libuv stream's data field. It's optional because it might still be **nil** when we first access it, and also because we want to be able to set it to **nil** (which will release the current context):

```swift
var _context: StreamContext? {
    get {
        return unsafeFromVoidPointer(stream.memory.data)
    }
    set {
        let _: StreamContext? = releaseVoidPointer(stream.memory.data)
        stream.memory.data = retainedVoidPointer(newValue)
    }
}
```

Finally, we can create a wrapper around the _context property that either returns the context or sets the _context property to an empty value if it's **nil**:

```swift
var context: StreamContext {
    if _context == nil {
        _context = StreamContext()
    }
    return _context!
}
```

Of course, we could have combined both _context and context into one property, but this way, what happens is clearer. Finally, to clean up the context, we need to change the implementation of closeAndFree to include a line that sets _context to **nil**, which will release the current context object.

Writing the TCP Server

We now have all the ingredients to write a TCP server that works with Swift callbacks. We'll first extend Stream once more with a bufferedRead method. It uses the read method we defined earlier and appends each chunk to an NSMutableData instance. When the end of the stream is reached, the callback is called with the full buffer:

```
func bufferedRead(callback: NSData -> ()) throws -> () {
    let mutableData = NSMutableData()
    try read { [unowned self] result in
        switch result {
        case .Chunk(let data):
            mutableData.appendData(data)
        case .EOF:
            callback(mutableData)
        case .Error(_):
            self.closeAndFree()
        }
    }
}
```

We can wrap up all these parts in one function that sets up the TCP server and runs it. The function is configured with a callback that, given some data, can write a response. In our example, we just close the socket after the data is written out:

```
typealias RequestHandler = (data: NSData, sink: NSData -> ()) -> ()
```

With these extensions, our final wrapper function is relatively short. First, we create a socket, bind it, and start listening for new connections. When a new connection comes in, we create a socket for the client. We try to let the server accept the socket, and we read out the data in a buffered way. When all data has been received, we handle the request with our callback. Finally, we close the socket if anything goes wrong during accepting, reading, or writing data:

```
func runTCPServer(handleRequest: RequestHandler) throws {
    let server = TCP()
```

```
let addr = Address(host: "0.0.0.0", port: 8888)
server.bind(addr)
try server.listen(numConnections) { status in
    guard status >= 0 else { return }
    let client = TCP()
    do {
        try server.accept(client)
        try client.bufferedRead { data in
            handleRequest(data: data, sink: client.put)
        }
    } catch {
        client.closeAndFree()
    }
}
Loop.defaultLoop.run(UV_RUN_DEFAULT)
}
```

Let's write a simple echoing server that reads out a string and echoes it back to the client. We run the server, and in the callback, we create a string out of the data. We then print that to the debug console and echo it back to the client:

```
try runTCPServer() { data, sink in
    if let string = String.fromCString(UnsafePointer(data.bytes)),
        let data = string.dataUsingEncoding(NSUTF8StringEncoding) {
        print(string)
        sink(data)
    }
}
```

To test that it works, we can use the nc command on OS X to send data to the server:

```
echo "Hello" | nc 127.0.0.1 8888
```

This concludes our chapter on interoperability. We've looked at C function pointers and why they cannot capture any state. If we want to use Swift closures in place of C function pointers, we either need to make them non-capturing, or we need to use a C API that provides an extra argument for storing data (such as the thunk pointer in the qsort_r function).

As we saw in the previous chapter, wrapping C types using classes is straightforward. We can use **deinit** to perform any cleanup. Yet, as we have seen in this chapter, things become complicated when dealing with asynchronous code, because a C pointer might outlive the wrapping class.

Thus, we need to be very careful with memory when wrapping an asynchronous library: we don't want to release memory too quickly, but we also don't want to introduce memory leaks. By carefully considering memory, we can write a wrapper that exposes a minimal API. This way, clients of the API do not have to worry about memory management. For example, the runTCPServer function only takes a function as its argument, and all the wrapping of libuv is hidden.

53965804R00199

Made in the USA
Charleston, SC
22 March 2016